THIS CRAZY WORLD
OF CHESS

ABOUT THE AUTHOR

Larry Evans is an international grandmaster, the highest title awarded by FIDE, and a legend in the world of chess. He won the USA national championship five times (starting at 19), the USA Open four times, and was a member or captain of nine Olympic teams, capturing several gold and silver medals along the way. He was also Bobby Fischer's second during his heyday as world champion.

Evans has drawn or beaten six world champions (Euwe, Fischer, Karpov, Petrosian, Smyslov, Spassky) as well as dozens of the world's top players. His syndicated newspaper column, "Evans On Chess," has won countless awards and he was named Chess Journalist of the Year in 2000. In 1972, he covered the Fischer-Spassky match for *Time* and ABC's *Wide World of Sports*, later serving as senior commentator at the Kasparov vs. Short title match in 1993, and at Kasparov vs. Kramnik in 2000.

Evans has written more than twenty chess books, including the classic, *New Ideas In Chess*, *The 10 Most Common Chess Mistakes*, and a British reprint of *Modern Chess Brilliancies*. He also collaborated on Fischer's *My 60 Memorable Games*, *Chessmaster*, the best-selling computer program, and revised the monumental 10th edition of *Modern Chess Openings*, which is commonly known as the "Chess Bible."

In 1994, Larry Evans was inducted into the Chess Hall of Fame.

Fischer (left) with Evans in Las Vegas, 1964

THIS CRAZY WORLD OF CHESS

By
Grandmaster Larry Evans

Cardoza Publishing

Cardoza Publishing is the foremost gaming publisher in the world, with a library of over 200 up-to-date and easy-to-read books and strategies. These authoritative works are written by the top experts in their fields and with more than 9,000,000 books in print, represent the best-selling and most popular gaming books anywhere.

FIRST EDITION

Copyright © 2007 by Larry Evans
- All Rights Reserved -

Library of Congress Catalog Card No: 2007932748
ISBN: 1-58042-218-7

Interior Design by Melissa Silberstang

Visit our web site—www.cardozapub.com—or write for a full list of books and computer strategies.

CARDOZA PUBLISHING
P.O. Box 1500, Cooper Station, New York, NY 10276
Phone (800) 577-WINS
email: cardozapub@aol.com
www.cardozapub.com

TABLE OF CONTENTS

INTRODUCTION

"Ultimately chess is just chess. Not the best thing in the world and not the worst thing in the world, but there is nothing quite like it."
—W.C. Fields

Chess is the greatest mind game ever invented, and because of this—or perhaps due to this—the game has attracted fascinating behind-the-scenes intrigues and shady dealings that were unknown outside of a small circle of players. And so, for the first time in book form, I decided to release all the investigative notes and inside escapades in one compelling volume. After reading this book, and learning what really goes on, you'll never look at chess the same way again!

Because of my close relationship with Bobby Fischer and many of the game's stars over the last 50 years, I was in a unique position to know of the scandals, machinations, and controversies in the world of chess—and expose them. The dispatches in this book contain the date they appeared in my syndicated newspaper column, "Evans on Chess." Some were enlarged and updated to reflect recent occurrences and throw more light on events, but little of substance has changed in the crazy world of chess since they were first published.

These 101 dispatches from the front line of chess blend instruction with entertainment. They run the gamut from humorous to bizarre, contemporary to historical. Some dominant figures in these stories include Garry Kasparov, arguably the strongest player who ever lived, his great rivals Anatoly Karpov and Vladimir Kramnik, and of course, the enigmatic legend, Fischer, whose many zany antics are revealed here. We'll also look at a host of fascinating characters and chess-playing celebrities from movie greats, Charlie Chaplin and Humphrey Bogart, to musicians Ray Charles and Artie Shaw, to vicious killer Charles Bloodgood. Along the way we'll meet the new Asian stars, 12-year-old grandmasters, and famous players who have been a central part of the chess landscape.

Hang on tight, you're in for a wild romp through the back door of chess.

1. FISCHER LETTER TO MARCOS
October 11, 2004

Bobby Fischer explained his position to Philippine President Ferdinand E. Marcos, who offered a $5 million purse to stage a title match with Anatoly Karpov in Manila in 1975. To the best of our knowledge, this letter dated January 27, 1975, has never been published.

> Dear Mr. President,
> How are you? It's been over a year now since we met and I want to thank you and your gracious wife for the wonderful time I had in your country on my last visit. I hope to see you again soon.
> I know you asked me to write the last time I saw you just before I left Manila for Japan. I apologize for not having done so but I really didn't know what to say under the circumstances–I'm not used to writing letters to Heads of State–I think you can understand what I mean. I haven't done too much this last year except for a couple of quick trips to Las Vegas. I've kept to the Los Angeles area.
> As you can imagine I'm quite excited about your extremely generous offer to play the Karpov Match in Manila and can assure you that if the match does indeed come off I'll be delighted to play in the Philippines. I think Campo is an excellent organizer and I'm sure the Cultural Center (developed by the First Lady) will be an excellent site.
> I also want to assure you that any kind of "scandal"–whoever is to blame for it is unthinkable in this match especially now since the President has put his own power, prestige and authority behind this match. You see Mr. President that's why I'm being so firm in what I feel are my rightful and fair demands with FIDE. I want to have every detail of the match agreed to by FIDE, the Russians and the organizers worked out in advance and signed by all the parties many months before the match takes place. This will head off any trouble between me and the

Russians and give the organizers plenty of time to work out all of the organizational problems and details in tranquility, assured that the match will indeed take place.

Last time in Iceland I never even signed any agreement because I was dissatisfied with some of the conditions. Contrary to what the press reported I was unhappy about the confusion that developed last time, and I have no desire to go through something like that again. That's why I resigned my FIDE title in the Summer of 1974 after FIDE rejected my basic match regulations, ie: the first player to win ten games (draws not counting) and if each side has won nine games (draws not counting) the match is declared drawn with the prize fund split equally.

By resigning my title I wanted to make it crystal clear to all that I was going to head off the kind of situation that developed in Iceland last time. If the Russians don't want to play me on my terms they can have the title by forfeit and there will be no match. Simple! And I feel certain that I made the right decision because I feel calm and satisfied about it.

By the way I'm writing this letter to you on a beautiful Philippine Chess Table that Campo just airmailed to me the other day to help me prepare for the match.

Also I want to wish you continuing success in building the "New Society." I picked up today's paper (the L.A. Herald Examiner) and there's an article about the upcoming referendum on February 27th. I'm sure you'll win–the article was very favorable to you.

What else have I been doing? My suit with the cameraman from the Iceland match [Chester Fox] is still dragging on and I'll be starting a suit of my own against someone who has written an incredibly boring book about me [*Bobby Fischer vs. the Rest of the World* by Brad Darrach] that's being pushed as "the most deliciously indiscreet biography ever written." I think it should be called the most inaccurate biography ever written! But we can't expect much accuracy from the press.

The article about you that I have before me states that "last year production rose 7% and the nation had a $96 billion balance of trade in its favor." I think that would be a bit high even for the Arabs!

Well, I guess that's all Mr. President and I just want to tell you again how pleased I am with your offer to hold the match in the Philippines. I like the climate, I like the people and I like the President, so I don't see how things can fail to work out!

I hope you're in the best of health and the First Lady also. Give my best regards to Mrs. Ford and her party the next time they're in town.

Best regards,
Bobby Fischer

FIDE and the Russians accepted most of his demands but Bobby didn't budge. His selfmate, alas, was a tragedy for him and a tragedy for chess.

2. WHY FISCHER FORFEITED
November 28, 2005

Bobby Fischer became world champion by beating Boris Spassky in 1972; afterward, Fischer stopped playing. It's still a hot topic and fans keep asking me why FIDE waited a full three years before stripping Fischer of the title for refusing to defend it against Anatoly Karpov in 1975.

The answer is simple. In those days a champion had to defend his crown every three years with no required activity in the interim. Technically speaking, however, Fischer wasn't stripped of the title. He resigned in a cable to FIDE president Max Euwe on June 27, 1974:

> "As I made clear in my telegram to the FIDE delegates, the match conditions I proposed were non-negotiable. Mr. Cramer informs me that the rules of the winner being the first player to win ten games, draws not counting, unlimited number of games and if nine wins to nine match is drawn with champion regaining title and prize fund split equally were rejected by the FIDE delegates. By so doing FIDE has decided against my participating in the 1975 world chess championship. I therefore resign my FIDE world chess champion title.
>
> Sincerely, Bobby Fischer"

The basis of Fischer's demand for counting only wins originated over 100 years ago with Wilhelm Steinitz. While defending his title against Isidor Gunsberg he noted in his *International Chess Magazine* (December 1890):

> "At the time of my writing I have secured half the championship with two games ahead and only two more games to play. I have only to draw one to maintain my title. If I lose both, there will be a partnership in the championship. But I may say in the meanwhile that I never intend to play again a championship match in which the number of games to be played is absolutely fixed, for under such conditions I have practically to give the large odds of the draw to any claimant of the title."

To avoid this dilemma, Bobby insisted that only wins should count with no restriction on the number of games. The only edge he sought was to retain his crown in case the score reached 9-9, which gave his challenger a better break than FIDE's 24-games-with-a-rematch clause in case the champion lost. "You can't even compare the rematch clause with Fischer's demands" said Garry Kasparov. "It's impossible to win two matches in a row. I did it, but even today I don't know how it was possible."

Even if all his demands were met, would Fischer have played Karpov? Nobody knows. When FIDE voted to restrict their tilt to 36 games—in effect nullifying his open-ended match of ten wins with draws not counting—Fischer vowed never again to play under FIDE jurisdiction. This meant spurning a purse of $5 million offered by president Marcos in the Philippines. FIDE relented and finally agreed to an unlimited match, but this time around they balked at his 9-9 tie clause.

"Thus Fischer relinquished his crown and joined Howard Hughes and JD Salinger in the great American void of absent legends," noted *The Guardian*.

Bobby in better days

Ever since 1948, when Mikhail Botvinnik won the title under suspicious conditions, the system was designed to protect Soviet supremacy by making it almost impossible for an outsider to wrest the title from behind the Iron Curtain. Botvinnik had draw odds in a 24-game series, an edge that enabled him to keep the title on a 12-12 tie in his first two defenses with David Bronstein in 1951 and Vasily Smyslov in 1954.

In addition, Botvinnik had the insurance of a rematch clause which he invoked successfully after losing his next two matches with Smyslov in 1957 and Mikhail Tal in 1960. FIDE finally struck the infamous rematch in 1963 before Botvinnik lost to Tigran Petrosian.

In return for ditching the 24-game format in favor of the first player to win six games, FIDE restored the rematch clause in 1978 as a sop to Karpov, a favorite of the Kremlin, against Soviet defector Viktor Korchnoi whose family was held hostage inside the USSR.

This dirty deal disgusted Fischer. He vanished in the California sunset, a period often described by Fischer watchers as his "wilderness years." He emerged in 1992 to trounce his old nemesis Spassky in an unofficial rematch for $5 million, the largest purse in chess history. It required 30 games for him to win, and the final score was 10-5 with 15 draws. This victory earned Bobby $3.35 million and an indictment for violating president Bush's embargo against Yugoslavia. Spassky returned to France without penalty.

I believe the champion should have no edge whatever. My main objection to Fischer's conditions was that the match could become a test of stamina instead of a test of skill. Indeed, the first Kasparov-Karpov marathon was aborted by FIDE president Florencio Campomanes at 5-3 (with 40 draws) when neither player could post the required six wins in 48 games in over five months.

Campo's action was akin to a boxing referee stepping in before the last round to save an exhausted champion who was shaky on his feet. He went on a whistle-stop tour around the world to justify his intervention, claiming he did it for medical reasons. At the Marshall Club in New York, *Chess Life* photographer Nigel Eddis asked which doctors he had consulted. Campo replied it wasn't necessary to consult doctors because he came from "a medical family."

When Kasparov finally dethroned Karpov in 1986, he promptly struck a blow for chess justice by voluntarily renouncing the rematch clause. But he didn't strike the second blow. The format for future title matches returned to the best-of-24 games with draws counting. In 1987 he barely saved his title against Karpov on a 12-12 tie. Kasparov gave two reasons for sticking with this system at a symposium we both attended in Madrid:

1. Since he had to overcome draw odds when he was the underdog, he saw no reason why the challenger shouldn't have to vault the same obstacle.

2. Organizers must have a definite budget and solid dates when they book a playing hall, which isn't possible in an open-ended match.

NO MORE TITLE MATCHES?

Kasparov's argument makes sense, yet Fischer's point is still valid. Only wins should count. This way, a champion can't cling to the title by playing for draws. But apparently the issue is now moot because FIDE plans on using tournaments rather than matches to determine its future champions. Or maybe not!

In a statement on November 9, 2005, Joel Lautier, president of the Association of Chess Professionals, chastised FIDE's decision:

> "Dropping the entire tradition of final matches for the title of World Champion is a decision with far-reaching consequences. What has made chess popular in the mainstream media are the great duels of the past, the Fischer-Spassky, Karpov-Kortchnoi and Kasparov-Karpov showdowns have brought chess in the limelight. The San Luis tournament [2005] was successful from the purely technical point of view, with an abundance of fascinating chess games, however its media impact worldwide was clearly lower than previous head-to-head matches. Certainly, opinions may differ on this complex topic, but once again, such a decision should be weighed carefully beforehand and not taken with such haste. Ending an almost 120 year-long tradition (even previous FIDE knockout world championships featured a final match) will have strong effects on the media popularity of chess, and it is highly unclear whether these will be beneficial to chess in the long run."

3. FISCHER STALEMATED
February 14, 2005

It seems incredible, but Bobby Fischer languished in a Tokyo cell for eight months without bail while Japan decided whether to deport him to America or Iceland, which had offered him asylum. His passport was confiscated but the USA did not demand extradition because Japan doesn't regard his offense as criminal.

"He's not a robber, he's not a killer, he's not a traitor. All he did was play chess," said his lawyer. So just what did Bobby actually do apart from yapping about the Jews and praising terrorists for 9/11?

A new book, *Bobby Fischer, The Wandering King* (Batsford, 2004), based on a Dutch TV documentary, notes, "Practising his art became criminal because George Bush pére issued an executive order in 1992."

Fischer violated that order by playing a $5 million rematch with Boris Spassky during a civil war in Yugoslavia. He was indicted by a Grand Jury 13 years ago and faces 10 years in jail plus fines, the only person ever prosecuted for defying Bush's economic sanctions.

The book quotes former *Chess Life* editor Larry Parr, who said, "The issue is not whether Fischer broke a law (so have all of us) but whether he is a criminal as opposed to someone who has fallen afoul of the federal regime. Americans today are largely sold on the State as the new god, but in 19th century England, juries often would not convict for minor theft because the punishment –hanging– was utterly disproportionate to the crime."

Canadian chess journalist Jonathan Berry observed, "It has been reported that President Clinton in his memoirs said the embargo was ignored by all, even the USA government, and it was only enforced to the extent that arms were not sent to Serbia. Yet arms were sent with impunity to other factions, and other contacts with Serbia were okay. If true, the whole incident appears doubly pointless."

A reader replied, "It's even worse than that. Serbia allegedly received missiles produced in the USA via Israel which makes it grotesquely hypocritical to punish Fischer for his 30 games against Spassky."

While his case is on appeal, Fischer gives interviews from his cell over the phone. One of the weirdest was his reaction to a *Time* magazine description of him as less than a babe magnet. He defended his virility by pointing out that he wears "size 14 wide shoes, just keep that in mind when they say I'm not a dreamboat."

After recounting an episode at a hot nude bath in Japan where two customers seemed in awe of his "size," Fischer accused America of persuading authorities to lock him up in a facility close to a nuclear plant to "make me impotent." In July 2007, an earthquake caused a severe radioactive spill into the sea, raising alarms about the safety of these plants in Japan.

In an interview, author James Michener stated, "In my lifetime I have met only two geniuses. One was Bobby Fischer, the chess player, and the other was Tennessee Williams, who simply looked at life and drama and the human condition differently from the way I do and that anybody else I know does. Both men found that to be the vessel housing genius was an intolerable burden, and each was destroyed by that burden."

4. FISCHER IS FREE
March 28, 2005

"Chess is not something that drives people mad; chess is something that keeps mad people sane."
—British IM Bill Hartston

The fugitive and former world champion Bobby Fischer is free at last, except from his own demons, that is. After a nine-month detention in Japan and a fight against deportation to America, he was saved when tiny Iceland miraculously granted him a passport and asylum.

Japan no longer had any legal basis to hold him after the oldest existing parliament ignored stern American warnings by voting 40-0 with two abstentions to make Fischer a full citizen. Legislators noted that the statute of limitations had expired on his violating an Executive Order forbidding him to play chess in Yugoslavia in 1992 where he won $3.35 million.

"My alleged 'crime' is not a crime anywhere else. So America made this detour around it by claiming I had an illegal passport. It was going to be a kangaroo court and they would murder me. They didn't touch me in neutral Switzerland but waited until I was in Japan where the United States is in control. I was kidnapped," snarled Fischer.

So it looks like we can thank Japan for providing what little bit of justice there was to be had in this case.

The case against him was so weak that America instead is pressing to extradite him for tax evasion. "We are disappointed by Iceland's decision but still want him to stand trial in his homeland," said a frustrated diplomat.

But fans view Bobby as a living legend, and he enjoys widespread support in a brave little nation that hosted his landmark title match with Boris Spassky in 1972.

"I don't like to dwell on the past. I won't sit in my rocking chair thinking about what I did long ago," said Bobby, 62. "I'm working on a new clock and trying to make chess a more exciting game."

Iceland loves chess and Bobby is now their tenth grandmaster, yet

18

many observers believe he will soon wear out his welcome. "He remembers every cut but he doesn't remember every kindness," lamented a colleague.

Surprised by arriving to a tumultuous hero's welcome in Reykjavik, Fischer told a midnight crowd that he plans to stay there. "If the people get tired of me, they can take away my citizenship later," he said.

So far he has kept a low profile, but some observers are wondering when he will bite the hand that freed him.

In a letter from congressman Christopher Shays to a constituent in Connecticut in 2005, he stated:

> "I do not believe that the United States should stop their pursuit and prosecution of Bobby Fischer. A warrant was issued for his arrest but never served since he has never returned to America. After his arrest in Japan he also accused President Bush and Japanese Prime Minister Koizumi of conspiring against him and said, 'They should be hanged.' The bottom line is Mr. Fischer broke the law and should be returned to the United States where he can be tried for the crimes of which he is accused. However, earlier this year, Iceland's parliament granted him asylum and citizenship for bringing attention and honor to the country in 1972 for beating Spassky there."

5. I REMEMBER BOBBY
January 5, 2004

"Bobby Fischer was the greatest genius to have descended from the chessic sky."
—Former world champion Mikhail Tal

Genius is a starry attribute, but posterity often finds a genius easier to bear than his harried contemporaries. I was a friend and competitor of Bobby Fischer during his rise to the top. In 1967 we collaborated on his *My 60 Memorable Games,* but his magnum opus almost never saw the light.

One day Bobby scratched out all of his notes before returning the proofs to Simon & Schuster. This left only my introductions to his games, which killed the deal. He cancelled the contract by paying back the advance to our publisher. I didn't find out the reason for his decision right away.

Time passed. He got a notice from Simon & Schuster asking whether he wanted to pay storage or destroy the plates. Bobby figured he could save money by having it shipped to his walk-up flat in Brooklyn. He asked my advice and I warned that these lead plates weighed a ton and might crash through the floor and kill tenants below.

"Oh well, the world's coming to an end anyway," he sighed. "Maybe I'll let 'em publish it."

At that moment I realized he had suppressed the manuscript because he feared giving away too many secrets. By now his opening innovations were common knowledge, so we added 10 more games to make the book more timely. That's how 50 became *60 Memorable Games* when it was finally published in 1969.

In 1972, Bobby finally became world champion at age 29, but his refusal to defend the title against Anatoly Karpov in 1975 proved to be a tragedy both for himself and the chess world. It was still the height of the Cold War and fans, who expected him to crush the darling of the Kremlin, wondered if he was crazy for spurning millions to play their match in the Philippines. Everyone was disappointed.

A mathematician found that Bobby's demands—10 wins, but retaining the title on a 9-9 tie—gave Karpov a better break than a 24-game tilt where the champion had draw odds. A French playwright depicted our hero as "a persecuted poet who defends human dignity." A psychiatrist stated, "A paramount theme is his refusal to compromise his principles." Diehards blamed it on a Commie plot. Recently GM Pal Benko stated, "Bobby was afraid that if he had defeated Karpov the Russians would have had him murdered."

This claptrap only encouraged Bobby to dig his own grave. I tried to persuade him to set a shining example by not seeking any advantage, but his selfmate handed the title to the Soviets without a fight. He promised not to seek any edge in future matches if he got his way just this once. Reasoning with him was absolutely futile.

"But when you were the challenger, you didn't think the champion should have any edge," I argued in vain.

"That's beside the point!" he insisted. "The Russkies always made their own rules and got away with it. Let's give 'em a dose of their own medicine."

Later I wrote, "It makes no difference whether Bobby obeyed his conscience or was afraid of losing. He shirked his duty by not defending his title under fair conditions. He refused to negotiate or compromise and his obstinacy killed the match—nothing or nobody else."

After Karpov took the title by default, he met Fischer several times around the world but never reached an agreement. Karpov later suggested he wanted to play but was under pressure from the Kremlin to avoid making any concessions.

Bobby was furious when FIDE, the Soviet-controlled world chess body, gave Karpov the gift of an even bigger edge than FIDE had denied him. He vowed to take revenge and became a recluse who grew a beard and handed out anti-Semitic leaflets in the street. In 1982 he wrote "I Was Tortured In The Pasadena Jailhouse!" a 14-page account of his overnight ordeal. It sold for a dollar and was signed Robert D. James (professionally known as Robert J. Fischer or Bobby Fischer, The World Chess Champion).

In 1992 he won a rematch against Boris Spassky and pocketed $3.35 million without paying any taxes. Some of it vanished when he naively deposited it in the sponsor's shaky bank, yet Bobby claims he kept most of the loot. America promptly indicted him for violating its embargo on war-torn Yugoslavia. France, however, took no action against Spassky.

Bobby fled to Hungary for about ten years. Now he hates America and applauded 9/11 by praising the terrorists in his interviews over the radio when he was living in the Phillipines. "Fischer appears to have become a complete madman who could no longer deal with the monster of his own madness," wrote the editor of *Chess Life*.

Alas, Bobby can't come home again.

6. FBI FILES ON FISCHER
June 23, 2003

The person who brought glory to America by humbling the Soviets at chess during the Cold War was spied on by the FBI. Although Bobby Fischer detested the "Commies" and beat them at their own game, the FBI kept tabs on him and his mother, who had studied medicine in Moscow for five years from 1933–1938. Her husband, Gerhardt Fischer, was denied admission to America when Regina and her one-year-old daughter Joan returned in 1939. During World War II he lived in Chile. They were divorced in 1945.

"They once believed she might be a Soviet spy, and that Moscow might have tried to enlist young Bobby as well," reported the *Philadelphia Inquirer* on its front page (11/17/02).

The heavily censored 900-page file suggests his real father was Paul Nemenyi, a Hungarian physicist who worked on the atomic bomb project in Chicago, where Bobby was born in 1943. Nemenyi met Regina Fischer a year earlier when he taught at the University of Denver, and he paid child support until his death in 1952.

High tuition fees and limited vacancies prevented Regina from becoming a doctor. She worked as a nurse and moved to Brooklyn with her children to study at New York University, then left in 1960 and finally got a medical degree in East Germany. She remarried and walked to Moscow in a radical antiwar peace demonstration.

I only saw Regina a few times and have a fleeting memory of a dark-haired, slim, intense woman. Joan later said her mother had great intellect, boundless energy, spoke over six languages, and was "a professional crusader."

When I collaborated with Bobby on his *60 Memorable Games* in 1967, his shabby flat in Brooklyn was roach-ridden and jammed with chess books, many written in the nineteenth century. "I don't like people in my hair, so I had to get rid of my mother," he said. Later they reconciled.

One day his mother, who was Jewish, tired of his tirades against the Jews. "What makes you think you're so pure?" she snapped. As fate would have it, Bobby later learned that his real father was also Jewish.

22

An FBI report from 1959 states: "A review of this case fails to reflect that the subject has been involved in Soviet espionage, and actually, there has been no allegation that she has been so engaged."

HANDWRITING ANALYSIS

"At the Leipzig Chess Olympiad in 1960 Miguel Najdorf asked for Bobby Fischer's autograph. Bobby agreed, but for one dollar," wrote Yugoslav journalist Dmitrije Bjelica.

This tale may be apocryphal, but it made me wonder how much Fischer's signature is worth today. Recently the bulletin cover of *Bled 1961* signed by him and most of the other players sold at an eBay auction for $2,025, according to Lawrence Totaro in the 57-page booklet *Fisching for Forgeries*, which undertakes the task of separating fact from fiction.

Prices for Fischer memorabilia have soared on eBay—but buyers beware. Sheila Lowe, a noted graphologist, contributed a chapter diagnosing him based solely on his handwriting. Here are some of her comments:

• His name as a chess genius was the full extent of what I knew about the man. The consistency and quality of the writing tells us that he has remained much the same over time, and that the many experiences and events he has undergone over more than 45 years have not touched him deeply at the core. He is still the person he always was.

• His handwriting suggests someone who has the ability to strip away any non-essential data and is able to see through to the bottom line of an issue. He is not the sort who will sit and listen to a lengthy explanation of whys and wherefores of something that doesn't interest him. He just wants to know what is.

• At some point in his young life probably as early as the first two years he decided that emotions were too painful to deal with and as a result began to cut off his emotions. Close relationships are a major challenge for Bobby. It's really difficult for him to trust anyone enough to allow intimacy to develop properly. The closer someone gets, the more vulnerable he feels. He is constantly on the alert for anyone who would try to manipulate him using flattery. Thus, he probably has a small circle of carefully selected friends who have stood by him over a long period of time.

• Mostly, though, he fights through his fears with great courage, pushing himself forward even when he feels as if he's walking through a desert filled with land mines. It is this internal fortitude that allows him to keep coming back, seemingly against the odds.

7. NEVER ON SUNDAY
April 17, 2006

A curious incident marred the Twelfth European Cup at Budapest ten years ago. In a field of 18 teams an Israeli squad withdrew to protest its 6-0 forfeit to a Tatar team that refused to alter the playing schedule from 2 p.m. to 10 a.m. on Friday in order to finish their games before sundown. Orthodox Jews are forbidden to work or even to write down chess moves on their Sabbath, which lasts from sundown Friday to sundown Saturday.

"It's the first time Israel ever lost a battle without a fight," said their captain, who claimed the organizers reneged on a pledge to respect their religious scruples.

HISTORY REPEATS ITSELF

Samuel Reshevsky, an orthodox Jew, never played on his Sabbath. He was America's greatest star for decades, the touchstone against which my generation measured its progress. Art Bisguier said that we would all beat him in a few more years when he got old. Meanwhile we got old waiting for him to get old.

Not to be outdone by Sammy, Bobby Fischer joined the Church of God in California and demanded the same Sabbath as his archrival. There was bad blood between them ever since Bobby forfeited their unfinished match in 1961 over a scheduling dispute with the score tied after 11 games.

Another fracas occurred in 1966 at the Seventeenth Chess Olympiad in Havana when the USSR was paired with the USA at 4 p.m. on a Saturday. The organizers had pledged to respect Fischer's holy day, but world champion Tigran Petrosian wouldn't delay the start of his game on first board for two hours until after sundown. Our team arrived at 6 p.m. to discover the Russians had already been awarded a 4-0 forfeit. Their manager treated our captain to a lengthy, irrelevant anti-American harangue. Why must the whole world pamper this spoiled brat who accused the Russians of cheating? The incident made international headlines.

Four days later arbiters from six nations urged Russia to reschedule the match in view of the fact that other teams had accommodated Fischer. Yet it took another five days, after checking with the Kremlin, for Russia to back down. This decision was promptly hailed by Castro's newspapers as "a noble gesture."

Russia replaced the cautious Petrosian with Boris Spassky "for tactical reasons." The reason for resting Petrosian became clear when he won the gold medal on top board with 88.46 percent vs. Fischer's 88.23 percent. Fischer faced tougher opposition and played four more games. If he had drawn with Petrosian, then Fischer would have captured the gold.

Our team did well by finishing second behind the USSR among 52 nations. Russia won our match 2½-1½. I drew with Lev Polugaievsky and Pal Benko drew with Leonid Stein, but Mikhail Tal beat Robert Byrne. Fischer, alas, with plenty of time at his disposal, missed a win against Spassky with 36 Bxe5! At the end, Spassky stood slightly better.

FISCHER vs. SPASSKY
Ruy Lopez, Havana, 1966

1 e4 e5 2 Nf3 Nc6 3 Bb5 a6 4 Ba4 Nf6 5 0–0 Be7 6 Re1 b5 7 Bb3 0–0 8 c3 d6 9 h3 h6 10 d4 Re8 11 Nbd2 Bf8 12 Nf1 Bd7 13 Ng3 Na5 14 Bc2 c5 15 b3 cxd4 16 cxd4 Nc6 17 Bb2 g6 18 Qd2 Bg7 19 Rad1 Qb6 20 Nf1 Rad8 21 Ne3 Qb8 22 Bb1 Qb7 23 Rc1 Kh7 24 a3 Bc8 25 Bc3 Bd7 26 Qb2 Qb8 27 b4 Kg8 28.Rcd1 Nh7 29 Ba2 Ng5 30 Nxg5 hxg5 31 dxe5 dxe5 32 Nd5 Ne7 33 Nxe7 Rxe7 34 Qd2 Bf6 35 Qd6! Kg7 36 Qxa6? Rc8 37 Rd6 Rxc3 38 Rxf6 Be6 39 Rxe6 fxe6 40 Rd1 Qb7 41 Qxb7 Rxb7 42 Bxe6 Rxa3 43 Kh2 Ra4 44 Rb1 Rc7 45 f3 Ra6 46 Bb3 Ra3 47 Rb2 Ra1 48 Kg3 Kf6 49 Kg4 Rc3 50 Bd5 Raa3 51 h4 gxh4 52 Kxh4 Ra1 53 Rd2 Raa3 54 Kg4 Rd3 55 Re2 Rac3 56 Ra2 Ra3 57 Rb2 **Draw**

8. BOBBY'S SHORTEST GAME
May 22. 2006

The shortest game Bobby Fischer ever played—indeed, the shortest game on record—took place on the island of Mallorca during the final round of the Eighth Interzonal tournament in 1970. He made just one move and Oscar Panno resigned!

Thereby hangs a tale.

Probably my hardest job as Bobby's second in Palma was getting him to the games on time. Rounds began at four in the afternoon with games adjourned after nine hours if still unfinished by move 72. Fortunately, few of them lasted that long.

In 1972 the top six in a field of 24 would advance to a series of matches to determine at challenger for world champion Boris Spassky. Bobby clearly dominated the tournament, ending a full 3½ points ahead of Efim Geller, Robert Huebner, and Bent Larsen, who was responsible for Bobby's only defeat.

Going into the last round, Panno still had a slim chance to qualify in the unlikely event that he could beat Fischer with Black. Panno protested that all games should begin at the same time so nobody would have an unfair advantage.

The organizers were at fault for scheduling this round on a Saturday when both Fischer and Samuel Reshevsky, due to their Sabbath observances, could not begin before sundown at 7 p.m.

All the other games started at 4 p.m. Duncan Suttles of Canada agreed to play Reshevsky at 7 p.m. and their lonely vigil was drawn in 23 moves. Bobby also came at 7 p.m. and played 1 c4 but Panno was nowhere in sight. The rules stipulate that if a player doesn't show up in the first hour then he forfeits the game.

Loathe to accept a forfeit, Bobby rushed over to Panno's hotel to try and talk him into playing. Alas, this gesture was in vain. Panno stood behind his principles, arrived after the hour was up, and signed "resigns" on his scoresheet.

Incidentally, Bobby's shortest loss occurred while he took on all comers barnstorming America on a cross-country tour in 1964. Such offhand games are usually not published, but this one versus Robert Burger is special.

FISCHER vs. BURGER
Two Knights' Defense, San Francisco, April 13, 1964

1 e4 e5 2 Nf3 Nc6 3 Bc4 Nf6 4 Ng5 d5 5 exd5 Nd4 6 c3 b5 7 Bf1 Nxd5 8 cxd4 Qxg5 9 Bxb5+ Kd8 10 0–0 exd4 11 Qf3 Bb7 12 Qxf7?? Nf6!
White Resigns

Final Position

Black threatens 12...Qxg2 mate. If 13 g3 Bd5! snaring the queen (stronger than 13...Qxb5). Curiously, seven years later David Bronstein fell into this same trap against Levente Lengyel in an actual tournament at Sarajevo!

THE LONG AND SHORT OF IT

While on this subject, I should mention that Bobby's longest tournament game took place in 1956, at the Canadian Open in Montreal, against Hans Matthai when Bobby was 13. I shared first with Daniel Yanofsky and Bobby tied for 6-9 in a field of 56. Afterwards he asked me to drive him back to New York, which began a long and sometimes turbulent friendship.

Fischer overlooked a way to draw by 45 Qh1! but escaped with one anyway after his opponent missed 104 Rfd5.

FISCHER vs. MATTHAI
Sicilian Defense Canadian Open, Montreal, 1956

1 e4 c5 2 Nf3 d6 3 d4 cxd4 4 Nxd4 g6 5 Nc3 Bg7 6 Be3 Nf6 7 f3 Nc6 8
Qd2 0–0 9 Bc4 Bd7 10 h4 Rc8 11 Bb3 Qa5 12 0–0–0 Nh5 13 g4 Nxd4
14 Bxd4 Bxd4 15 Qxd4 Nf4 16 Kb1 Ne6 17 Qd2 Rfe8 18 f4 Nc5 19
h5 Nxb3 20 axb3 Bxg4 21 Rdg1 f5 22 hxg6 hxg6 23 b4 Qxb4 24 Rxg4
fxg4 25 f5 Rxc3 26 fxg6 Rh3 27 Qxb4 Rxh1+ 28 Ka2 Kg7 29 e5 dxe5
30 Qxb7 Rhh8 31 Qe4 Kf6 32 Qxg4 Reg8 33 b4 Rxg6 34 Qf3+ Kg7
35 Qe3 Re6 36 Qxa7 Rd8 37 Qg1+ Kf7 38 b5 Rdd6 39 c4 e4 40 c5
Rd2+ 41 Kb3 e3 42 Kc3 Rf2 43 c6 Rf5 44 Qb1 Kf6 45 Kd3? e2 46 c7
Rc5 47 b6 e1Q 48 Qxe1 Rxe1 49 b7 Rxc7 50 b8Q Rd7+ 51 Kc2 Re2+
52 Kc3 Re3+ 53 Kc2 Rd6 54 Qh8+ Kg5 55 Qg8+ Kf4 56 Qg2 Re5 57
Qh2+ Kf5 58 Qh5+ Ke6 59 Qg4+ Rf5 60 Qe4+ Re5 61 Qg4+ Kd5 62
Qf3+ Re4 63 Kd3 Ke5+ 64 Kc3 Rdd4 65 Qh5+ Kd6 66 Qg6+ Kc7 67
Qg7 Rd6 68 Qh7 Re5 69 Qg7 Re3+ 70 Kc4 Re4+ 71 Kc3 Kd7 72 Qf7
Re5 73 Kc4 Ra5 74 Kb4 Rdd5 75 Kc4 Rac5+ 76 Kb3 Re5 77 Qg6 Rf5
78 Qg7 Rce5 79 Kc4 Rg5 80 Qh7 Ref5 81 Kd4 Ra5 82 Ke3 Ra3+ 83
Kf4 Rga5 84 Qf7 Rc5 85 Ke4 Rg5 86 Kf4 Rga5 87 Ke4 R5a4+ 88 Kd5
Ra5+ 89 Ke4 Rh3 90 Kf4 Kd6 91 Qg6+ e6 92 Qe8 Ra4+ 93 Kg5 Rg3+
94 Kh5 Ra5+ 95 Kh4 Rga3 96 Qd8+ Ke5 97 Qc7+ Ke4 98 Qc4+ Ke5
99 Qc7+ Kf6 100 Qf4+ Rf5 101 Qd4+ Kg6 102 Qe4 Ra6 103 Qc4 Rd6
104 Qc8 e5? 105 Qg8+ Kf6 106 Qf8+ Ke6 107 Qe8+ Kd5 108 Qb5+
Draw

Final Position

In 1966 he coauthored *Bobby Fischer Teaches Chess*, possibly the biggest selling chess book ever. Basically, he just corrected the proofs and put his name on it. Frank Brady, his biographer, noted, "The book lacked color or even a fleeting glimpse into the real way Bobby's mental processes work. It was not therefore one of the great introductory chess treatises of modern times."

Later we worked together on Bobby's classic *My 60 Memorable Games* (published by Simon & Schuster in 1969). I wrote the introduction to each game and convinced him to include several of his losses. When a friend asked him about my role in this book, Bobby shrugged and said, "Oh him? He just does the typing!"

9. FISCHER AT 24
March 22. 2004

Bobby Fischer's legend seems to grow even as he sinks into obscurity. When we worked together on his *My 60 Memorable Games*, he was unsure about competing in the Sousse Interzonal and I wrote an article about his baffling behavior to pressure him into playing. He went, but dropped out while leading.

Chess Life published my article in June 1967 with a curious disclaimer stating, "The opinions expressed are those of Larry Evans, or his quoted sources and do not necessarily reflect the views of the United States Chess Federation, *Chess Life*, or its Editor." It took several months before I could persuade the editor—who feared offending Fischer—to publish the article.

Bobby never complained about what I wrote, and in 1970 he asked me to be his second at the Mallorca Interzonal. The authors of *Bobby Fischer Goes To War* (2004) explain why we parted company shortly before he dethroned Spassky. "Evans refused because of Fischer's twin demands that he abstain from journalism and leave his wife at home." The book mentions what happened later:

> "Fischer stated that he would not shrink from defending his title; on the contrary, he would regularly take on challengers. Few expected him to be knocked off his throne for a decade or more. One exception was his former second Larry Evans who explained to *The New York Times*. 'I probably have more influence on him than anybody else, and that's exactly zero... I just had the feeling he would never play competitive chess again.'
>
> Warner Brothers had the idea of making a Christmas LP in which Fischer would record some basic chess lessons. Two producers had been dispatched to Iceland during the match to try to agree on terms. Fischer was too busy to grant them an audience. Nevertheless, money was considered no object in the LP's preparation—the potential spoils were forecast to be

massive. Larry Evans was contracted to assist with the script for a handsome fee. He asked the president of Warner Brothers whether Fischer had actually signed a contract and was told no, but this was a mere formality. All the particulars had been agreed to in principle. Said Evans, 'In that case, I'd rather be paid in advance.' He was."

Incidentally, Bobby backed out of the deal and never made the record. I never found out why, but someone told me he didn't like the way his voice sounded.

OUR HERO: FROM *CHESS LIFE* IN 1967

Ever since Robert Fischer became the hero, though not the winner, of both the 1966 Piatigorsky tournament and first board at the Havana Olympic—as well as the U.S. titleholder for the eighth time—he has been treating the chess world to new examples of his unique behavior. Presently, among other things, he is demanding that the next U.S. Championship become a double round robin—or else! His willful absence from serious competition for almost two years after winning the title in 1964 (with a perfect score) certainly did not improve his game. Apropos of this, Korchnoi pointed out in 1965, with reference to the Belgrade chess congress:

> "Fischer made his participation conditional on an extra honorarium of $1,000—a sum equal to first prize in the tournament! I think the organizers were right in not accepting his terms. Of course it is too bad that the chess world was deprived of the possibility of comparing the play of the talented American with that of the recognized masters of the old world. But Fischer himself suffered: without contesting with players of one's own strength, it is hard to improve. If Fischer continues to conduct himself so arrogantly in the future, he will be running a grave risk."

Similarly, but for unstated reasons, he did not take part at the Interzonal in Amsterdam (1964) even after the world championship qualifying system had been changed, essentially to nullify his printed accusations that the Russians had colluded against him. Former world champion Max Euwe, in the November 1964 issue of Ogonek, sought an explanation for Bobby's puzzling boycott:

> "Why did he refuse to play at Amsterdam? On this score, no reasonably satisfactory explanation has been given. In fact,

no explanation whatsoever. Fischer himself was satisfied with a curt 'no comment.' From several quarters he received offers that would have taken care of him with a sum expressed in thousands of dollars. Fischer turned them all down. So it was not a question of money.

What then? Was Fischer scared? No, the young grandmaster is never scared. His faith in himself is boundless. The contrary is the sooner case: he LACKS fear because he tends to exaggerate his own possibilities. Remember, for example, that several years ago he proposed to play Botvinnik, who was World Champion at the time, a match for the Championship with Botvinnik given two points at the outset! [Note: In 1972 Fischer overcame a two-point deficit at the start of his title match with Spassky.]

So it is not a question of dollars or fear—and all the same, Fischer refused to play. What is the reason? We proceed from the supposition that there IS an explanation, though given the immature character of the young U.S. Champion one cannot affirm that it exists in his mind. In my opinion, the cause of Fischer's refusal to take part in the Candidates' Tourney is the following: he takes into consideration (like most young people) first of all, and perhaps exclusively, his own opinion.

'There exists a worldwide chess organization,' he reasons 'which sets conditions for winning the world championship. Of course, this is well and good, but much more important and significant is what I, Robert Fischer, consider to be right. If a chess player has far exceeded the average level of accomplishment, he is above the usual rules. He has no need to stubbornly make his way up the steps of competitive events leading to a match for the title of World Champion. He can be given direct access to a match.'"

After reviewing Fischer's record, particularly his 'relative failure' in the Challengers' Tourney at Curacao in 1962, Euwe concludes:

"Fischer (even overlooking the FIDE rules) can hardly declare himself to be the first in line to challenge the World Champion. All the same, he is ready to bring up an additional argument. We know he has proposed that a match be organized between him and one of the five strongest USSR players. And he has forcefully stressed that this match will have no connection with the question of the World Championship. It is clear, though, that Fischer hopes, in the event of a possible and, still more, a convincing victory, to gain new arguments for a direct encounter with the World Champion. And again: he hopes, wherever possible, to circumvent the procedures set up by FIDE when he does not consider them right in the given case."

Bobby assured me that Euwe was wrong on one point. He said nobody had offered him anything to go to Amsterdam. This surprised me, since Benko, Reshevsky, and I were each given $500. It seems unlikely that Bobby was offered less, since for some years now, for other tournaments, he has always received more. And in reply to my recent question about offering Botvinnik two points in a match, Bobby said, "Don't you think I could have done it and won?" I told him no, whereupon he looked pained.

As for the FIDE rules, his ideas for improving the machinery for the qualifying procedure and the title match itself were set forth in a letter to President Folke Rogard that I helped him prepare last summer. These proposals were taken up at the FIDE congress in Havana during the course of the 1966 Olympics. Fred Cramer, our delegate, invited Bobby to amplify his views for the benefit of the congress; but Bobby, after due deliberation, did not appear. His proposals were voted down.

For years, the manner in which Bobby's attitude has made itself apparent has provoked comment throughout the chess world. Keres was moved to say of it:

> "In my opinion, and not only mine, Bobby Fischer's greatest failing is lack of objectivity toward his achievements, his ability, and the playing strength of his opponents ... disparaging the performances of his adversaries will not improve his own results. In the August 1965 issue of Shakhmatny, Botvinnik opined: 'Fischer is a very talented player. What is the nature of his talent? A chess player calculates elementary functions and from these he arrives at further, likewise rather elementary functions, and so forth. Fischer calculates these elementary functions very well indeed. For this reason he finds his way fast and confidently in tactical complications. But when the game takes on a more indefinite character, and one must first of all attack questions of planning and of subtle positional considerations, Fischer's game is weaker. He is also obviously hampered by his emotions. When there is nothing to calculate, he is not infrequently thrown at the mercy of his emotions and loses control.'" [Note: In a lifeless position he grabbed a tainted pawn in his first match game with Spassky instead of taking an easy draw with Black.]

Bobby attributed his bad start in the 1966 Piatigorsky Cup to "rustiness and poor chess nerves." Among other examples of those chess nerves was his complaint (after a few early losses) that the chessmen were too large. The tournament committee promptly supplied a smaller set. He also found it necessary (to insure greater tranquility) to change hotel rooms. A photographer at Santa Monica, Art Zeller, grumbled about Bobby's difficult temperament:

"His unbelievable comeback made me forgive him everything as he emerged the hero of the tournament [½ point behind Spassky in a field of 10]. I cheered for him with the rest. But I had to shoot under duress. Fischer put pressure on Mrs. Piatigorsky and she on me. At first he objected to flash. Then he said the click of the shutter distracted him and so did cameras pointing in his face. But when I moved to the very back of the room with a 400mm lens and tripod, where he could neither hear not see me (without trying hard) and he still objected—that was obnoxious. From there on I had to sneak every shot. No other player objected to any of the above. Fischer even prevented Petrosian from taking any photos! Once Mrs. P. caught me sneaking a shot and got all excited. I told her that she would be glad to have these pictures when the games were over. The thought seemed to strike home and she only half-heartedly tortured me thereafter." [Note: Shades of Reykjavik 1972, where cameras nearly scuttled his title match with Spassky.]

This calls to mind Fischer's explanation for his dismal showing at the great Buenos Aires tournament in 1960. "Poor lighting." Will Bobby be plagued in future competitions by such small matters? Disturbed enough to be put off his game? So far that hasn't appeared to be the case, because he did win decisively at Monaco despite the fact that the tournament had not been run entirely to his satisfaction.

Toward the end of the first week of play he telephoned New York (collect) to complain that the organizing committee had broken their agreement with him. Although to satisfy his religious scruples they had scheduled no games for him on his holy day, as agreed, they had scheduled the round for everyone else. Bobby seemed to think that all the participants should also observe his holy day. In fact, since they didn't, he declared that he was going to drop out. It took $60 worth of dimes to convince him of the faulty reasoning of such a move.

FISCHER'S 10 BEST LIST

Bobby's opinions about the game have provoked as much controversy as his exploits over the board. For example, the brouhaha occasioned by his selection of Morphy, Staunton, Steinitz, Tarrasch, Tchigorin, Alekhine, Capablanca, Spassky, Tal and Reshevsky as the ten greatest chess players of all time. This list appeared in the first issue of the now defunct *Chessworld* which noted:

> "In naming the ten greatest masters in the history of chess, Bobby (who, in the editor's opinion, belongs in the list himself) gives decisive significance to the quality of their play, not to their successes and results. This may explain the exclusion from the list of such players as Lasker, Botvinnik, and others."

That Bobby considered Staunton, for example, as stronger than either Lasker or Botvinnik, was curious indeed. He justified his choice saying, "Just because a man was champion for many years doesn't mean that he was a great chessplayer, just as we wouldn't necessarily call a ruler of a country great just because he was in power for a long time."

A thundering rebuke from the veteran Edward Lasker (not to be confused with Emanuel, in whose defense he wrote) appeared in the following issue:

> "Fischer has a lot of growing up to do before he can create works of art like the Ruy Lopez Lasker won from Capablanca (at St. Petersburg 1914) or the game he played with the Black pieces against Alekhine's Queen's Gambit in New York 1924. Even Alekhine himself willingly admitted that in the course of two decades, beginning with the victory over Steinitz, Lasker had no equal in the art of the endgame...I predict that, despite his youth, which gives him a tremendous advantage, Fischer will never become World Champion."

However devoutly one may hope this prediction will not come to pass, there is no question that—ability apart—Bobby must clear certain emotional hurdles before he can achieve his ambition. Further along in the already quoted Ogonek article, Euwe analyzes the striking absence of Botvinnik and Petrosian from Fischer's list, as opposed to the inclusion of Spassky and Tal (all contemporaries):

> "Certainly, everyone has the right to his favorites, and to his

opinion on the strength and talent of this or that chessplayer, though Fischer's commentaries could be seriously criticized. But what does this list mean? If one considers that Botvinnik, and Petrosian even more, are in Fischer's eyes his direct rivals (1964) while Tal and Spassky can be his rivals only in the more or less distant future, then one can conclude that Fischer consciously or unconsciously downgrades his direct rivals. In this respect it is typical that Fischer, during the period when Tal was World Champion, expressed himself to the effect that the Champion was a weak player while now, on the contrary, when Tal is a little further removed from the highest of titles, Fischer counts him among the best. In the words of the proverb, Fischer is contemptuous about wolves in the forest. But what will happen if the forest wolves break into the garden?"

CAPABLANCA ON LASKER

Confirmation of Edward Lasker's view of Emanuel (as opposed to Bobby's) may be found in a recently published book, *Last Lectures*, by Bobby's acknowledged hero, Capablanca:

"No other great master has been so misunderstood ... It was often said of Lasker that he had rather a dry style, that he could not play brilliantly and that his victories were chiefly the result of his uncanny endgame skill and of his opponent's mistakes. That he was a great endgame player is unquestionable; in fact, he was the greatest I have ever known. But he was also the most profound and imaginative player I have every known.

Even toward the end, during the great Nottingham Tournament (1936) when he was 68, his quick sight of the board was still notable. In this connection I am reminded of the following incident: I had just won a very important game and was on my way back to the hotel. During the course of the game my opponent built up a magnificent position. At a certain point he saw an opportunity to win the Exchange, and did so. Yet he lost the game! Some of the world's greatest masters, who were present, began to study the game. All of them began their investigations from the point where my opponent had won the Exchange, for they assumed that this had been the proper course, and that his error must have occurred later on. They spent a good deal of time on the game, and meanwhile Lasker came in. They told him how the game had ended and played it over for him; but when they came to the point where my opponent had won the Exchange, he interrupted them and said, 'Oh no, that move can't be right!' The aged master had realized at once what the others had failed to perceive: that the win of the Exchange was an error which lost not only the advantage, but the game itself. Lasker saw that it was not my opponent who had made a combination but I! Several hours later he met me in the hotel and said, 'You must have been relieved when your opponent swallowed the bait,' Then he added, 'These players are not so strong as most people think.'"

And so Lasker had been the only one who had correctly appraised the position and had been fully aware of the possibilities it contained.

GROWING PAINS

Of course, no one—not even a champion performer—is expected to be an insightful critic. It is said that Bill Tilden, the tennis great, could never pick a winner in any match. Bobby's judgment, or lack of it, may not affect the quality of his play. But his performances away from the board are, for the most part, interesting because of what they tell us about him as a human being; they shed little light on Bobby the chess master.

Still, the master lives in the man—not the other way around. Ironically, it was Emanuel Lasker who emphasized that chess involves a struggle of the total human personality in which the rounded man and not necessarily the better player is eventually bound to triumph. Perhaps in a few years we may feel, looking back, that many of his statements and much of his behavior simply reflected growing pains.

10. HELP, MATES!
August 22. 2005

If you don't solve this puzzle by grandmaster Pal Benko, you're in good company. Bobby Fischer once bet he could solve it in a half hour and lost. (Solution at end of chapter.)

White mates in 3 moves

Bobby then bet Benko he could find a second solution (called a cook) if he could study it overnight. He lost again. There is one and only one key move.

Benko no longer competes very often. Today he is a major problem composer whose specialty is "helpmates" where both sides collaborate to find the shortest way to mate. In other words, Black must help White to checkmate the Black king.

These unusual exercises are ingenious and infuriating. Solving them forces us to think backwards to envisage a mating pattern and then reach it the shortest possible way.

Here's how Benko explains this strange art form:

"The helpmate does not conflict with existing rules of play. The solver must find the only variation leading to mate—which should be cleverly hidden by the composer!—and do this with the cooperation of both sides. Black always moves first and must cooperate in finding the only sequence leading to checkmate."

Helpmate in 2 moves

Benko gives this simple example requiring underpromotion. The solution is 1 b2! (remember, Black always moves first) Kb3 2 b1/B! Bc3 mate. Okay?

Now substitute a White rook for the bishop on b4. The solution now is 1 b2! Kc3 2 b1/R! Ra4 mate. In each case Black had to help seal his own doom.

Solution: 1 Bc4! Kf6 (better than 1...Ke4? 2 Qd5 mate; or 1...Kf5 2 Qh5+ Kf6 3 Qg5 mate) 2 Qd6+ Kg7 (or 2...Kf5 3 Qe6) 3 Qh6. Composed by Pal Benko.

I I. KASPAROV RETIRES
June 20, 2005

Garry Kasparov, arguably the greatest player in history, stunned fans by retiring after he won a major tournament in March in Linares, Spain. It's the end of an era. We may never see his likes again, but he left the door open:

> "I won't quit completely. I'll write books, play exhibitions, but what else can I accomplish? I proved to myself I'm still the best. Twenty years as number one is good enough. I'm a man who needs a goal, and who wants to make a difference. My accomplishments and contributions are for others to judge, but I feel that I am no longer playing an essential role in chess. With reclaiming the unified world championship out of reach due to political chaos in the chess world, I am reduced to unfulfilling repetition."

Hikaru Nakamura, a 17-year-old who recently won the USA championship, summed up the mood of many rivals when he said, "Chess is dead."

But with Kasparov out of the way, FIDE gleefully invited eight stars to a tournament to crown its next champion. Vladimir Kramnik, who dethroned Kasparov in 2000, turned it down but offered to face the victor in a title match.

Meanwhile Kasparov, 42, threw his hat into the chaotic Russian political arena by chairing a group that opposes Vladimir Putin's reelection in 2008. At a Moscow rally someone asked for an autograph and then conked him over the head with a wooden chessboard. A while later, when he protested outside the court before oligarch Mikhail Khodorkovsky was convicted, Kasparov barely escaped a scuffle with the police.

"I doubt he's in real danger," an aide told me. "Everyone in Russia knows his name, but voters only take him seriously at chess. The Kremlin can use him to pretend that democracy is still alive and well in Russia." Kramnik noted, "I don't think he is in any personal danger. There are lots of people who speak out against Putin and nothing happens to them. A large part of the Russian press is oppositional, but they continue to exist and nobody does anything against them."

KASPAROV ON FISCHER RANDOM CHESS

"From my viewpoint, Fischer Random is entirely acceptable. But instead of 960 possible positions, most of which are poison to your eyes, downsize the number to 20 or 30. Simply pick one and play it for a year. Next year a different one. It goes without saying that a year later this whole theory that has developed will be of no use to anyone: move a single piece and the entire position changes radically. But at the same time, to entirely exclude opening preparation is unimaginable. In that case chess will turn into a very strange spectacle."

**Kasparov arriving for his last game
vs. Veselin Topalov**

KASPAROV'S LAST GAME?

In his first article for *New in Chess* (2005 #4), Kasparov stated:

"Although you will find few of my games in future editions of this magazine, for me chess is neither out of sight nor out of mind. This column will focus on contemporary goings-on, but I would like to begin with a look back at the place where my professional career ended: Linares."

With first place sewed up before the last round, Kasparov needed only a draw. Yet his mind was elsewhere and he let a rival catch him by missing

21...Qd8 22 Nf3 Qb6 23 d4 Qxb2 24 Rb1 Qxc3 25 Rxb7 Kd8 with good chances to hold. Later 27...h6! might still draw. Kasparov continued, saying, "In my final game against Topalov I lost all sense of danger. I knew I had won the event, which is what I came to do, and I played in a trance."

TOPALOV vs. KASPAROV
Sicilian Defense, 2005

1 e4 c5 2 Nf3 Nc6 3 Nc3 e5 4 Bc4 d6 5 d3 Be7 6 0-0 Nf6 7 Nh4 Nd4
8 g3 Bg4 9 f3 Be6 10 Bg5 Ng8 11 Bxe7 Nxe7 12 f4 exf4 13 Bxe6 fxe6
14 Rxf4 Kd7 15 Nf3 Rf8 16 Rxf8 Qxf8 17 Nxd4 cxd4 18 Ne2 Qf6 19
c3 Rf8 20 Nxd4 Nc6 21 Qf1 Qxf1? 22 Rxf1 Rxf1 23 Kxf1 Nxd4 24
cxd4 d5 25 Kf2 Ke7 26 Kf3 Kf6 27 h4 g6? 28 b4 b5 29 Kf4 h6 30 Kg4

Black Resigns

---

12. PASSING THE TORCH
Monday, October 24, 2005

"I guess many chess fans are starting to recall the last game Kasparov played before his retirement from professional chess—his loss to Topalov in the last round of Linares 2005. This game is getting a new (quite symbolic!) meaning—it's like Kasparov passed a torch to his successor in that game!"

—GM Alex Finkel

After Veselin Topalov, 30, captured the FIDE world championship in a field of eight stars at San Luis, Argentina, Garry Kasparov, 42, proclaimed, "The schism in the chess world is over. Now that Topalov is the best player in the world, the matter can be closed."

Not so fast! Classical World Champion Vladimir Kramnik, 30, declined his invitation to this tournament on principle, just as Kasparov himself declined to compete in FIDE's so-called title events. Many observers believe that a match with Topalov is now required to unify the title and heal the schism created by Kasparov when he broke away from FIDE in 1993.

Kasparov anointed Kramnik the rightful heir to his throne after losing to him in 2000. He called Kramnik the fourteenth world champion in a line extending back to Wilhelm Steinitz in the nineteenth century. Kasparov said only a match between the two best players could produce a legitimate titleholder, but now he has changed his tune. Maybe he's still miffed because Kramnik never agreed to a rematch.

A link with the past will be broken without a Topalov-Kramnik match. Topalov's manager said they would play, but Topalov ducked out a week later.

He argued that Kramnik's recent results did not make him a worthy challenger and he won't put his title on the line against someone rated 60 points below him. "That is a different class altogether," he said. Nonsense. This gap is trivial, and Kramnik was 79 points below Kasparov when he deposed him five years ago.

"If Topalov thinks he is stronger, let him beat me in a match," taunted Kramnik, who has a big plus score against the Bulgarian.

YES, NO, MAYBE

Everyone knows there is a vast difference between tournament play and match play. If a sponsor coughs up $2 million, a title match could happen next year—otherwise Kramnik will be left out in the cold (which seems to suit Kasparov).

All this wrangling reminds me of an old joke about the difference between a diplomat and a lady: If a diplomat says "yes," it means maybe. If a diplomat says "maybe," it means no. If a diplomat says "no," he's no diplomat. If a lady says "no," it means maybe. If a lady says "maybe," it means yes. If a lady says "yes," she's no lady.

FINAL STANDINGS

1. Veselin Topalov 10
2. Vishwanathan Anand 8½
3. Peter Svidler 8½
4. Alexander Morozevich 7
5. Peter Leko 6½
6. Rustam Kasimjanov 5½
7. Michael Adams 5½
8. Judit Polgar 4½

13. IS CHESS DYING?
October 3, 2005

The first computer world championship was held at Stockholm in 1975. That's ancient history. Artificial intelligence is still in its infancy, but hand-held programs already can find the best move in a split second. Nowadays there are two crowns: one for us and one for them.

In the early days of automation, Canada's Nathan Divinsky, a math professor and chess master, predicted:

> "Machines can certainly solve the mysteries of chess. As soon as this happens the game will vanish. It will become another mathematical theorem locked away in a cold book. Few will look at the body as it is buried. Few will know the details of the inhuman calculation. They will only know that a good and warm friend has perished."

Who knows what the future will bring? The speed of cars hasn't killed racing, and the agility of fish hasn't daunted swimmers. Still, many chess pros fear they might become obsolete. Who will pay to watch a contest that machines can do far better than humans? Perhaps the only sporting interest left for spectators will consist of comparing the move chosen by masters with the one recommended by computers.

Chess is the only game that spans the centuries and vaults all national borders. But today Bobby Fischer has abandoned what he calls "the old chess" and is pushing a random version that starts with a new lineup each game. Machines are addressing this challenge and it's just a matter of time before they unlock its secrets.

We are still learning new things even about basic endings. Contrary to conventional wisdom, machines proved that two bishops can defeat a lone knight 91.8 percent of the time—but most lines run afoul of the automatic 50-move draw rule.

What will happen on the day when two invincible machines clash? A draw is likely; yet just maybe White has a forced win. Nobody really knows.

This year endgame databases reached another milestone: they now can solve any position with up to six pieces on the board! GM John Nunn studied the result for *New in Chess* and was flabbergasted:

> "The impact proved to be far more substantial than I expected. The most remarkable discovery is that Black can draw in the diagram with his king in front of the pawns. Admittedly the defense is not easy, but from a normal starting position the side with the pawns cannot win. This result is utterly astonishing and counter-intuitive."

Only one move draws for black!

Solution: Many players would resign here with Black. It's hard to believe a powerful computer found the only defense. 1...Qb6!! 2 Kg5 Qh6+ 3 Kf5 Qf8+ 4 Qf6 Qc5+ 5 Ke4 Qb4+ 6 Qd4 Qe7+ 7 Kf3 Qf7+ 8 Qf4 Qb3+ 9 Qe3 Qf7+ 10 Kg3 Qc7+ 11 Kh3 Qc6 returning to a good square and White has not improved his position according to John Nunn who composed this endgame study.

14. LOSING BATTLE
August 1. 2005

"Grandmasters admit the odds are against them. So why keep tilting at windmills trying to beat machines?"

—*New York Times*

"It took thirteen years of brute-force computer analysis to examine all 500 billion billion possible board positions, but on July 19, 2007 researchers at the University of Alberta in Canada formally announced that they had finally solved the centuries-old game of checkers. It's a draw with best play."

—Associated Press

Before losing a close six-game match to an IBM supercomputer in 1997, Garry Kasparov claimed he was defending the honor of the human race.

"It's like landing on the moon," enthused the lead programmer who wrote a book entitled *Behind Deep Blue*, about this landmark in artificial intelligence. A documentary film *Game Over* also covered this epic encounter.

Angry and frustrated, Kasparov vowed to avenge this defeat. "I'll play again for all or nothing, winner take all, just to show it's not about money!" Since then he has held his own despite huge leaps in artificial intelligence, but clearly it's a losing battle.

Nowadays it's all about money, as computer firms shell out big bucks to hype their products. In June, FIDE champion Rustam Kasimdzhanov, 26, faced the Accoona Toolbar at ABC's Times Square studio in Manhattan. The Uzbekistan star was lured to the Big Apple by the challenge plus a fat fee.

"New York looks very normal, like any other place," said Rustam. "Until you look up! That is where the city is."

His silicon foe was a Fritz 9 prototype that can be installed as a browser on your hard drive at Accoona.com within seconds; and you can set the chess engine at different levels of skill. It learns from mistakes because each game played against users on the Net is sent to a central server that gets stronger as time goes by.

The program in this game ran on a simple, off-the-shelf notebook computer capable of analyzing more than a million positions per second to a depth of 15 moves, equipped with endgame tablebases enabling it to play perfect chess if there are five or less pieces on the board.

Three hundred spectators and a dozen cameras watched Rustam launch a slashing attack. Most experts thought he could win, yet the machine calmly forced a draw.

"I used too much time and could not overcome the terrible precision of this machine," he explained. "But I think sport is more about developing your inner qualities than about reaching a result. The gap between the strength of a human and a computer is not yet so big as the gap between a person trying to race a car."

Still, the days of machines vs. humans may soon be a thing of the past. A week later a different program named Hydra crushed Britain's leading grandmaster Michael Adams, ranked #7 in the world. He drew one and lost five! "Hydra proved to be far more powerful than anyone expected. There were only a few times where I was really in the game at all," he lamented.

KASIMDZHANOV vs. FRITZ ACCOONA
Ruy Lopez, June 21, 2005

1 e4 e5 2 Nf3 Nc6 3 Bb5 a6 4 Ba4 Nf6 5 0-0 Be7 6 Re1 b5 7 Bb3 d6 8 c3 0-0 9 h3 Na5 10 Bc2 c5 11 d4 Qc7 12 d5 Nc4 13 a4 Bd7 14 b3 Nb6 15 a5 Nc8 16 c4 Bd8 17 Nc3 b4 18 Ne2 Nh5 19 g4 Nf6 20 Ng3 h6 21 Be3 Re8 22 Kh2 Rb8 23 Qd2 Kh7 24 Rg1 Ne7 25 g5 hxg5 26 Nxg5 Kg8 27 Qe2 Ng6 28 Nf5 Bxf5 29 exf5 Nf4 30 Qf3 Qe7 31 Bxf4 exf4 32 Ne6! fxe6 33 fxe6 Rf8 34 Qd3 Rb7 35 Rg5 Qe8 36 Rag1 f3 37 R1g3 Kh8 38 Rxf3 Rg8 39 Rg6 Rf8 40 Rg5 Rg8 41 Rg6 Rf8 42 Rg5 **Draw**

---

15. GAME OVER
September 23, 2003

Garry Kasparov's landmark loss to Deep Blue in 1997 captured headlines and even caused ripples in the stock market. On the next day IBM stock rose 15 percent and their machine was soon converted to other uses.

Kasparov promptly accused IBM of cheating. The petulant world champion told reporters he was defending the honor of the human race, and he has been crying the blues ever since. Was he just a sore loser or was Deep Blue yellow?

In an open letter on the Net, IBM's lead programmer Feng-hsiung Hsu indignantly stated, "Unfortunately, Kasparov repeated his groundless and false accusations, changing from one conspiracy to another as time wore on. I took it as a personal insult, and I doubt that any corporate officer would think otherwise...It is a shame there won't be a new match, but the two previous ones were the most exciting experiences in my life. Kasparov, our worthy opponent, played the central role in these experiences."

A joke made the rounds at the time: Q. How do you know when Kasparov's plane has arrived? A. The engines stop, but the whining continues.

An editorial in the *New York Times* opined, "Maybe no one feels threatened by the humdrum number-crunching of computers that figure payrolls or mimic wind tunnels. But chess programs are invading the special human domain of creativity. Soon new gambits and openings will be named after programs, not people. Is that a victory or defeat for human intelligence and creativity?"

Game Over: Kasparov and the Machine made its debut September 2003 to rave reviews at the Toronto Film Festival. The full-length documentary was directed by Vikram Jayanti, who won awards for *When We Were Kings* (about the epic Foreman vs. Ali bout in Africa) and *The Man Who Bought Mustique*.

Jayanti intersperses archival footage with interviews of computer nerds and chess geeks. "This suspenseful film doesn't disguise its sympathy for

49

Kasparov...It has less to do with the advance of computer science and more to do with a nasty mix of bruised egos and corporate arrogance run amok. It speculates on the limits of the human mind and how truth can never be fully known," observed one reviewer.

The *Washington Times* noted, "There is a conspiratorial tone to this probing film with tracking shots that stalk through dark corridors, hushed narration and seditious score. And there is Kasparov, still fiercely bitter about the outcome. It's an incisive overview of the most notorious chess match ever played, an ultimately unfriendly contest delving into psychological warfare, paranoia, accusations and defenses. 'I'm a human being. When I see something that is well beyond my understanding, I'm afraid,' said a dispirited Kasparov."

Kasparov collapsed in the sixth and last game, claiming he felt "ashamed" of an obvious mistake. Perhaps the real reason he lost is that intimidation, which works with human opponents who fear him, proved futile against a machine that couldn't be intimidated. This time it was the other way around.

16. WAR FOR THE CROWN
June 27, 2005

"Chess is a dirty game," declares Dominic Lawson in his book, *End Game: Dispatches from a War for the World Chess Crown*, about a thrilling bout between British challenger Nigel Short and Russia's Garry Kasparov sponsored by the *Times of London* for $2.5 million in 1993.

All 20 games are cited without analysis because the focus is on the *Inner Game* (its British title). Lawson's story is candidly told from inside the Short camp where he was privy to the treachery and intrigue taking place behind the scenes at a pivotal moment in chess history.

Garry Kimovich Kasparov, the thirteenth world champion, was born in the oil city of Baku in 1963, the only child of an Armenian mother and Jewish father. In 1985 he fought his way to a title match with Anatoly Karpov.

FIDE tried to stop Kasparov, but he won the rematch and vowed to take revenge on "the chess Mafia." His chance came in 1993 when he and Short audaciously created the PCA (Professional Chess Association) to seize the title, FIDE's main source of income. FIDE retaliated by purging the two rebels from its rating list.

The story of this failed revolution was told by Lawson, an astute eyewitness. He rightly wondered whether Kasparov could convince his colleagues that he was a more desirable despot than FIDE president Florencio Campomanes.

For two months Kasparov and Short were like "two prisoners locked in the same cell" in this grueling test of willpower and stamina. Short put up a great fight before succumbing 20½-7½, but it pained him when top British players he thought were friends attacked him publicly for joining Kasparov's crusade.

The book chronicles his sense of betrayal upon hearing the tape of a secret meeting with Kasparov and his advisors. "He's not a man of principle. Of course, it's my own fault for doing a deal with one of the most unpleasant people in the chess world," said Short bitterly. After the match began, Lawson describes Short's agony in having to discard his mentor Lubomir Kavalek, an act Short described as "parricide."

"I have attempted to describe much more than just the moves that the greatest chess players make on the board," writes Lawson. "I have also tried to reveal the psychological tricks of their trade and how such men set up their defenses in advance against the low mental blows of their enemies."

The author succeeded admirably. His book can be relished even by someone who never pushed a pawn.

17. TURNING POINT
March 27, 2006

When the World Trade Center went down in 2001, it was a grim reminder of the Kasparov-Anand match for the PCA World Championship held there in 1995. An instant book aptly titled, *On Top of the Chess World*, omitted such basic information as a round-by-round score table.

FIDE got no cut of the prize money and did not recognize the victor as world champion. The $1.5 million duel, sponsored by Intel, began with a record string of eight draws as tension mounted in this best-of-20 series.

"We both basically agreed with each other that we didn't have a clue what was going on," said Anand, who accepted a draw in game six during a complex battle after only 28 moves. Their games weren't dull, just abandoned too soon. Fans who made a special trip to New York and bought tickets felt cheated.

The 1966 Petrosian-Spassky match began with six straight draws. "When am I ever going to win a game?" moaned challenger Spassky. "Lose one first," quipped savvy ex-champ Botvinnik, who figured it would either demoralize Spassky or "stir the passion that whips the blood" (as Emanuel Lasker put it). Petrosian defended his title in that match but lost it to Spassky three years later.

Garry Kasparov, then 32, was the first to lose a game (#9) against challenger Vishy Anand, then 25. Kasparov heeded this wake-up call with a dazzling victory in game 10 to even the score at 5-5 at the halfway mark. Since Kasparov would keep his title on a tie, each draw now nudged him closer to victory.

Game 11 was the turning point that quashed Anand's dreams of glory. Kasparov surprised him by adopting the Dragon Variation of the Sicilian Defense for the first time. Anand refused a draw after move 19 and gained an advantage before going astray. Kasparov compared it with game 47 of his epic first match against Anatoly Karpov who also declined a draw in an equal endgame and then lost.

Anand failed to exploit a subtle error by Kasparov (26...Rb8 was called for) and then missed a chance to snare a pawn with winning chances by 28 Nxe7! Re8 29 b4 axb4 30 axb4 Rc4 31 Nd5 Bxd5 32 Rxd5 Rxb4 (no better is 32...Rec8 33 c3! Rxc3 34 Re2) 33 Kc3 Rc4 34 Kb3 Rec8 35 Re2.

Instead Anand fell for a trap by 30 Rb6? (even now 30 c3! Bxd5 31 Rxd5 Rxc3 32 Re2 holds a draw) and threw in the towel because 32 Rxc2 Rb3 33 Ka2 Re3 spells fini.

The outcome of the match never was in doubt after this fiasco. Kasparov surged ahead with 10½-7½ and the last four games were drawn without much fight. The average length of all 18 games was fewer than 30 moves!

Ten years later, at 42, Kasparov retired from tournament chess to enter Russia's risky political arena. He is arguably the greatest player in history and it's unlikely that his phenomenal record ever will be surpassed.

"My life is very busy. I'm writing books, politics takes a lot of time, and I'm doing speeches for banks and corporations about decision-making. I travel probably even more than when I played chess," said Kasparov recently.

ANAND vs. KASPAROV
Sicilian Defense #11, New York, 1995

1 e4 c5 2 Nf3 d6 3 d4 cxd4 4 Nxd4 Nf6 5 Nc3 g6 6 Be3 Bg7 7 f3 0–0 8 Qd2 Nc6 9 Bc4 Bd7 10 0–0–0 Ne5 11 Bb3 Rc8 12 h4 h5 13 Kb1 Nc4 14 Bxc4 Rxc4 15 Nde2 b5 16 Bh6 Qa5 17 Bxg7 Kxg7 18 Nf4 Rfc8 19 Ncd5 Qxd2 20 Rxd2 Nxd5 21 Nxd5 Kf8 22 Re1 Rb8 23 b3 Rc5 24 Nf4 Rbc8 25 Kb2 a5 26 a3 Kg7? 27 Nd5 Be6 28 b4? axb4 29 axb4 Rc4 30 Nb6?? Rxb4 31 Ka3 Rxc2 **White Resigns**

---

18. KASPAROV TIES MACHINE
March 24, 2003

It's just a matter of time before computers beat the best humans. Technology is advancing so fast that in a few years the chess skills of machines will be far ahead of ours.

In 1997 a 16-year-old Japanese student was seeded into FIDE's first qualification event for the crown in Holland but he was surprisingly denied school leave because his principal said chess was no longer a serious pursuit after IBM's Deep Blue beat world champ Garry Kasparov 3½-2½ by crushing him in game six.

This February in New York, Deep Junior, a $50 software program that runs on Windows, tied the top rated star 3-3. Kasparov earned half a million dollars for showing up and split another half million with the machine. He won the first game, lost the third, and drew four others.

"I had one item on my agenda: not to lose. I'm quite satisfied with this performance," said a cautious Kasparov, promptly declaring that Deep Junior was even stronger than the program that beat him in 1997.

Game Five, the shortest one, was his last chance to win with White. The audience gasped at a dubious sacrifice on move 10 that came as a real blow. A critical line to avoid repetition of moves was 16 g3 Nh2 17 Kf2 Ng4 18 Ke1 Qh3 19 Rg1 Nd7 20 Kd1 Ndf6. White is a piece up with no clear win and problems untangling his pieces.

Kasparov dared not risk this line over the board and said he was also worried about 16...Qh2 cutting off his king's escape and leaving it vulnerable for the rest of the game.

KASPAROV vs. DEEP JUNIOR
#5 Nimzo-Indian Defense, 2003

1 d4 Nf6 2 c4 e6 3 Nc3 Bb4 4 e3 0-0 5 Bd3 d5 6 cxd5 exd5 7 Nge2 Re8 8 0-0 Bd6 9 a3 c6 10 Qc2 Bxh2!? 11 Kxh2 Ng4 12 Kg3 Qg5 13 f4 Qh5 14 Bd2 Qh2 15 Kf3 Qh4 16 Bxh7 Kh8 17 Ng3 Nh2 18 Kf2 Ng4 19 Kf3 Nh2 **Draw**

---

19. THE FIRST BYTE

June 19, 2006

"Machines are in the saddle and ride mankind."
—Ralph Waldo Emerson (1841)

In California in 1988 grandmaster Bent Larsen acquired the dubious honor of being the strongest player ever to lose a tournament game to a computer. Deep Thought tied for first with GM Anthony Miles to earn a 2598 rating, but USCF rules disqualified it from winning prize money.

That was only the first byte. In 1988 Deep Thought also shared first in the U.S. Open and captured the Pennsylvania State Championship, a grim harbinger of things to come.

A group called WOCIT (We Oppose Computers in Tournaments) persuaded the USCF not to force players to face machines if they put it in writing before the tournament began. A growing number of refuseniks included ex-world champ Mikhail Tal.

"I didn't know there was a list I could sign not to play it," moaned Larsen.

When news of Larsen's loss reached England, GM Nigel Short exclaimed, "My God! Why are computers trying to ruin chess? Maybe I should start to look for a second career."

Instead of destroying chess, machines made it more popular than ever before. But will public interest decline if they consistently beat the best humans? Although still in their infancy, computers already are so strong that world champions are glad to draw with them. Just ask Garry Kasparov or Vladimir Kramnik.

Deep Thought was named after a super-computer created by aliens in Douglas Adams's cult sci-fi novel The Hitchhiker's Guide to the Galaxy. Deep Thought morphed into Deep Blue when IBM hired the team that vanquished Larsen.

Other big firms like Intel and Microsoft jumped on the bandwagon. Pepsi even aired a commercial with Kasparov during the Super Bowl.

As sales of chess machines soared, the *Wall Street Journal* reported a new problem: "The people who make chess computers may be checkmating themselves by making the gizmos too good. The computers are getting so strong that people won't buy them, because they'd never be able to beat them."

Sid Samole of Fidelity Electronics, a pioneer in the field, said he was "terrified" that potential buyers might be scared away. But what to do about it? Realizing it was smart to be dumb, his ingenious solution was to let buyers adjust the level to match their own skill. Sid passionately loved chess, and his son constructed the Chess Hall of Fame in Miami as a tribute to his father's memory.

Syndicated columnist Charles Krauthammer, an avid player whose game room contains a game by Napoleon framed on the wall, wrote an article about Larsen's defeat. "Machines beat man in just about every field of endeavor, and we will get used to that in chess too. What is troubling about Deep Thought beating Larsen is not that man lost to another species (one which we created, remember). It is that art and intuition lost to brute mechanical force."

Larsen bytes the dust in this historic encounter. It could have gone either way until he missed 26 Rhg1! or 27 Kb1! on the next move to provide sanctuary for his bishop on b2.

LARSEN vs. DEEP THOUGHT
English Opening Software Toolworks Open, California, 1988

1 c4 e5 2 g3 Nf6 3 Bg2 c6 4 Nf3 e4 5 Nd4 d5 6 cxd5 Qxd5 7 Nc2 Qh5 8 h4 Bf5 9 Ne3 Bc5 10 Qb3 b6 11 Qa4 0-0 12 Nc3 b5 13 Qc2 Bxe3 14 dxe3 Re8 15 a4 b4 16 Nb1 Nbd7 17 Nd2 Re6 18 b3 Rd8 19 Bb2 Bg6 20 Nc4 Nd5 21 0-0-0 N7f6 22 Bh3 Bf5 23 Bxf5 Qxf5 24 f3 h5 25 Bd4 Rd7 26 Kb2?! Rc7 27 g4? hxg4 28 Rhg1 c5 29 fxg4 Nxg4 30 Bxg7 Rg6 31 Qd2 Rd7 32 Rxg4 Rxg4 33 Ne5 Nxc3 34 Qxd7 Nxd1+ 35 Qxd1 Rg3 36 Qd6 Rxd7 37 Nd7 Re3 38 Qh2 Rh7 39 Nf8+ Kh8 40 h5 Qd5 41 Ng6+ fxg6 42 hxg6+ Kg7 43 Qh7+ Kf6 **Black Resigns**

---

20. HAIL THE UNKNOWN!
August 30, 2004

The wonderful thing about chess is that just one game can make you famous. Even if you lose.

"Where individual genius will come from is totally unpredictable. Occasionally we come across a game that bears the unmistakable stamp of real creative genius," said Reuben Fine in *The World's Great Chess Games*.

Losers bask in the reflected glory of negative immortality because great games live forever. Today, William Ewart Napier is chiefly remembered for his brilliant loss to Emanuel Lasker at Cambridge Springs in 1904. Napier considered it the finest game he ever played.

At an obscure tournament in Argentina in 1980, Gustavo Mahia, a 19-year-old unknown, created a gem destined for the anthologies. His victim, Miguel Quinteros, had been an aide to Bobby Fischer.

Nobody heard of Mahia again. In the words of Gray's Elegy, "Full many a flower is born to blush unseen, and waste its sweetness on the desert air."

Mahia's combination is dubious, but who cares? It's beautiful. 15 Bf6! steered into treacherous waters. The move had been played before and Quinteros prudently declined to capture this bishop by 15...gxf6. He went astray later when 17... Bc5! refutes the attack.

Still, White's fantastic sacrifice on move 24 elevates this game to greatness. It's always wondrous to behold a thunderbolt that shatters the enemy on the spot.

As Keats observed, "A thing of beauty is a joy forever."

MAHIA vs. QUINTEROS
Sicilian Defense, Los Polvorines, 1980

1 e4 c5 2 Nf3 d6 3 d4 cxd4 4 Nxd4 Nf6 5 Nc3 a6 6 Bg5 e6 7 f4 Qb6 8 Qd2 Qxb2 9 Rb1 Qa3 10 e5 dxe5 11 fxe5 Nfd7 12 Be2 Bb4 13 Rb3 Qa5 14 0–0 0–0 15 Bf6!? Nxf6 16 exf6 Rd8 17 fxg7 Rxd4 18 Qh6 Qe5 19 Ne4 Qxe4 20 Bh5 Rd7 21 Rd3 Bc5 22 Kh1 Bd4 23 Rg3 Nc6 24 Bg6!! Qxg6 25 Rxg6 Ne7 26 Rxf7 Kxf7 27 g8/Q Nxg8 28 Qxh7 **Black Resigns**

---

21. WAR GAMES
June 14, 2004

Nobody knows the origin of some ancient board games. One myth has is that a Buddhist priest sat down one day and invented chess as a bloodless substitute for war.

FACT OR FICTION?

"How about a nice game of chess?" asks the computer in the movie *WarGames* after a hacker nearly starts World War III by accident.

Recently, the Australian Defense Force conducted a 2½-year study to see if chess strategy really is a useful guide in warfare. "Those familiar with Harry Potter and the Philosopher's Stone would know just how important chess can be," stated their official newspaper.

SCIENTISTS PLAY WAR GAMES

A team led by mathematician Greg Calbert played thousands of computer-generated games "to mimic the fog and friction of war." Some games began in an equal position, usually not the case in real life, but others added "asymmetries," in which one side either had no queen or had an extra rook. Options also allowed machines to make several moves in a row or pieces were hidden from the enemy to test the value of stealth.

"The opposition could have greater resources, but we found that good planning and tempo will nearly always win," said Calbert, who also factored in the quality of troops, loss of life and the level of political support at home.

One of his goals was to teach computers how to get smarter on their own "to provide a better understanding of the future battlefield" and defeat enemies who have greater force. Calbert used a cluster of Apple Xserve computers to crunch the numbers.

"They can mimic humans and learn from experience," he said. "America also is applying this model to other areas from ecology to economics. It's limitless."

Skeptics may wonder if this work is valid or practical, but it's a great way to get more funding. Let's hope—for now, at least—that *WarGames* remains just a movie and doesn't become a reality. Its essential message is "The only move is not to play."

22. DILEMMA OF PROFESSIONAL CHESS
August 23, 2004

"Chess is my profession. I am my own boss. I am free."
—Danish GM Bent Larsen

This controversial article appeared in the April 2004 issue of *Chess Life*, where part of it was omitted for lack of space. It was recently voted the year's Best Editorial by the Chess Journalists of America. Here is the complete 3,500-word text.

AH, FOR THE GOOD OLD DAYS!
"It has become abundantly clear that men and women of good conscience can no longer support FIDE in the face of its hapless organizational bungling and callous destruction of professional careers."
—American GM Yasser Seirawan (2003)

What happened to the unification match that was supposed to produce one world champion as called for at the vaunted Prague Agreement in 2002? Why is international sponsorship drying up? How did the chess world become so divided? I will attempt to answer some of these questions here.

The Professional Chess Association (PCA) was launched on February 26, 1993, by world champion Garry Kasparov and Nigel Short before their $2.5 million title match sponsored by the *London Times*. "So it's to be Short and it will be short," quipped Kasparov upon learning the name of his challenger (who eliminated Anatoly Karpov and then Jan Timman, to reach the top).

In his book *End Game* (1993), Dominic Lawson reported on a meeting he attended between both players in London a day before their press conference announcing the PCA. "Kasparov launched into a lengthy description of how the PCA should be run. 'The world champion,' he pronounced, 'should of course have the dominant role.' Nigel, who had been nodding patiently up till then, interrupted. 'If I have been nodding, Garry,' he said, 'that does not mean I necessarily agree with you. It just means I understand what you say.' Kasparov leapt up from his chair. 'Oh! Oh! Now we have crisis! Major crisis!' I suddenly felt sorry for Nigel. It was bad enough to play chess for two months against Kasparov. But to do business with him looked to be, if anything, more unpleasant."

Their games were exciting and hard-fought, and Kasparov won decisively. He has done more to popularize chess than anyone else, yet some rivals detest him. Short referred to him as an animal: "He's not a man of principle. Of course, it's my own fault for doing a deal with one of the most unpleasant people in the chess world. He does all this staring, pacing up and down the tournament hall like a baboon. He can't deal with people at all and has no normal relationships. It's master-slave; that's all he can understand."

"I beat a lot of people and made a lot of enemies," shrugged Kasparov.

SLAYING THE DRAGON

FIDE retaliated by purging Kasparov and Short from its ranking list. They were both restored after a worldwide outcry pointing out that ratings were supposed to measure performance, not punish dissenters. It was clear FIDE couldn't even be trusted to maintain the integrity of the rating system, so the PCA established its own list (now defunct).

Incorporated in the United States by Wall Street lawyer Bob Rice, the organization entered into a $6.5 million contract with Intel. Hopes ran high and PCA Commissioner Rice waxed ecstatic: "It's a modern sophisticated sports marketing contract, allowing for the participation of other sponsors under specific terms and conditions. The chess world has never seen anything like it. Basically, Intel has put chess on the map with other professional sports."

Kasparov stated in a prologue to *A New Era* (Ballantine Books, 1997): "I believe that within a few years we'll be able to build the heart and guts of a new professional world of chess. Under our new setup, there is no relationship between the PCA and FIDE. None of the directors of the PCA was paid. No one controlled the PCA, including me. We created a board in which my voting rights were equal to those of any of the other four members. Today our organization unambiguously declares that rapid chess is our priority activity!"

Kasparov, and many others including Reuben Fine and Bobby Fischer, pointed out that a Soviet-dominated FIDE had mismanaged the title ever since it assumed control after Alekhine died in 1946. At first I applauded Kasparov for slaying the dragon of FIDE. "The PCA is for grandmasters what the Emancipation Proclamation was for slaves," I noted at my induction into the U.S. Chess Hall of Fame in 1994.

"It might appear that Kasparov and Short were on a somewhat short fuse and perhaps overreacted to the decision of the World Chess Federation to place the match without properly consulting them," wrote British GM Raymond Keene. "However, this judgment would overlook the long history of friction between top players and FIDE which culminated in the current breakaway."

Keene went on to explain why FIDE president Florencio Campomanes and Kasparov were at odds: "Had the umpire in any other sport stepped in, as Campo did in 1985 to halt the Kasparov-Karpov match without result at its most interesting and climactic stage, that unfortunate official would undoubtedly have been lynched. FIDE got away with this act of dubious prestidigitation, but inevitably there were consequences."

Indeed, Kasparov contemplated a split with FIDE after he won the title and created the Grandmasters Association (GMA) in 1986. He asked this writer and GM Keene to prepare a document to justify this radical course of action. We submitted 64 reasons why FIDE is unfit to govern chess, one for each square on the board. When we three met in Madrid in 1988 during a rapid chess match between Russia and the Rest of the World, Kasparov agreed with our points but decided the time wasn't ripe to start the revolution without backing from the GMA board of directors.

The GMA was cofounded by Kasparov and Belgian impresario Bessel Kok and lasted from 1986 until 1989. And the organization was discontinued after staging an impressive Grand Prix series offering the highest prizes ever seen in chess tournaments. On the way out of a frustrating meeting with the FIDE leadership, Kok whispered to Kasparov, "I've never seen so many people in one room who hate chess so much." Alas, the GMA perished after a falling out between Kasparov and Kok that had tragic consequences for professional chess.

"We missed the opportunity to reform chess in 1989," lamented Kasparov. "As Jan Timman has correctly written, FIDE was our common enemy. Kok negotiated with FIDE; I directly opposed such a move. If the GMA had not proceeded down the path of compromise with FIDE in 1989, chess history might have turned out quite differently. The political strength of the GMA on its own was so imposing that FIDE would have been unable to do anything to oppose it. Because it accommodated FIDE, the GMA lost its influence and its battle for leadership in the chess world."

TROUBLE IN PARADISE

After the birth of the PCA and the deal with Intel, it became apparent there was trouble in paradise. GM Valery Salov, who was ranked in the top ten, accused the PCA of excluding him from its lucrative series of rapid tournaments in Moscow, Munich, New York, Paris, and London. The PCA also unveiled a Code of Conduct supposedly based on disciplinary measures in tennis and golf with fines for violations ranging up to $25,000. "Some rules raised the eyebrows and the ire of a few observers," noted *Chess Life*:

• "Players must speak positively about all sponsors and the PCA when talking to the press or public."
• "Players and members of their delegations must not slander or libel PCA officers, organizers or sponsors. Players are responsible for the actions of acknowledged members of their delegation."
• "At public appearances, correct dress must be worn at all times; jacket, shirt and tie; no jeans or sneakers. This applies both to players and their delegations."

These rules were cooked up by the "democratic" PCA without any input from the top players. The dress code particularly irked a chess fan in Minneapolis who sent me a copy of an indignant letter he wrote to the editor of *Chess Life*:

"Chess is changing, but is it changing for the better? In chess as in other sports, change is too often dictated not by what is good for the game but by what is profitable. We play our best when comfortable in our attire. It's nothing short of amazing that many people still make an issue out of trivial external characteristics. Is it really asking too much for chess to remain above the mindset that article of clothing A is somehow better than article of clothing B? Suits and ties probably translate into more money, and this is the bottom line. Money talks, and it talks a lot louder than integrity and the well-being of chess."

THE GAG RULE

Other portions of the code were blasted by this writer and FIDE champion Karpov, who disliked the odious provision that punished players for acts committed by their delegation. GM Yasser Seirawan, a frequent critic of Kasparov in those days, also sounded an alarm in his regular *Inside Chess* editorial:

"There are a number of issues at stake here. One is 'Free Speech.' The second is, 'Who determines proper behavior?' If Kasparov makes annoying faces during my game with him, can I calmly call for an arbiter and tell him that Garry's next smirk should cost him at least $50? A pleasant prospect, but difficult to enforce."

The first victim of the gag rule was 21-year-old Gata Kamsky. In 1995 he balked at signing the code before playing 25-year-old Vishy Anand, who won their match to become Kasparov's next challenger atop the ill-fated World Trade Center in Manhattan. At a press conference Kamsky complained that the PCA sliced its $200,000 purse in half. He was fined $1,500 on the spot.

"Kamsky's treatment was truly despicable," opined former *Chess Life* editor Larry Parr.

"Oh, yes, I know that his pugnacious father angers people; but the job of the PCA is not to get even with him by punishing his son. I interviewed Kasparov a number of times, but friendship did not cloud my judgment or blind me to his egotism. He is a chess genius, but the gag rule and blacklisting players is the kind of thing we had come to expect of FIDE, not the PCA. How has the PCA demonstrated its moral superiority to FIDE?"

Even three-time USA champion Lev Alburt, a pal of Kasparov, told the *New York Times*, "Kamsky probably said a number of unpleasant things, but I don't think the PCA treated him very fairly. An organization that conducts championships must be objective, show no favorites, no bias. To build it around the world champion just doesn't look right to me, doesn't look like it has a future."

The PCA shackled top players with silly rules instead of tackling problems such as prearranged draws or the impact of big money on speed games. Perhaps the newly created Association of Chess Professionals led by French GM Joel Lautier will deal with these issues as well as the burning question of whether pros must submit to drug tests in order for chess politicians in certain countries to remain eligible to receive funds from their national Olympic committees. It's a safe bet that none of it will be used to provide grandmasters with health care or retirement benefits.

"This intolerable situation, where we can see our sport crumble to pieces with every traditional tournament that disappears and the media interest in our game dwindling dramatically, has prompted us to act and create a new organization," said GM Lautier. "Matches for the reunification have been announced and cancelled several times over the past year by the FIDE President. The final result looks like a joke: the official FIDE World Champion, Ruslan Ponomariov, is now offered a spot in the first round of a knockout tournament while his challenger Kasparov has somehow taken his place since he will only play the final match against the winner of the knockout tournament. Not even in the troubled boxing world do you see such an absurd situation where the current champion has to qualify to gain the right to meet his 'challenger'! I'm certain that Kasparov himself finds that situation a little strange, to say the least."

In an interview with *New in Chess* (2003, #7), Garry Kasparov stated: "We live in the shadows. I hope chess players recognize that unless you get corporate sponsorship the game will die. Now if FIDE wants me to play a match, I will insist on a deposit of the loser's share before I sign any contract again. Also I was a bit upset that FIDE president Ilyumzhinov broke his own rules. Because FIDE, with all its bad things, always stuck to one principle, that the title was theirs. They disqualified Fischer and Kasparov, but they stumbled with Ponomariov who, with all respect, doesn't have the same status as Fischer or Kasparov. He was given five deadlines over six months and eventually FIDE didn't even take away his title. According to the Assembly in Bled and the FIDE presidential board, he was supposed to be replaced with Ivanchuk. But they couldn't because of political intrigues and Ukrainian money and this inability of FIDE to disqualify Ponomariov shows the misery of present day chess."

END OF THE LINE

In January 1996 Kasparov announced that the deal with Intel was dead. "I am fed up with being an Intel slave for the benefit of other players. I'm going to play [IBM's] Deep Blue. Intel doesn't want that match to be played," he said, running afoul of his gag rule by criticizing a sponsor.

There never was a public accounting of PCA finances or how much any of the directors received for their services. "Everyone worked essentially without pay for the good of the organization," insisted Kasparov. "$6.5 million represents the exact amount that was spent on chess. And if people want to try to calculate the amount spent—even Grandmaster Valery Salov or Rustam Kamsky, the father of American Grandmaster Gata Kamsky—they should take out their calculators and start punching keys to learn how much it costs to put on one tournament."

In 1997 the PCA collapsed.

WAR WITH FIDE

After declaring Spanish IM Ricardo Calvo persona non grata because of a letter he wrote to *New In Chess* in 1986 criticizing Campomanes, FIDE pushed for a "Code of Ethics." Under this abominable code, truth would be no defense for "insults" uttered by players away from the board. This gambit violated FIDE statutes and was quashed, but that didn't stop Campo from abusing his authority by stepping into the 65th square.

At India in 1995, during the Kamsky-Salov qualifying match to find a challenger for FIDE champion Karpov, Campo fined Kamsky for "inappropriate utterances" made by his father, who accused the organizers of welshing on expense money. "I had a big fight with Campomanes, who is almost as dirty as Kasparov," said Kamsky aide GM Roman Dzindzichashvili. "He is a dangerous maniac who makes new rules all by himself and then immediately executes them."

Campo left FIDE on the brink of bankruptcy and later was convicted of embezzlement. Kalmykian dictator Kirsan Ilyumzhinov replaced him in 1995 and poured over $30 million into chess. "If he spent it on a Federation Intent on destroying chess the result would not be worse," stated AP reporter Robert Huntington in an open letter to the chess world. "Corporate sponsors don't see incompetent scheduling or his misguided attempts to get chess into the Olympics. Instead, they see stories of corruption coming out of Kalmykia, endless investigations concerning vanished millions by authorities in Moscow, his ties to Saddam Hussein, the murder of Larisa Yudina, and they look for something more reputable to sponsor. It is obvious what must be done is to get rid of Ilyumzhinov even if it means bankrupting FIDE."

Chess czar Kirsan gets what he wants because FIDE now depends upon his largesse for its survival. A journalist once described the spectacle of FIDE insiders standing in a receiving line while Kirsan handed out jars of caviar, his autobiography (*Crown of Thorns*) and gold Rolex watches.

"What a shame that FIDE is run by a wealthy lunatic and a horde of beggars," observed IM Jack Peters, chess columnist for the *Los Angeles Times*.

Kirsan changed time controls several times without consulting the grandmasters that were at the mercy of his whims. He also created a permanent medical commission with the power to ban players who refuse to be drug tested even though there are no steroids of the mind. Clearly chess is not an athletic sport, but his pretext for testing (including out-of-competition tests!) was to get chess into the Summer or Winter Olympics. When the International Olympic Committee flatly rejected chess, as expected, that didn't deter Kirsan's ongoing dope-testing campaign. It probably will succeed—in driving players away from a game where machines, which don't have to be drug tested, can now beat almost everyone.

TRADING KINGS

Kasparov, who turned 41 this April, has been rated number one for almost twenty years, a feat unprecedented in modern times. Along the way he lost only two matches; one to a machine, the other to a human. "Deep Blue was not obnoxious. It was simply nothing at all, an empty chair—not an opponent but something empty and relentless," he said, then promptly accused IBM of cheating.

After dethroning him in 2000, Vladimir Kramnik observed: "Kasparov needed an opponent for a world championship match. I did not ask for it. They ignored Shirov, who had earned the right to play and then asked Anand, who did not agree to play. Then they asked me. Nobody really expected me to win. Now things have changed."

Despite these setbacks, most experts consider Kasparov the greatest player in history. The rap against him is that after blasting Campo for years as a fiend incarnate, as "the leader of the chess mafia, a man who will do anything for money," he betrayed his supporters and destroyed his own credibility by twisting arms to get his old foe a fourth term as FIDE president. Here's what happened.

Campo was not on the ballot as a candidate, so the FIDE Congress at Moscow in 1994 needed to change its rules at the last minute. It all depended on what stand America took. Kasparov phoned USCF Executive Director Al Lawrence in New York to demand that the American delegate, the late Fanueil Adams, change his vote and support Campo. Lawrence immediately contacted most of the board members who reversed their policy on the spot. Campo gloated, but not for long. A year later in Paris, Adams forced his ouster.

By choosing opportunism over principle, Kasparov became a general without troops. Sponsors grew wary and colleagues distrusted him. "I admit I had some sympathy with Kasparov in 1993, though when he supported Campomanes in 1994, that sympathy vanished," said a chess fan on an Internet newsgroup. "It's clear the PCA stands for Kasparov's Personal Chess Association and his credibility is already wearing thin, especially with the defection of Short back to FIDE," observed another fan.

Acutely aware of his predicament, Kasparov later offered a murky justification for his U-turn: neither of the two announced candidates suited him! "It might appear that my relationship with Campomanes has been inconsistent, but an internal logic was always present. The PCA supported him for president because we felt he was the only one who was experienced in finding sponsors and collecting money for chess at FIDE. I believe it was important for FIDE and the PCA to present a united front, especially so that commercial sponsors would not be confused or put off by our internal misunderstandings. Unfortunately, FIDE rejected our proposal outright."

In 1995 they went ahead and elected Kirsan Ilyumzhinov and his castles in the sky.

All of Kasparov's flip-flops and intrigues contributed to the demise of the PCA in 1997. Now he made a deal to play the next FIDE champion a match for the FIDE title. Will Kramnik, who beat him fair and square, be left out in the cold?

Today there are distressing signs that FIDE is returning to its old ways. In February FIDE Vice President Ignatius Leong stated: "Players in the FIDE cycle who also play in another should be expelled from FIDE. Players in events which involve the expelled players shall also be expelled. I'm not a dictator, but if a player doesn't love FIDE, I don't see any reason why FIDE should be so sympathetic towards him. By these, I also mean stripping off titles and ratings."

Ironically, after accusing Campo and Ilyumzhinov of making rules without consulting top players, Kasparov did the same thing himself.

Why trade one king for another?

23. SUSAN POLGAR VS. FIDE
January 24, 2005

Nowadays lawyers seem to be replacing good moves over the board. FIDE, at war with several top players who refuse to submit to vacuous drug testing, is being sued by a Jewish grandmaster who was prevented from competing at the "judenfrei" knockout championship held in Libya last year.

History repeats itself. In 1999 FIDE stripped Anatoly Karpov and Susan Polgar of their men's and women's crowns respectively. They both sued FIDE at the International Court of Sports in Switzerland. Karpov was awarded $50,000 and Polgar $25,000, but their crowns were not restored.

In March 2001 the court found that FIDE erred by precluding Susan from defending her title because there was no compelling reason not to accommodate a new date after she had a baby. Her Web site reported:

> "Polgar agreed to accept a lesser amount in a spirit of goodwill. In order to lessen the damages, FIDE claimed it's a non-profit organization without any money at all! Another unfortunate revelation to the court was FIDE's claim that it had to spend 'several hundreds of thousands of dollars for its legal defense.' It is strange that FIDE can plead poverty and ask for mercy in one breath and then justify these pleadings by explaining the immense costs of its legal defense with its next.
>
> One of the main reasons Polgar did not play was because FIDE failed to find a sponsor for her match with Xie Jun. In hindsight, it would have been cheaper for FIDE to sponsor that match to begin with."

An editorial in *Inside Chess* noted why FIDE has lost so much credibility:

> "All players should be able to make the leap of logic that if women's world champ Susan Polgar can be treated so callously,

anyone's rights as a player are similarly worthless. The USCF should call for the collective resignation of FIDE's executive body and work toward the creation of a new governing body for chess. It has become abundantly clear that men and women of good conscience can no longer support FIDE in the face of its hapless bungling and callous destruction of professional careers."

The Polgar sisters, who are Jewish, have long been a thorn in the side of FIDE, which is clearly an anti-Semitic organization. For an account of how every woman in the world except Susan Polgar got 100 free rating points, see "Rigging Ratings." This scandal took place at the Chess Olympiad in the United Arab Emirates in 1986 where a team from Israel was banned.

In 2004 Susan led the USA women's team to a silver medal. She was the individual high-scorer on board one, and then was singled out for a humiliating "random" dope test, which she dared not refuse on pain of having her team's result erased. Thus FIDE made the USCF eat crow for publicly taking a stand against dope testing.

Susan and her sister Judit, who just had a baby (August 2004), are currently the two highest-ranked women in the world. Winning is the best revenge.

24. WHY SEIRAWAN QUIT
October 6, 2003

Chess has survived for a long time. It will probably survive the honorable men of FIDE.

GM Yasser Seirawan said the following in an open letter on the Internet urging leaders of the world chess body to resign: "The FIDE that exists today is barely alive. Its every announcement is met with doubt and suspicion. Its sole financial supporter is President Kirsan Ilyumzhinov. Is this a healthy institution? I suggest not. Indeed we can and must do better."

Recently GM Alexander Morozevich, 26, said he plans to abandon tournament chess, though he still continues his winning ways. Now *The Chess Journalist* sadly reports another defection:

> "We are distressed to learn that Yasser Seirawan, 43, former U.S. champion and publisher of *Inside Chess*, has announced his retirement from the game. It is difficult to disagree with his assessment of FIDE and the international scene—indeed, matters may have grown worse with the collapse of the planned Kasparov-Ponomariov match and Kramnik's repudiation of Brain Games/Einstein Group. Nevertheless, we continue to hope that Seirawan will reconsider his decision in the days to come."

In citing reasons for ending his active career so soon, Seirawan takes his fellow grandmasters as well as FIDE to task. Some excerpts:

> • FIDE has injured the prestige of its title with inane time controls that have spoiled the quality of games.
> • Now players have to be tested for drugs—as if a drug problem exists in chess? Players know the most important part of their body is the brain and would be loath to take any drugs that might injure themselves. In my 31 years as a player I have not encountered a single case of an accusation that an opponent had won because drugs had been consumed.

• Many top pros can't earn a living. Their departure does not seem to be of concern to FIDE, whose answer is to give out grandmaster titles with the ease of passing out raffle tickets.

• In their often bitter competitive struggles, players have killed top chess. It appears that selfishness has no bounds.

• In February 2002 I launched my Fresh Start proposal (to unify the world championship). Through a difficult birthing process the Prague Agreement was reached...but not implementing concrete steps has led to the failure of this agreement.

• It is painful to witness such events unfolding. Indeed, I'm filled with dread by the prospects of ever further injurious actions. So, I have decided to stop playing. Of course, I love chess very much and will continue to follow it from afar.

25. SWAN SONG?
November 17, 2003

"Chess should not be indulged in to the detriment of other and more serious avocations—should not absorb the mind or engross the thoughts of those who worship at its shrine."

—Paul Morphy (1859)

Morphy, the premier player of his era, cringed when people called him a chess professional and then eventually quit altogether. Instead, he became a lawyer who despaired when clients kept pestering him for advice about chess.

Today the royal game is more popular than ever but can only support a handful of superstars. "It's the very best and most enjoyable waste of time that you'll ever experience in your entire life," noted one fan.

But many pros are fed up with the governing world body, which recently decreed that players in "all FIDE competitions" are subject to mandatory drug testing—even though the International Olympic Committee has flatly rejected chess as an Olympic sport.

"If Stephen Hawking can do it, it's not a sport," quipped a critic. But nothing seems to have stopped FIDE from establishing a Medical Commission that is hungry to grow with the power to destroy the careers of players who refuse to pee in a cup or provide their whereabouts for out-of-competition testing.

Grandmasters such as Artur Yusupov and Jan Timman are boycotting events that require random testing, and the list is growing. Yasser Seirawan recently cited this roadblock as an important reason for packing it in. (See "Why Seirawan Quit.")

Why submit to an absurd and costly test when no drug has ever been proven to help anyone win chess games? Frankly, I can't think of a better way than drug testing to kill chess promotion even more in the United States.

The chorus of critics is growing louder. "FIDE has one overriding agenda. I know because they told me so when I visited them. They are paranoid about player discipline and control. Ask why they demand useless drug tests when everyone knows that illegal substances (steroids of the mind?) only harm your game," said GM Raymond Keene in the *London Times*.

"Chess officials are, by and large, failed players and incompetent administrators. Some get their kicks from bossing around masters. Very few have the game's best interest at heart," sneered Jack Peters of the Los Angeles Times.

Alexander Morozevich, at age 26, despite a stunning victory at the thirty-sixth annual chess festival in Biel, Switzerland, announced his plans to abandon a professional career in chess. Just a few months later he tied for first in the fifty-eighth Russian Championship. Is that really his swan song?

"I still earn my living from chess and it's a great pleasure, but I can't find any objective to spur me on," he said. "My decision is final unless there's a miracle. There is no real cycle for the world championship, no chance to fight for the title. So I study chess less and less, no more than four or five hours a week."

Morozevich was undefeated with six wins and four draws at Biel, leaving five other grandmasters in his wake. He made short shrift of the great Viktor Korchnoi, 72, whose last chance to fight for a draw was 17... Nxe5! 18 Nxe5 Bxb5 19 Rc3 Bc4 20 Bxc4 dxc4 21 Rxc4 Rhd8 22 Rxc5 Rxd2 23 Rxd2 Rxc5.

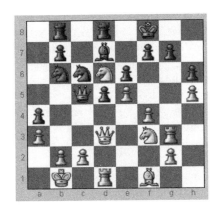

Final Position

MOROZEVICH vs. KORCHNOI
French Defense, 2003

1 e4 e6 2 d4 d5 3 Nc3 Nf6 4 Bg5 Be7 5 e5 Nfd7 6 h4 c5 7 Bxe7 Kxe7 8 dxc5 Qc7 9 f4 Qxc5 10 Qd2 Nc6 11 Nf3 Nb6 12 a3 a5 13 h5 h6 14 0-0-0 Bd7 15 Kb1 a4 16 Rh3 Rac8 17 Nb5 Rhd8? 18 Nd6 Rb8 19 Rg3 Kf8 20 Qd3! **Black Resigns**

Black threw in the towel due to the quiet but deadly threat of 21 Qh7. If 20. .. Kg8 21 Nxf7! Kxf7 22 Qg6 Ke7 23 Qxg7 Ke8 24 Qg6 Ke7 25 Qf6 Ke8 26 Rg8 mates.

Morozevich is still active in the international arena and is currently ranked fifth in the world at 2758 (July 2007).

26. THIRTY-SIXTH CHESS OLYMPIAD
December 20. 2004

The times they are a-changing. *The West Wing*, a popular TV series, featured a president who plays chess instead of golf, and the front page of the *International Herald Tribune* reported that for the first time Amazon.com listed a chess program as its best-selling software product for kids this Christmas.

But some things never change. Politics reared its ugly head at the Thirty-Sixth Chess Olympiad in Calvia, Spain, where the Ukraine captured the gold ahead of Russia and Armenia among 129 teams. The USA took fourth, its best showing in years, but the entire 6-man squad including the captain consisted of Russian immigrants. A wag called it "The Russian B Team."

The USA women's team silver medalist Susan Polgar also earned a gold medal for the best individual result on board one. New York State Governor Pataki with Kasparov in the center gave her a plaque. Hungary's Polgar led the USA women's team to a silver medal behind China but ahead of Russia among 87 nations. After the last game she was singled out for a degrading urine test even though no known drug has ever enhanced chess performance.

Chess is supposed to be a pocket of beauty in a noisy world, but it doesn't always work out that way. At the closing ceremony, a top FIDE official was wrestled to the ground, handcuffed, beaten and arrested for trying to crash his way to the stage.

IranMania.com reported that four of Iran's top players were banned from future events for refusing to compete in this Olympiad. "Their behavior does not conform to our country's chess norm. We will never forget this immoral conduct," lamented an Iranian official.

POLITICALLY FORBIDDEN PAIRINGS

Andy Soltis noted in the *New York Post*:

"Organizers refuse to pair players against opponents who fear retribution from their government. This is so routine that computers, which make pairings at major Swiss system events these days, are programmed to avoid matchups between Israelis and players from certain federations. At the biggest international of 2004, the Aeroflot Open in Moscow, the pairings for one round had to be thrown out at the last minute when the arbiter found what he called a 'politically forbidden pairing.' So all pairings had to be recalculated, causing a massive delay."

The Chess Olympiad began in 1924 when FIDE was created with the motto "gens una sumus" (we are all one family). The USSR first entered a team in 1952 and won easily every time until 1976 when it was held in Haifa, Israel. The USA took the gold in field of 48 nations when the Soviet bloc boycotted this event. In 1986 the motto again was flouted when an Israeli team was excluded from the Olympiad held at Dubai in the United Arab Emirates.

Nowadays FIDE is run by a bunch of thugs and does about as much for promoting chess as the United Nations does for stopping war. Yet the games go on because it's a place where players can gather and fraternize every two years regardless of their nations' conflicts and squabbles.

27. NOT KEENE ON TESTING
August 26, 2002

Never in history has any illegal substance enabled anyone to win a single game of chess. Yet FIDE is now pushing for universal drug testing on the pretext of getting chess into the Olympics, thus making it eligible for government funding in many nations.

The Spanish Chess Federation, for example, receives about $320,000 a year from the Council of Sports for testing 20 players at random. More than 100 substances are banned, including excess levels of alcohol, cannabis, and coffee.

Frankly, I can't think of a better way to drive people away from chess than by compelling them to pee in a cup in order to compete in tournaments. Branding chess as an athletic endeavor is ludicrous, and the United States Olympic Committee had the good sense to reject this hobby as a sport.

FIDE GOES BESERK

Although chess is unlikely ever to become an Olympic sport, that doesn't stop the bureaucrats from imposing their silly regulations. "FIDE has made its decision, and players who do not accept drug testing will not be able to play chess," wrote Dr. Stephen Press, vice-chairman of FIDE's medical commission.

"It almost made me cry, for I realize that from now on no kindred soul, no young intellectual with any self-respect will ever contemplate a career as a professional chess player," noted Dutch grandmaster Hans Ree. "It is hard to say who are more despicable, the FIDE bosses who invented this horror, the chess federations that saw it happen but did nothing to prevent it, or those players who will meekly submit to these senseless humiliations."

"The Olympics are for physical sports, not board games. Their motto is 'Faster, Stronger, Higher.'—not Cleverer," noted an outraged amateur. "Certain drugs can significantly improve athletic performance, while at the same time often harming the athletes who take them. No such problem has been established in chess, and chess players are therefore properly suspicious and even resentful when told they have to be drug tested. I have no sympathy with the people who claim they are fighting to get chess into the Olympics; and I have actual animus toward officials who try to impose controls on chess with the excuse that the Olympics requires drug testing."

Ray Keene, Britain's leading chess authority, argues that the real agenda is to control the careers of players. Some excerpts from his article in the Spectator:

- Performance enhancing drugs—steroids of the mind as it were—are not and never have been a problem in chess.
- Although chess bureaucrats are enthusiastic about these new regulations, players as a whole are neither ready nor willing to submit to wholesale drug testing.
- FIDE's initiative is designed to extend bureaucratic control over players who are inconveniently insubordinate rather than to stamp out any real abuse in chess.
- Why do chess officials waste their time on this kind of nonsense when it is clear that their constituencies have absolutely no interest in it?
- This syndrome is absolutely rife in politics. I have seen it so many times before. FIDE Delegates imperceptibly at first cease to represent the views of their own country—instead they start to represent FIDE's views to their country, thus becoming a kind of fifth column! That is why nation states continually revolve their ambassadors before they 'go native' in the quaint phraseology of the British Foreign Office.
- The key is often insidious hospitality. Once the naive backwoods chess politician starts rubbing shoulders with the FIDE bigwigs, invitations to dinner start coming in, exclusive gatherings of top people. It's not so much gifts and bribes as corruption by association.
- We know what's best for Ivan and Ivan should shut up and take his medicine. After all it's good for him and good for chess. Discipline—that's what Ivan needs.

28. JUST TESTING
February 7, 2005

Two players had their scores erased at the 2004 World Team Championship in Calvia because they refused to comply with a "random" drug test demanded by FIDE. Yet many people wonder why there is any need to enforce Olympic restrictions now that both the International Olympic Committee (IOC) and the USA Olympic Committee (USOC) have flatly rejected chess as a sport.

On August 20, 2001, Larry Parr and I wrote a position paper for the FIDE Advisory Committee of the USCF. We argued that FIDE initiated drug testing knowing full well that chess was a nonstarter in the summer or winter Olympics for the simple reason that it's not an athletic sport and we analyzed FIDE's real motives.

Our main points still stand, though there are some anachronisms. Jim Eade no longer is our zonal president and the new rules, though shorter, refer all questions to WADA regulations which are even tougher than those we cited. Therefore, the net result is that the situation is even worse than what we concluded.

For example, in a press release of January 13, 2005, the Association of Chess Professionals (ACP) singled out Article 3 of the FIDE Anti-Doping Regulations as an object of scorn: "Out of competition: In accordance with WADA requirements FIDE will form a Registered Testing Pool consisting of the world's best chess players determined by ELO rating revised annually according to January ELO list (45 top rated male players and 5 top-rated female players). It will be the responsibility of these players and their National Federations to provide FIDE with whereabouts information."

Our article ends with a series of policy proposals that the United States Chess Federation should adopt in defiance of FIDE.

THE CASE AGAINST DRUG-TESTING IN U.S. CHESS
by Larry Parr and GM Larry Evans

"FIDE has made its decision, and players who do not accept drug testing will not be able to play chess. At the moment, I would have to freely admit there are drugs which theoretically COULD affect cognitive performance, but we have NO real scientific proof that anything can positively affect cognitive performance and consequently, chess."
—Dr. Stephen Press, vice-chairman FIDE Medical Commission

Let's get one thing straight right off the bat, shall we?

There is no demonstrable drug problem in chess. There is not even a claimed drug problem in chess. There is not even, as we shall see, a claim that there could be a drug problem in chess. There is only a claim that IF there might someday be a drug that affects cognition, then there could possibly be a drug problem in chess.

We have a "could" conditioned on an "if." Wow!

The decision about whether to support or to oppose drug testing is not a question to be resolved by specialists exchanging discrete bits of arcane knowledge. The question is how USCF interests are served by accepting and promoting drug testing in tournaments in the vain hope that chess may someday become not only an Olympic event but that Olympic status will result in tangible gains for the royal game.

We believe that USCF interests are best served in making policy based on reason, and on respect for personal privacy and on a shrewd understanding of its business interests given the passionate and widespread opposition to drug testing among American players at all levels.

We hold that creating bureaucracies to solve nonexistent problems is an affront to reason and an open door for predictable problems that will bedevil the USCF. We hold that violations of privacy by third-rate, arrogant chess politicians will end in lawsuits and outrages that will drive Americans away from chess. We hold that extending the surveillance society and drug snooping to chess with unaccountable FIDE officials holding open the doors of toilet stalls and conducting numerous intrusive tests is both immoral and an invitation to assorted forms of blackmail. We hold that in this Internet age, inevitable horror stories about drug testing will spread quickly to USCF members in spite of attempted news blackouts in *Chess Life*. We hold that the USCF will suffer the loss of several thousand financially beloved "regular" members once the bad news circulates sufficiently. We hold that there is no benefit from drug testing posited by even the most enthusiastic pro-surveillance chess politician that will justify the entirely predictable consequences of player disaffection and of FIDE abuses. We hold that if drug snooping triumphs, then one day a grandmaster will win the U.S. Championship over the board and have his title revoked and be banned for years from international play because he took some home cold remedy.

We hold that, in the words of Ayn Rand, "Civilization is the progress toward a society of privacy. The savage's whole existence is public, ruled by the laws of his tribe. Civilization is the process of setting man free from men." We hold that Caissa's precious realm has been historically amicable to individuals leading free chess lives without a mammoth caste of bureaucrats, and we hold that this freedom is more precious than the pipe dream of chess reaching the Olympic Games in some dim distant future.

SCREW REASON

Millions of games have been played in tens of thousands of tournaments "From California to the New York Island, from the Redwood Forests to the Gulf Stream waters." Yes, yes, there have been millions of games, and there has not been a single complaint (not even a bogus complaint) that someone won or drew a game because drugs were ingested.

Reasonable men will conclude there is no problem.

Reasonable men will argue that catastrophes occur when solutions for nonexistent problems are forced upon unwilling players and USCF customers.

Reasonable men will conclude that human and financial resources should not be lavished upon FIDE's unaccountable Medical Commission—an international bureaucracy that exists to create a problem rather than to waste time on a nonexistent problem.

Reasonable men of prudent disposition will suspect that the not-so-hidden FIDE agenda is to funnel political and financial perks to appointees and officials of national federations so as to further corrupt the decision-making processes of these federations and to exert greater control over players and tournament organizers.

84

Reasonable men will conclude that a vague promise of Olympic recognition is being used as a lever to open the doors of our toilet stalls and the skin of our veins to a permanent FIDE medical bureaucracy. Finally, reasonable men will conclude that FIDE poses a mortal threat to USCF business interests. Why?

In a memo to FIDE member nations, president Kirsan Ilyumzhinov added meat to the bones of his dream of world-chess control. He called for all tournaments to be required to receive prior approval from FIDE (defiant organizers would be blackballed) all prize money flowing to a bank to be chosen by FIDE, establishing "Press Commissars in all FIDE countries" (he wrote it, not us!) issuing a FIDE-VISA credit card. And he called for the rating of players down to 1000 and making them pay membership dues directly to FIDE to get ratings.

To deny FIDE's designs against the USCF and other national federations is an affront to reason.

U.S. Zonal President Jim Eade wrote in an e-mail to Larry Evans:

"I do think it plausible to suggest that some people think amphetamines [or a bottle of fresh orange juice] might enhance chess performance over the short term. I think it plausible to suggest that people actually used them in the highest levels of competition. I think it plausible to suggest that it is reasonable to test for them so that nobody does that ever again."

They want to test so nobody does what "ever again"? As I've previously stated, in the entire history of chess in these United States, nobody has ever documented an instance of a single game won or drawn because of drug use. Notice the Zonal president's statement, that he "thinks" it "plausible" to "suggest" (though not insist) that "some people" might "think" that amphetamines "might" enhance chess performance over the short term. What we have here is an argument for a permanent FIDE medical bureaucracy on the basis of what he thinks is a plausible suggestion about what others might think about what may or may not happen if there were a drug that could affect chess cognition positively.

What we do not have is a demonstrated problem, a claimed problem, or even a claim that there could be a problem. But, of course, we have a solution.

"Drug testing in chess," writes Dutch GM Hans Ree, "is a perfect example of officialdom drumming up a problem that did not exist before their intervention."

Utterly astonishing. And, yes, an affront to reason.

THE SCHACH-DOCS

The U.S. Zonal president writes, "Whether illegal substances or legal ones enhance performance at chess is hardly the issue. The issue is abiding by the rules of the IOC until such time as they can be modified to make more sense in terms of chess competitions." The translation here could be, with respect to Tennyson: "Theirs not to reason why, Theirs but to do and die."

Note his phrase, "until such time." This may mean "never." Or a decade. Or a century. But most probably never. Dr. Press, as always, is candid in a grisly way, "We are at present still classified as a sport, not separated as a mind sport, and that, i.e. the idea of presenting to the IOC to create a separate category, is fraught with all sorts of potential minefields for FIDE at the moment. It is something being considered for the future [our emphasis]."

If chess were reclassified and if drug testing were disallowed, then there would be no justification for a permanent FIDE Medical Commission and for handing business to the Schach-docs at around $300 a pop. To imagine that the politicos at the FIDE Medical Commission will try to become unemployed by convincing the IOC to reclassify chess is, yes, an affront to reason.

What does Dr. Press mean when he writes that reclassifying chess as "a mind sport" is "fraught with all sorts of potential minefields for FIDE"? Could he possibly mean that basic vitamin supplements and herbal helpers such as Gingko Biloba (thought to make Alzheimer's less likely) would be outlawed? Could he possibly be suggesting that substances that aid human health would be proscribed and that chess players who wish to promote their health will face lengthy playing bans? Could he possibly be implying that American chess players will be told not to fortify themselves with health-giving substances if they wish to fulfill whatever dreams they may have in chess? Could the rationale behind drug-testing in a mind sport become this perversely subversive of both human well being and USCF financial health?

Oh, yes. Writes Dr. Press:

86

"However, be aware that it [chess classified as a mind sport] will open up the field of drugs for which we have to test to then include nicotine, and may make presently legal substances like Ginko Biloba, commonly used by chess players for an advantage perceived by them, to first be studied, and if it actually works, it may then have to be first banned due to our new status, and consequent new banned list...We have to carefully think if we are placing ourselves in a bigger problem if we open this can of worms."

The principle, as clearly framed by Dr. Press, is that if the functioning of a brain is improved by a given substance and even if this substance is not detrimental to health or even if it aids general health, it might be banned according to the destructive logic behind the move to make chess an Olympic sport. Yet if someday a drug is found that improves cognition without harmful side effects, why shouldn't it be made available to everyone?

Notice the reference to nicotine. Many smokers continue to play in USCF tournaments even though they must leave the tournament room to smoke. Drug testing for nicotine will finally drive them from rated USCF play. One doubts that many would bother to renew their membership in this age of Internet chess news and play.

Banning health-giving substances and waging war against USCF customers is not an affront to reason. It is the rape of reason.

IS IT INEVITABLE?

One of the most insidious arguments used by drug-testing advocates is the appeal to inevitability based on force majeure. "[W]e believe," writes someone from the FIDE Medical Commission on FIDE's Web page, "that the governments of the World will ultimately hold us to conform to these or similar rules at some point in the near future anyway."

This is nonsense, at least in the United States and many free Western countries. But the argument amounts to "Let's do it anyway because it is inevitable." This idea is allied with a certain intellectual embarrassment that can also be found in a statement issued by the FIDE Medical Commission:

"Please understand that this Commission does not create the rules under which FIDE is required to perform doping controls. That is the function of the World's Sports Community, in association with all the agency's and under pressures caused by the problems in our society today. The rules are the result of a collaboration of the UN, the IOC, the WHO, the Council of Europe, the US Drug Czar's Office, every International Sports Federation, every National Olympic Committee, and etc., etc., etc. In other words, society as a whole."

TRANSLATION: We may not be able to defend our practices with reason, but we can appeal to the argument that everybody's doing it. As for "society as a whole," the list given includes a bunch of government agencies and semi-governmental sports federations. Only a bureaucrat down to the warp and woof of his soul would confound society with an alphabet soup of agencies.

In other words, this is yet another affront to reason.

SCREW PRIVACY

"1.5. Notwithstanding the foregoing, the FIDE Medical Commission shall have the right to request, without justifying the reason therefore, that any competitor undergo a doping control at any time during the relevant competition."
—From FIDE's antidoping disciplinary regulations

"1.1. The procedures which follow are those applicable to FIDE Competitions. In other competitions, as well as in out-of-competition testing, if the FIDE Medical Commission shall determine that out-of-competition testing shall be introduced, the same procedures shall apply, mutatis mutandis."
—From FIDE's anti-doping disciplinary regulations

"Anyone with a material condition requiring use of any prohibited substance, should contact the FIDE Medical Commission Secretariat office ASAP, to obtain a waiver from the IOC Medical Commission. Documentary evidence provided, should include AT A MINIMUM [our emphasis], records of tests taken, affidavits from prescribing physicians, consultants' reports, etc."
—From the Web page of the FIDE Medical Commission

IT CAN'T HAPPEN HERE

Part of the soft-soap peddled by drug-testing advocates in the United States is that intrusive knocks on the toilet door are meant only for those who will compete in the Olympiad, and that there is no intention on the part of the honorable men of FIDE—including the widely reputed killer Kirsan Ilyumzhinov and the shadowy Armenian Artyom Tarasov—to abuse any power by engaging in medical and financial blackmail of unruly players.

But FIDE's antidoping regulations grant the FIDE Medical Commission the power to test every single player at the U. S. Open, if it so decides. Section of paragraph 1.1 is a blank check.

Read it:

"The procedures which follow are those applicable to FIDE Competitions," 1.1 begins. But, "In other [unspecified, undefined] competitions, as well as in out-of-competition testing [a knock on your door at home], if the FIDE Medical Commission shall determine that out-of competition testing shall be introduced, the same procedures [more about the procedures in a moment] shall apply." Moreover, the Commission need not provide any reason for demanding testing at, say, the U. S. Open. "The FIDE Medical Commission," states 1.5, "shall have the right to request, without justifying the reason therefore, that any competitor undergo a doping control at any time during the relevant competition." Further, "without justifying the reason," the Commission may require blood and urine tests "on more than one occasion during the competition (1.6)."

An unfavored grandmaster may be tested at ruinous expense on multiple occasions, including having blood drawn repeatedly during a tournament if the Commission, "without justifying the reason therefore," so decides. An unfavored organizer, given contracts with participating players, may have to pay for an enormous number of drug tests.

In paragraph 1.1, we quoted the phrase "the same procedures" that could apply to all national and local tournaments, if the FIDE Medical Commission so decides "without justifying the reason." What do these procedures, which are stated to be applicable to all FIDE events and which even could be applicable to non-FIDE events, encompass?

In paragraph 1.2, the FIDE Medical Commission will decide the number of competitors to be subjected to doping control per day in each competition, subject only to "available capacity of the laboratory." National federation officials (who may or may not get a cut of the swag from medical testing) and tournament organizers have no veto here. Their role is only one of cooperation or facilitation.

In paragraph 1.3, the FIDE Medical Commission and a representative of the national chess federation (who may or may not draw pay from the FIDE medicrats) shall determine the number of competitors in each competition to be tested "in accordance with the total number agreed upon under paragraph 1.2."

These regulations, as written, grant the FIDE Medical Commission unlimited power to intervene in any tournament on earth—a power only limited by available resources and the amount of resistance arrayed against these regulations. These regulations permit any interference by the FIDE Medical Commission on behalf of one national organizer against another national organizer, allowing FIDE a foothold in political and business struggles within national federations.

Yet we have assurances that none of the above will happen because none of the above is meant to happen. Testing will only be at the highest levels. That's a joke.

IT BEGAN AT THE LOWEST LEVEL

Which is why, of course, drug testing began at the lowest level, at a world youth tournament in Argentina in May 2001. Parents and participants arrived without any prior notification that there would be drug testing—an example of the kind of wooden arrogance that will eventually embroil the USCF in ruinous legal actions if we permit it to gain a toehold in the United States.

Still, we are assured that children will be exempt. That's another joke.

The following addendum to FIDE's antidoping code provides no guarantees of any kind: "FIDE will NOT, for the time being, and subject to IOC/WADA regulations, test competitors under 16 years of age." The phrase, "for the time being," is clear enough.

Will one's eight-year-old daughter have to undergo intrusive, humiliating, perhaps psychologically damaging public urination, defecation or emotionally grinding blood testing? The FIDE Medical Commission may so decide, given its stated procedures, "without justifying the reason" if it shall also decide that "for the time being" no longer applies.

The above is what the regulations say. But are they to be taken seriously or are they just window-dressing for the International Olympic Committee? The answer is that the regulations will be taken as seriously as an unaccountable FIDE Medical Commission, a bureaucracy hungry to grow, wish them to be.

Logic, prudence, and any reading of history leave no rational doubt that the FIDE executive and its arms will wish to increase their "area of competence" so as to extend their control over national federations and rebellious players.

Certainly, FIDE's public statements leave no room for doubt. "The Board also resolved," reads one recent release, "to fully adopt the IOC Medical Code as the only basis for the FIDE Anti-Doping Code with effect from 1 July 2001." We have already read that the procedures for implementation grant the FIDE Medical Commission unlimited power to destroy the careers of professional and amateur players—a power that need not even justify itself.

Another aspect of the IOC Medical Code is that Draconian punishments ensure that athletes or, as FIDE would have it, grandmasters may be smashed to professional smithereens if they refuse compliance. A key weapon here is that "presumption" may substitute for proof. "Presumption" may, if the FIDE Medical Commission so decides, end the career of any dissident.

ONCE AGAIN, LOOK AT THE REGS

Article 3 of FIDE's antidoping regulations covers penalties for both unintentional and intentional violations. The penalties are—not so surprisingly, if one understands bureaucratic logic— quite similar. The penalty for a first unintentional offense ranges from a warning to "a fine of up to US $100,000." Given the limited economic wherewithal of our chess world, such a fine is, in effect, a career-ender. It is no different than a formal lifetime time ban for intentional doping. A player such as an unwanted Karl Robatsch or a much-hated Miguel Quinteros would be told to find something else to do with his life.

Is it possible for a FIDE medical official, after an unexpected midnight tap on the door, to demand testing of a top player and his GM analytical entourage during the middle of a coffee-laced night of opening analysis? Here, the regulation is unambiguous (Article 3.5):

"The penalty for an offence committed by a competitor and

detected on the occasion of an out-of-competition test if the FIDE Medical Commission shall determine that out-of-competition testing shall be introduced as determined by the FIDE Medical Commission shall be the same, mutatis mutandis, and shall take effect from the date the positive result was recorded or the date on which the final judgment further to an appeal is pronounced, whichever is the more recent."

Is FIDE a body with a long tradition of obeying its own regulations and of operating under a strict rule of law? Or is FIDE a body likely to plot obvious entrapment set-ups and prejudicial use of its powers to test at any time or in any place? We believe that the answers to both questions are self-evident, given the sad record of this lawless organization. We note that this antidoping code went into effect on July 1, 2001, yet intrusive, unannounced testing began in Argentina in May. FIDE is an organization that was so anxious to establish a precedent for testing anyone—right down to young girls, possibly humiliated in front of male officials—that it transcended its own regulations by instituting mandatory testing without official regulations.

Lawless? FIDE cannot even stay within its own Draconian edicts.

Lest anyone imagine that FIDE will have to prove a case before ruining the lives of unwanted players, there is Article 4.1. "Intentional doping can be proved," reads this paragraph, "by any means whatsoever, including presumption." TRANSLATION: If the FIDE Medical Commission says so, a Joel Benjamin or a Yasser Seirawan will not play international chess again. "Presumption" is sufficient.

Is there a role for USCF officials, a possible way to cut themselves in on the drug-testing swag? Indeed. Article 5.4 reads:

"At all other events (except where doping control is carried out under the rules of another sporting body) the NCF [National Chess Federation] conducting the controls or in whose territory an event is held shall be responsible for conducting doping control and shall adopt the procedures set forth in these Regulations and shall report the results thereof to the FIDE Medical Commission."

Among the "procedures" set forth in the FIDE regulations

is the power to test during out-of-competition moments and the power to demand extensive medical documentation and the power to demand both blood and urine tests of any competitor. Hated political opponents at the U.S. Open may be presented with ruinous testing bills or be forced to withdraw or face permanent ban from play for refusing to take drug tests.

Have there ever been USCF politicians who would have attempted to exercise such power against, say, a much-hated Lev Alburt back in 1985 or 1986? Did several such USCF politicians attempt to connive with anti-Semitic Soviet officials to keep GM Alburt off the American team in a contemplated USA-USSR "Summit Match"? Would these politicians have used the power of drug testing to wage a war of publicity against GM Alburt so as to discredit him at that unhappy time?

Even if one answers these questions with a vigorous no—in, we believe, dishonest denial—such power should not reside in any chess political figure.

Against the backdrop of these regulations, we have assurances that the good men of FIDE would never exercise such power, given that they would be restrained by…whom? Kalmykian president Ilyumzhinov, who proudly boasts a one-party state without opposition newspapers? Kalmykian dictator Ilyumzhinov, whose associates murdered dissident journalist Larisa Yudina and whose brother Vyacheslav was sighted at the murder scene by a witness who has since perished in an automobile "accident"?

In the March 2001 *Chess Life*, American FIDE representative Bill Kelleher gave readers the anodyne "probably" analysis. American local tournaments will "probably" be exempt. Urine rather than blood tests will "probably" be sufficient. Drug testing will "probably" not have a great effect on the players.

Since then, given the FIDE antidoping regulations of July 1, we have learned that the Medical Commission is free to enforce testing at any tournament it wishes—subject, once again, only to availability of resources and the degree of resistance offered.

Mr. Kelleher also wrote soothingly with a view to reassure and, perhaps, to blunt budding opposition, "Beta-blockers are also on the list of proscribed drugs. Players who take them for medical reasons will need a letter from their doctor."

Just a "letter" from the good ol' family GP. Innocent and fuzzy enough, right?

Wrong! The small print on the Web page of the FIDE Medical

Commission is far franker. The Schach-docs will not find a "letter" from the good ol' family GP or even a "letter" from a highly expensive specialist to be anywhere near compliance:

"Anyone else with a material condition requiring use of any prohibited substance, should contact the FIDE Medical Commisson Secretariat office ASAP, to obtain a waiver from the IOC Medical Commission. Documentary evidence provided, should include, at a minimum, records of tests taken, affidavits from prescribing physicians, consultants' reports, etc."

The minimum documentary evidence required is stated. But what is the maximum? We have no idea. The FIDE Medical Commission may bar unwanted grandmasters from competitions without ever making a finding that doping has occurred through the bureaucratic device of demanding endless expensive expert medical reports.

SCREW THE USCF, IF NECESSARY
The most striking aspect of the politician-led campaign for drug testing in chess is neither the attack on reason nor the attack on privacy. After all, power and money usually trump reason and privacy. Getting gain by inflicting pain is to be found in politics everywhere, though Third World despots such as Ilyumzhinov have a freer hand than politicians leashed by Western constitutional protections and traditions.

For us, the most striking aspect of the campaign is the enormous dangers that the advocates of drug testing are willing to visit upon the USCF in exchange for insinuating chess into the Olympic Games—somewhere, alphabetically, between bobsledding and curling—during one of the coming decades. The sheer disproportion between the enormous damage created and the unlikely benefit to be produced is thought provoking, if nothing else.

Assaults on reason, violations of sexual and health privacy, permanent bureaucracies, unrestrained power in the hands of unaccountable international officials, and entirely predictable USCF customer disaffection and later legal actions weigh no more in the minds of these drug-testing advocates than a diaphanous tail feather of a hummingbird. Their lead weight on the scales is the vague dream of Olympic participation at some level during some future decade.

In the view of certain USCF leaders for whom chess has long been a resumé and social-enhancer as well as an income-supplementing avocation, the Federation is either on its last legs as the leading force in American chess or on its last legs, period. Indeed, few would deny that the USCF is shrinking as a company and that numerous Internet chess businesses, which can't drug test, are occupying a market vacuum.

The smart idea is to use the cachet of USCF office as a bridge to other chess endeavors in the future. The important point for politicos who dream of quasi-diplomatic glory as Olympic officials hobnobbing among those who have favors to dispense is that there be a chess umbrella organization that will protect their status as accredited Olympic chess officials.

WHAT BETTER WAY TO KILL CHESS?

What will be the reaction of American chess organizers to the imposition of costly drug testing and to the prospect of losing tens of thousands of tournament entrants who wish to have nothing to do with signing commitments to take whatever drug tests that the FIDE Medical Commission may elect to impose? What will those players, who look forward to certain major tournaments as annual vacations, decide to do if even their hope to recoup a portion of their expenditure by winning a class prize becomes dependent on passing a drug test or several drug tests during a single competition? Will they continue to attend tournaments in which they could forfeit class prizes or have to pay for expensive drug tests before they can get prize money?

Bill Goichberg, America's largest tournament organizer writes the following:

"When FIDE issued its startling pronouncement at the end of 2000 that, with about one week notice, all FIDE rated tournaments were required to use the 'new FIDE time control,' I received several emails from players asking if CCA tournaments advertised as FIDE rated would use the new control. I replied that I didn't think it was really required and that if it was, we still wouldn't use it. Likewise, let me assure everyone that there will never be 'anti-doping tests' at any CCA tournament. We will hold our [tournaments as we] always have, and submit them to FIDE for ratings and sometimes title norms because there is nowhere else for players to go who wish to become GMs or IMs, but we fully expect our events to be rejected by FIDE within a year or two because we will not accept their control."

Under FIDE regulations, the USCF could face penalties for continuing to do business with Mr. Goichberg and other tournament organizers, who understand that fast time limits and drug testing spell business death for them. We do not believe these organizers will pass quietly into the sweet night of income oblivion. They will establish a competing rating system instead.

SCHISMS BREWING?

There will be numerous absurdities. "As a grand climax," writes Mr. Goichberg without (in truth) much necessary foresight, "perhaps at the closing ceremony [of a given tournament] the official FIDE antidoping service will announce that the GM who apparently won the event has been disqualified for puffing on his asthma steroid inhaler."

Yeah, it will happen.

Lawsuits? Numerous American antidiscrimination laws are there to be violated. "Any competitor," says the fine print on the FIDE Medical Commission site, "who is a Diabetic using Insulin, those with Exercise Induced Bronchospasm (Asthma), or a Cardiac condition requiring Beta-Blocker medications, should file the following form prior to competition with the FIDE Medical Secretariat Office." Tournament directors will need to have legally vetted legal disclaimers for all players to sign and will require legal advice to establish elaborate procedures for guarding against legal actions from outraged tournament customers.

What will happen if one of the tournament assistants at, say, the U.S. Open fails to cover a legal base involving an asthmatic, who suffers an attack after an intrusive, nerve-wracking blood test—say, a second or third such test during a given competition? Impossible? Read Article 1.6 of FIDE's antidoping regulations.

With all the lawyers, forms, tests, etc., tournament costs will skyrocket and so will entry fees. As for the truly vicious Soviet absurdity of press "Commissars," this self-discrediting idea could only come from FIDE and its dictator-president.

WHAT IN THE NAME OF FIDE IS OUR POLICY?!

"Our desire to have the opportunity to raise the stature of chess to an Olympic sport outweighs our aversion to drug testing. It's not that we're for drug testing for the sake of testing, but if it's

required as part of the game of chess becoming an Olympic sport, then we see it as a necessary evil."
—USCF Executive Director George De Feis, USCF Press Release No. 38 of 2001

"The Delegates believe that drug testing is unnecessary in chess and urge FIDE to limit testing only to events where it is absolutely essential for qualification into the Olympic games."
—ADM passed by USCF Delegates at the 2001 U.S. Open

"USCF's FIDE representatives are instructed to actively campaign at all FIDE meetings against the practice of requiring drug testing at any chess tournament or match."
—ADM-64 passed by USCF Delegates at the 2001 U.S. Open

Mr. De Feis claims that "we" see drug testing as a "necessary" evil. But USCF Delegates, the controlling legal body of the USCF, see it as "unnecessary." The Delegates have also ordered our FIDE representatives to campaign "actively" at "all" FIDE "meetings" against "requiring drug testing" in "any" chess tournament or match.

We believe that the Delegates are on record as saying the following: Drug testing must, at the very least, be radically limited and that our representatives are to formulate and implement a campaign to stamp out such testing completely. Moreover, the campaign is to be "active" and to be pursued at "all" FIDE meetings.

The reaction of our Zonal president was that he intends to do as he will without such campaigning at "all" meetings and then submit his record to the Delegates. The political calculation is that the Delegates will ratify even bald defiance of their clearly stated policy.

The lawless spirit of FIDE has been one of the corrupting influences in USCF governance. Numerous American officials in FIDE have banked on their political clout to overcome resistance from Delegates, who often understood perfectly well that their resolutions were being flouted. An enormous amount of cynicism has undermined the vigor of governance and the morale of those Delegates involved.

We object to the Zonal president's frank avowal that a Delegate policy, which is ever so clearly stated and even demanded, will not be followed. We object to the notion that healthy governance is deliberately disobeying a policy in the expectation that a majority can be assembled to sustain such a violation. We argue that the perceived necessity by numerous American FIDE representatives to flout what they understand to be the will of the Delegates and of the USCF members at large has been a pernicious virus undermining the governance process.

29. IT'S ONLY A GAME
November 21, 2005

To most of us chess is only a game. But to the Soviet Union it showcased the glories of communism.

Chess is still as popular in Russia as baseball is in America. This tradition extends from the czars to Lenin, an avid player whose brother composed chess problems. Revolutionary leaders used the game as a political pawn to divert and educate the masses. For the first time in history, chess pros were subsidized by the state and Soviet stars were treated like royalty. But prize money was kept low to discourage competition from outsiders, mostly amateurs who had to earn a living from real jobs.

When the American team visited Russia in 1955 our interpreter quipped: "When we have troubles we play chess to forget our troubles. When we have no troubles, we play chess because there's nothing better to do."

While I was there, a dissident told me Russia was only good for two things: chess and ballet.

In 1972, after Bobby Fischer trounced Boris Spassky in Reykjavik, a Soviet grandmaster told me: "At home they don't understand. They think it means there's something wrong with our culture." You can just imagine the shock waves. Max Lerner wrote in the *New York Post*:

> "The Russians are in despair, as they should be. There were suspicions that Spassky might defect to the corrupt monied West. Their run of champions has been broken. Worst of all, it was done by a flamboyant, neurotic, authentic individual, against all the collective balderdash which says the individual is a cipher."

No longer honored as a Soviet hero when he got home, Spassky was castigated by officials who had urged him to walk out while he was leading 2-0 after the upstart American forfeited the second game. Spassky's good sportsmanship cost the USSR a crown it had held for a quarter of a century. He was no longer free to compete abroad and endured many indignities.

In the first test case of the Helsinki agreement, he caused an international outcry in 1976 that forced the Kremlin to let him marry a girl who worked for the French embassy in Moscow. The couple moved to a suburb of Paris.

Chess always was regarded as an extension of Soviet diplomacy. After World War II, their chess masters were sent on goodwill tours of neighboring states where Russia planned to increase her sphere of influence. Team matches with Hungary and Czechoslovakia preceded the actual takeovers of those nations. Where chess went, tanks followed.

Grandmaster Ludek Pachman, a good communist, was imprisoned in 1968 for protesting the Soviet crackdown in Czechoslovakia. Upon his release he was allowed to leave, but was forbidden to represent his country in international tournaments; Russia also boycotted events in which he competed. Pachman was the first chess player ever to be discriminated against solely on political grounds.

After this dangerous precedent, Russia succeeded in getting South Africa expelled from FIDE, the governing world chess body that then consisted of only 107 member nations. This move violated FIDE's own by-laws. The reason given was apartheid, although ironically sport was the chief area in which people of all races mixed and competed together in South Africa.

Korchnoi became the target of Soviet wrath when he defected in 1976. First they tried to disqualify him from a title shot on the grounds that he was stateless, but FIDE had the courage to declare that challengers represented themselves as individuals, not their nations. FIDE nonetheless bowed to Soviet pressure by forcing Korchnoi to accept a rematch clause that FIDE had stricken in 1963.

Then the Soviet Union refused to release Korchnoi's family and objected to his playing under the flag of his new country, Switzerland. During his 1978 title match, the Soviet press never mentioned his name, referring to him only as "the challenger" or "Karpov's opponent."

Korchnoi squawked that the deck was stacked against him even in a neutral country like the Philippines. Two members of his delegation were denied entry to the auditorium, but a parapsychologist with Karpov's entourage was allowed to roam freely in the audience while trying to hypnotize and unnerve Korchnoi.

Try as he might, Korchnoi could not get Dr. Zukhar removed. When Korchnoi appealed his loss in the final game of the match on the grounds that the hypnotist had broken an agreement by moving from the rear of the auditorium to the fourth row while play was in progress, FIDE not only turned down the appeal but went on to condemn the challenger for not conforming to "the sporting ethics of chess and general social obligations."

The matter did not stop there. The Soviet Union suddenly pulled out two of her players from the Nineteenth Lone Pine Open in America after learning Korchnoi was competing. Other tournament organizers were notified that if Korchnoi were invited, no Russians would come. His name was conspicuously absent from the list of the world's top ten grandmasters in 1979 competing at the $110,000 Challenge Cup in Montreal. Anatoly Karpov, who tied for first there with ex-titleholder Mikhail Tal, had been able to wield his influence as world champion in support of the party line, cabling the organizers, "If I could not refuse to face Korchnoi at Baguio, I am now entitled to expect organizers to respect certain conditions. Either they invite Korchnoi or me."

Not all the Russians joined the offensive against the expatriate. Spassky was one of three (but only three) Soviet grandmasters who refused to sign a letter of censure against Korchnoi. (Botvinnik and Bronstein were the other two holdouts.) Korchnoi's son was imprisoned in the USSR and beaten on the eve of his next title match with Karpov in 1981. After Korchnoi lost, his family finally was released.

Times have changed. Today Spassky is widely respected throughout the world and travels freely from France to Russia. Korchnoi, still going strong at 74, is also a welcome visitor to his homeland. Karpov is mentioned as a possible candidate for FIDE president. And Fischer is a fugitive from American justice who resides in Iceland to escape prosecution.

It's only a game.

30. CHESS POLITICS
December 29, 2003

You know the saying: The more things change, the more they stay the same. This column could have been written yesterday but was penned in 1987 by Mikel Petersen, who made an unsuccessful bid in 2003 for a seat on the 7-member Executive Board of the United States Chess Federation, which is now struggling to survive despite a record number of members approaching 100,000.

"Chess is the ideal game. Anyone can play. Anyone can enjoy. There can be no cheating over the board (well, almost). As a matter of fact it would be the best game in the world if not for one thing: politics.

I expect political fighting in government. It's what makes the world work, at least as we know it today. I even expect it in the business world. Anyone working for a major corporation understands that. But what I can't accept is the politicization of chess.

Why do I feel this way? Well, I was president of the Florida Chess Association three times. No matter what I did, it made no difference. One part of the state was always bickering with another part of the state. I finally gave up. The abuse I suffered at the hands of friend and foe alike just wasn't worth it - and I wasn't even paid!

Look what's going on in the chess world. First, there are constant machinations of the world championship matches. Years ago there was maneuvering to raise the ratings of all women on the world's rating list by 100 points—except for one woman (Susan Polgar). [See "Rigging Ratings."]

I guess what I'm trying to say is that the whole thing makes me sick. Seeing grandmasters having to fight for their rights as chess players pains me greatly. What can be done about it?

Man, even writing this column depresses me. I am watching

the game I love defiled by stinking, rotten politics, and I don't like it.

Do you?

Will chess experience more of the same in 2004? Right now the Prague Agreement of 2002 that promised to heal the rift and unify the title is in shambles. Vladimir Kramnik and Peter Leko haven't secured funding for their match. The victor was supposed to face the victor of Garry Kasparov vs. Ruslan Ponomariov, but this tilt also was scrubbed. Instead FIDE announced another knockout championship in six months or so."

Meanwhile AP reporter Robert Huntington stated in an open letter:

"AP informed me that they would no longer be covering most chess events. While they cited economic reasons, the timing of the decision leaves little doubt that FIDE's chronic inability to hold an event as scheduled was the catalyst....It is obvious what must be done in the first place: get rid of Ilyumzhinov even if it means bankrupting FIDE...If he had given his money to a federation intent on destroying chess, the result would not be worse...I can do little beyond advising all in the chess world to regard FIDE as anathema until he is gone and reforms are instituted."

This decade has witnessed other dangers to chess promotion such as FIDE's drive to speed up time controls and impose random drug testing even though chess was rejected as a sport in the Summer or Winter Olympics. Also the inexorable advance of computers poses new challenges to our ancient pastime.

While chess bureaucrats make new regulations and each nation fights for more titles and a bigger slice of the pie, players continue to exercise their creativity and create pockets of beauty in a noisy world.

Somehow, amidst all the strife, chess survives.

31. HOW AMERICA WAS BETRAYED
February 13, 2006

Former *Chess Life* editor Larry Parr recently noted that *Inside Chess* lasted from 1988 to 2000 and the one article that still stands out in his mind was one I wrote called "How America is Betrayed in World Chess." It prompted our FIDE delegate Don Schultz to sue me for $21 million, claiming in a sworn affidavit that I ruined his ambition to become president of FIDE. His case was tossed out of court. The controversial article is reprinted below from Volume 1, issue 4 (February 24, 1988). Updates are in brackets with subheads added for ease of reading.

In his book *Chessdon*, Don Schultz later explained:

> "In retrospect, I never should have filed the lawsuit. Aside from advising me to ask for such a ridiculous amount of money, my lawyer failed to fully consider that I am, for matters of chess, a limited public figure. Therefore, to win the lawsuit, three things needed to be proven, a) that Evans was lying, b) that he was doing it maliciously and c) that I incurred real damage. This is an almost impossible thing to do. Furthermore, for me to sue Evans would be like a president of the USA suing ABC newscaster Sam Donaldson for something Donaldson reported on. It took a long time to heal the wounds. In 1997 GM Larry Evans, his wife Ingrid, Larry Parr, Dato Tan, Teresa [my wife] myself and a few other friends met in Las Vegas and had a delightful dinner in a warm friendly environment."

HOW AMERICA IS BETRAYED IN WORLD CHESS

Any chess lover will tell you chess is the greatest game in the world. Kids can learn its simple rules. Duffers succumb to its temptation.

Chess even has its own world government called FIDE, founded in 1924, now a 125-nation giant [around 160 today]. Measured by number of nations, FIDE is the third largest world body, behind only the UN and ISA (International Soccer Association).

SOVIETS CONTROLLED FIDE

FIDE's initial purpose was to organize chess Olympiads, but the death of Alekhine left the chess throne vacant. In 1948 FIDE assumed control of the title and set up a three-year cycle to determine a new challenger. Yet already suspicions arose in the first match-tournament that the three Soviets (Botvinnik, Keres, Smyslov) might collude against the three outsiders (Euwe, Fine, Reshevsky). Reuben Fine just dropped out in disgust and devoted himself to psychiatry. Botvinnik, as expected, emerged victorious while Reshevsky cried foul, hinting that Keres had thrown some games. Keres later said that he felt obligated to Botvinnik, who had saved his life during the war.

Bobby Fischer, after a sour experience at Curacao in 1962, also accused the Russians of collusion. He said, "I had the best score of anyone who didn't cheat." This charge resulted in serious reforms, including the abolition of the rematch clause that Botvinnik had enjoyed for lo those many years. No longer did the challenger have to win two matches before the title [really] changed hands.

In 1975 FIDE stripped Bobby of the title [technically he resigned] then turned around and gave Karpov even more than Bobby had dreamed of asking for. FIDE restored the rematch clause with consummate ease for Anatoly Karpov. After Karpov lost to Garry Kasparov, he promptly invoked the clause and FIDE president Florencio Campomanes, in violation of his own rules, threatened to strip Kasparov of the title unless he agreed to play yet a third consecutive match with Karpov.

KARPOV-KASPAROV RIVALRY

Even before this match began, Kasparov renounced the infamous rematch clause, striking a real blow for chess justice in one stroke. But he still had draw odds in a 24 game-limit. This edge enabled him to hold his crown by 12-12 in his fourth match with Karpov last year [1987] for a $2 million purse in Seville, Spain. In the short space of three years, they faced each other in 120 games spanning four grueling title matches, with Kasparov holding a slim edge of one point.

[In 1990 Kasparov won their fifth and last match by the slim margin of one point after 24 more games. In 1993 Kasparov broke with FIDE to beat Nigel Short and then Vishy Anand in 1995. Vladimir Kramnik deposed Kasparov in 2000 outside of FIDE jurisdiction and then held his title on a tie against Peter Leko in 2004, before toppling Topalov in 2006.]

Kasparov never forgave Campo for conniving to save Karpov's crown in that first match. Although still leading by two points, Karpov had just lost two games in a row and was unfit to continue after 48 games that lasted almost six months. He tried for a postponement to preserve his lead, a ploy that backfired when his good friend Campo, under the glare of the international press, ordered a new match to start from scratch later in 1985.

The neutrality of FIDE officials was called into question from the outset. It was discovered that both Campo and Alfred Kinzel, a man he appointed to the match jury, had acted as financial agents for Karpov in a matter involving roughly half a million dollars in Karpov's foreign hard-currency bank account from royalties endorsing chess computers. Clearly, FIDE officials at the highest level had violated the cornerstone of sporting ethics and were implicated in a conflict of interest. Kasparov was livid, because it set the pattern for Karpov's preferential treatment by FIDE in subsequent matches.

During an interview Campo clammed up when I broached this touchy topic: "That is, that is, that is not chess, that is private business, and I will not go into private affairs with other people. Did the *Chess Life* editor put you up to asking that question?" he stuttered. [Campo deemed Larry Parr's coverage of FIDE too critical and pressured American officials into firing him.]

CAMPO'S SECOND TERM AS PRESIDENT

Campo runs FIDE as president Marcos ran the Philippines. He dispenses patronage like a Mafia godfather, as Kasparov put it, and merrily presided over four title matches, raking in $400,000 or 20 percent off the top of the last one in Seville. This year Campo became the first president in FIDE history to receive an annual salary ($70,000) plus an expense account that may easily exceed that figure. Under his regime FIDE is now in the red with money pouring out faster than it comes in, according to one accountant. But it is not easy to pierce the financial veil because Switzerland, where Campo moved FIDE headquarters, lacks stringent laws regarding full financial disclosure.

In a bitter election in 1986, Kasparov strongly backed a

reform slate headed by Lincoln Lucena of Brazil and Raymond Keene of England. Recalling that campaign with some relish, Campo, with a gleam in his eye, told me how a rival said: "You had it easy in 1982. This time we will try to make it interesting for you."

Campo is a crafty politician who honed his skills in the Philippines. "When I ask President Marcos for two million dollars, at worst he wants to know whether he should bring the money straightaway or whether I can wait for a check in the mail," he is quoted in Kasparov's book *Child of Change*. Campo controls the votes in FIDE with a fistful of proxies from grateful Third World nations. To get around a FIDE rule, he freely dispenses these proxies to his minions on the floor of the General Assembly.

DUBAI CHESS OLYMPIAD 1986

In 1986 Campo created a furor by awarding the Twenty-seventh Chess Olympiad to the United Arab Emirates, an oil-rich Persian Gulf state. There was one small catch: Israel was barred. Despite a worldwide outcry, Campo stuck to his guns and failed to find an alternate site despite a two-year search. A threatened boycott failed to materialize and only Denmark, Holland, Norway and Sweden stayed away. Lo and behold, a record 108 nations showed up in Dubai. America came, under protest, with instructions to walk out immediately if our FIDE delegation failed to strike a key FIDE statute allowing such boycotts. Our politicians failed, so they declared victory and stayed.

The USCF found funds to send four politicians to Dubai while claiming there was no money to send a team coach. One of our politicos was caught red-handed in padding his expense account, and this feeding frenzy may even have cost us the gold. We beat Russia in our individual match (where Seirawan downed Kasparov at top board) and were leading by a half point going into the last round (another Soviet scandal). Who knows, a coach might have put us over the top. This incident alone proves that USCF priorities are badly skewed. Politicians are kings; players are pawns. Shouldn't it be the other way around?

What happened in Dubai explains the mystery of why Campo was determined to keep the Olympiad there: it virtually guaranteed his re-election for four more years. Jon Tisdall of Reuters reported: "There was yet another controversy when it became known that the Dubai organizers had paid nearly one million dollars on air fares for small or distant federations to attend the Olympiad. Indeed, one of the chief organizers stated in the Abu Dhabi newspaper Al Ittihad that such spending was a sign of commitment to the Campomanes campaign."

In an article "One Bridge Too Far" for *New in Chess*, Spanish journalist and chess master Ricardo Calvo wrote: "The Arabs had sent free tickets to almost 70 carefully selected countries. The excuse of helping poor people was untenable. For instance, Spain received free tickets, but Portugal did not."

According to Calvo the election in Dubai could still have gone either way with forces evenly divided and some 20 nations undecided, waiting for Russia to make up its mind. Their own world champion was grimly opposed to Campo, whom he has repeatedly called "a man who will do anything for money." But when the USSR bucked Kasparov and threw its weight behind Campo, the opposition collapsed and Campo won by acclamation. The election was never held. [History repeated itself in 2002 when Ignatius Leong accepted a high post in FIDE (plus what else?) to drop out against Kirsan Ilyumzhinov.]

What price did Campo have to pay for this critical Soviet support? A small glimmer surfaced when FIDE voted unanimously to give 100 free rating points to every woman in the world—to every woman, that is, except Hungary's Susan Polgar, who had crept to the top of the women's rating list ahead of the Soviet titleholder. This action bumped Polgar to the #2 spot, another stunning example of democracy in action.

100 FREE RATING POINTS

In a syndicated newspaper column called "Rigging Ratings," I dared to suggest that the Polgar deal was not kosher and linked it to the Soviet support for Campo. It struck a raw nerve. FIDE retaliated with more disinformation, mailing out yet another of its famous self-serving presidential circulars which included a letter from Dr. Arpad Elo, now 84, chastising me by pointing out this rating recommendation originated with him.

The fact that FIDE struck back so hard and so fast only proved the charge had substance. How Campo must have laughed at our FIDE delegates. What chumps! Campo once again could thumb his nose at those fools in the West for going along with almost anything. And he knew he could make it stick because it had the imprimatur of Dr. Elo, who invented the rating system.

In a debate over Leisure Linc, a worldwide computer-chess network, Don Schultz said I was "all wet." He again spouted the party line: "Professor Arpad Elo of the USA actually made the proposal to raise women's ratings by 100 points. I called Arpad the other day to verify all this and he indicated he was fully satisfied with the action of the Qualification Committee. Yet you persist in promulgating the theory that there is some sort of collusion between the Soviets and Campomanes."

In their haste, the politicians forgot that Dr. Elo is a man of unimpeachable integrity. After the debate, he authorized me to release this statement: "I have nothing against FIDE, and my scientific dealings with them have always been honorable and correct. However, I am not altogether happy with the way my data was used in the Polgar matter. I see no reason to award 100 points to the three women (Cramling, Jackson, Fishdick) when I recommended lesser increments. All four of my recommendations should have been carried out rigorously."

Now the story began to unravel. To argue that there was no deal would be to argue that, if the situation had been reversed, FIDE would have fallen all over itself to topple a Soviet titleholder and move a Hungarian woman to #1. One sees that Dr. Elo's changes were accepted only in part, and that was the part that favored the Soviets. If there was genuine concern about women's ratings, all four of his recommendations would have been implemented.

So what does this all mean? The pieces of the puzzle begin to fall into place and the picture that emerges shows how Dr. Elo's data was perverted by Campo for political purposes. We now know that even objective, mathematical data, cannot be entrusted to this gang in power. FIDE used Elo to justify the Polgar fiasco, just as FIDE used Arnold Denker to chair a committee to study a censure against Dr. Calvo. It is truly amazing how Campo hoodwinks Americans into doing his dirty work.

THE CALVO SCANDAL

At the 1987 FIDE congress in Seville, an unprecedented motion was passed declaring Dr. Calvo persona non grata by 72-1 with two nations abstaining. At his victory press conference, Kasparov showed his contempt for FIDE by publicly embracing Dr. Calvo and using him as his translator.

"Just this title in my hands will kill this organization," said

Kasparov. "Because now we will discover a lot of people who hate this system. And they will do it themselves, just with my protection, the protection of my name."

The story behind this scandal deserves to be told because it reveals much about the inner workings of an organization that has good reason to be fearful of a free press. Calvo's article, "A Bridge Too Far," was about his trip to South America to campaign against Campo in the coming election. "My only weapon was a letter from Garry Kasparov giving me full powers to arrange a tour of simuls, exhibitions, and lectures to most Latin American countries," wrote Calvo.

Denker was outraged. "Calvo was guilty of election fraud and racial slurs. Even a ten-year ban would not have been out of line for what he did!" Denker said the following passage proved insulting to many FIDE delegates: "A girl must become a prostitute from 14 years on, or a boy must become a policeman of the dictator if they want to survive. In these situations, chess delegates are delighted with a small piece of the big cake of money, or power, or traveling away from their unhappy surroundings."

So, Calvo was really being punished for telling us that the civil war–scarred countries he visited in South America were so steeped in poverty that about the only thing people had left to sell was their soul. Calvo was telling us that empty stomachs are despoilers of human dignity. Yet he saw a ray of hope: "But I have also seen, in remote towns, chess players meeting for a lecture with shining eyes. And one is touched when the parents come with a 7-year-old boy with an Indian face, dressed with his best shirt, to ask to play a game against the boy, because he is talented and not many masters have visited the town."

Calvo also describes the sheer magnitude of his political task: "Sometimes it seemed to me that in the whole country there was only one single person favoring Campomanes but, in each case, this person was in charge of the delegation and with the tickets in his hands."

Denker's committee met for a few hours before recommending that the General Assembly ban Dr. Calvo for five years. Don Schultz explained: "I also saw Arnold right after I saw the draft of his committee report. There had been no mention of election misconduct in it. Unknown to Arnold it had been removed. Arnold protested strongly and the report was finally corrected."

But the first draft told the real story. Denker and Schultz, or Arnie and Don as they often are fondly called, realized that a charge of racial slurs would not play in Peoria. So this reference was deleted and the final report mentioned only "election irregularities" that will play in Peoria.

Sadly, it was only the forceful intervention of the Western democracies, frustrated by the lack of American leadership that substituted the persona non grata motion for the harsher penalty that would have passed overwhelmingly on the floor of the General Assembly. The ban motion was defeated, no thanks to Don and Arnie, who later took credit for softening the penalty!

In our Internet debate, I asked: "Don, don't American values hold that if you disagree with what someone writes you have three courses? Either you ignore it, or refute it, or sue. That's the way we do it in the West, remember? We don't set up star chambers packed with a person's enemies and then destroy his professional career in a few hours without due process."

Don replied: "There is not a single sports organization that fails to censure people for unbecoming conduct, and that is putting it mildly."

I retorted: "Calvo may have promised things to get votes for Lucena, but that's what politics is all about. Calvo's only bargaining chip was a letter from Kasparov. He didn't bribe anyone. He didn't offer anyone money. And there was no evidence presented before the Denker committee that he ever told anyone that if they didn't vote for Lucena, then Kasparov would not give an exhibition in that country."

Why do Arnie and Don still cling to the myth that Calvo engaged in election fraud? The answer is obvious. Once that prop is removed, it reveals the ugly reality that Calvo was punished not for his deeds but for his thoughts. So when the pretense is peeled away and we get right down to the nub, Calvo was being punished for exercising his right of free speech. This witch hunt exposes FIDE in all its glory as a world body reveling in a raw display of power, warning other chess journalists that the same thing or even worse might happen to them. We are rapidly approaching the point where a journalist might be declared persona non grata for writing about someone who threw a chess game.

Schultz now denies saying a word on the floor of the General Assembly in favor of the Denker resolution, and now even denies that he was going to vote for it! But there is a smoking gun, a

111

tape recording which belies these words. No wonder Schultz exhibits such hostility toward hard-nosed reporters and the free flow of information: He is a politician grasping at straws, trying desperately to restore his credibility and his tattered reputation. But every time I start to take pity, I think back to how he carried out Campo's orders in getting the *Chess Life* editor fired by knifing him in the back.

Now Schultz lashes out blindly, blaming the press for making Campo look like a bad guy. In the great tradition of Richard Nixon, he kicks the press rather than admit that his actions have betrayed American values such as free speech and the right to travel. A member of the Soviet FIDE delegation told a reporter he could not believe his eyes. The Americans were actually the driving force behind muzzling a free press.

[In *Chessdon*, Schultz later conceded, "If I had another opportunity, I would vote against any condemnation of Calvo. The world interpreted FIDE's censure as a rebuke for what he wrote and not election cheating. We should have recognized that and not allowed our vote to be interpreted as stifling freedom of the press."]

BANNING PLAYERS

For several years not a word appeared in *Chess Life* about an aborted USA vs. USSR summit match. For a purported fee of $20,000 Campo was a middleman in secret negotiations to exclude six ex–Soviet Jews from the USA lineup, including U.S. champ Lev Alburt. But the match fell through after Alburt leaked several classified USCF internal memos to the press. Alburt wrote: "The time has come for our chess officials to base their conduct on American values."

FIDE also flexed its muscle by banning Grandmaster Miguel Quinteros from tournament chess for three years for violating a ban on playing in South Africa. Needless to say, Don again went along with the tide. But once FIDE gets into the business of examining the moral credentials of its member nations, then it starts down a slippery slope. Why not also quarantine Russia for its gulags and invasion of Afghanistan, or America for its intervention in Nicaragua, or countless small nations that routinely violate human rights and torture political prisoners? Once you start, where does it end?

Chess players are artists whose careers should not be left to the whims of bureaucrats, who live to control rather than to create. Players should have the right to go anywhere in the world to play chess. That is a matter of individual conscience.

Isn't that precisely the meaning of FIDE's motto gens una sumus? FIDE was created to unify people, not separate them. The FIDE of today is a ghastly perversion of its original ideal to show the world that chess is a universal tongue that can travel without passport across all borders.

POWER BROKERS

FIDE politicians care more about power games than chess games. But now their dirty little secret is out, and people are beginning to wonder why we need all those huge international congresses where FIDE hotshots attend lavish cocktail parties in fancy hotel suites, like worms in the bacon, while real players struggle so hard. People might wonder why we need anything more than a chess board and a chess set. They also might wonder why we need a computerized rating system in an office somewhere to keep track of the "best" players.

People who believe that playing good chess is more important than playing FIDE politics don't need a world body to change an occasional rule. We know what the rules are. All we need is a few tried-and-true good men like Dr. Elo to settle disputes as they arise.

Gee, what kind of subversive talk is that? If others start talking like this, people might discover that they can dispense with the services of chess politicians. Players might discover they don't need to recognize the authority of parasites that strip Bobby Fischer of the title, a supreme insult to America that has never been avenged. Players might even discover that the scant money going into chess belongs rightfully to those who give their lives to the art.

When chess is infested with power brokers, anything is possible, any rule can be broken. Excellence becomes a secondary consideration. As Nikolai Krogius told a young Kasparov, "We already have a world champion. We don't need another one."

Long after FIDE has vanished, the games of great players will still be remembered and enjoyed. One Fischer is worth a thousand Campos. One Kasparov can excite the masses and make them wonder why a dull game like chess holds so many of us in its thrall. Ordinary people might discover what a great game chess really is and why a few fools fight so passionately to keep it clean.

GOING ALONG TO GET ALONG

Don Schultz recently boasted: "I feel I made many achievements in FIDE. The USA is held in far higher esteem in that body than when I started as delegate. At that time there was political speech after political speech against the USA. This exists no more. I made a short speech at the General Assembly in Dubai that resulted in an unprecedented standing ovation by Black African countries."

It's easy to get a standing ovation if you don't make waves and are willing to abandon your constituency. When asked how America can ever hope to win in FIDE, I replied: "I don't expect us to get our way. That's impossible in a forum where about 90 votes come from nations that support Campo. It is impossible to budge those votes. What we can do is stand up for American values, swim against the tide, take positions of principle and stick to them. We should lead the loyal opposition with the other Western democracies. If we stood up and blew the whistle, FIDE wouldn't be able to get away with all its dirty tricks."

Actually, what I meant to say is that America should call for Campo's resignation or else pull out. The one thing that Florencio Campomanes fears above all else is the wrath of America, a sleeping chess giant. [FIDE was nearly bankrupt in 1995 when our FIDE representative, Fan Adams, finally ousted him in a palace coup. Years later Campo was convicted of embezzlement yet still remained "honorary" president of FIDE.]

If America pulled out of FIDE, as Reuben Fine and Bobby Fischer advocated long ago, others would soon follow suit and organize a new world body where the players have a greater voice than the politicians.

That would be a switch, wouldn't it?

32. LIBYAN FIASCO
May 31. 2004

FIDE, a 163-nation world chess body, has awarded its next 128-player world championship to Libya. Jews are excluded.

This decision violates the spirit and charter of FIDE which says no event will be held anywhere that bars entry to eligible players. The announcement came with pictures of FIDE president Kirsan Ilyumzhinov playing chess with Moammar Al Qaddafi, who is offering about $2 million in prizes.

Qaddafi's son, who heads the organizing committee, stated: "We did not invite nor will we invite the Zionist enemy to the competition."

Boris Gulko, former champion of both the USSR and USA, is boycotting the event along with most top players: "Our magnificent and noble game does not deserve such a disgrace," he said.

It's not the first time FIDE has bowed to Arab money. In 1986 the Chess Olympiad was held in the United Arab Emirates where an Israeli team was banned.

But it appears FIDE is standing firm behind Libya. The FIDE fuehrer defended his policy and averred that "the main goal of FIDE is to popularize chess." He nixed a proposal by FIDE champ Ruslan Ponomariov of the Ukraine, who won't defend his title in Tripoli, simply to award the crown to the victor of a tournament among the world's six highest ranked players.

Instead, the victor in Libya is slated to play a match with Garry Kasparov. Then the winner is supposed to meet the victor of Vladimir Kramnik vs. Peter Leko to unify the title. Will it ever happen?

"FIDE's style of governance is increasingly founded on diktat with dissenting views brushed aside," stated the U.S. Chess Federation.

One grandmaster expressed the revulsion felt by many observers: "It's now abundantly clear that men and women of good conscience can no longer support FIDE in the face of its hapless organizational bungling and callous destruction of professional careers."

For decades FIDE has ignored the views of most pros and arrogantly stumbled into a series of scandals. Were FIDE to vanish tomorrow, who would miss it?

33. WHO KILLED ROUND ROBIN?

November 7, 2005

We all know that a true test of skill is a round robin tournament with a slow time limit where all play all at least once. And preferably twice—this is the main reason why the recent FIDE world championship in Argentina won by Bulgaria's Veselin Topalov, 30, in a field of eight stars is widely respected.

But such a format requires money and time, nearly three weeks for 14 rounds and 56 games. By contrast, Swiss tournaments with fewer rounds and several games a day can accommodate hundreds of players in a weekend. Winners weed out losers in a process of elimination until a victor emerges.

QUANTITY OVER QUALITY?

It's easy to see why the Swiss tournaments are so popular. Lose your first game and you can go home, if you wish, without incurring further expenses trying to snare a large prize.

Recently, U.S. champion Hikaru Nakamura, 17, complained about the new format for defending his crown at San Diego next March. Instead of a 64-player, 9-round Swiss, the field will be divided into two groups of 32 culminating in a playoff between both victors at the end.

"I think it's a horrible idea that will lead to a questionable winner. They don't have to play the same competitors or a level field. I hope the organizers are not sacrificing quality just to try and make chess more marketable," Nakamura wrote.

But this sacrifice was made years ago when the American Foundation for Chess raised a record $300,000 purse to make chess "democratic" by widening the field to 64 instead of adhering to the tradition of an elite round robin restricted to a dozen or so of the nation's top players. The AF4C also combined both the female and male titles in a single event.

The flaw in Hikaru's argument is that players never meet exactly the same opponents even in a pure Swiss-style game. Pairings vary with scores after each round. So what's wrong with creating two groups if the rating points in both are equalized? The drama of a shootout at High Noon between two gunslingers is made to order for TV.

Alas, there is no cure for Nakamura's other complaint about the dismal state of professional chess in America:

> "I remember when I first started playing chess that it was all about winning games and trophies. Eventually it was about winning and making money, but even though I've made my fair share of money over the last ten years, it is nowhere near enough to live comfortably. Everyone must fight to make a living, which leads to a lot of discord amongst players.
>
> With the chess pool as small as it already is, almost no one can succeed unless there is support. Unfortunately, our dog-eat-dog chess society does not pride itself on supporting up-and-coming chess talents. Why would anyone want to play chess forever if they have to deal with such issues? I know I wouldn't."

The sad fact is that it's next to impossible to make a living off of chess in America, even though he was just awarded the Samford Chess Fellowship which has a total value of $32,000. Hikaru, the nineteenth recipient of this annual grant to talented youngsters, was born in Japan and moved here when he was two. Now this teenage ace, the youngest player to hold our national title since Bobby Fischer, is eyeing greener pastures away from the 64 squares.

If he pursues his education to find a more stable and lucrative career, who can blame him?

In 2006 Hikaru lost the title to Alexander Onischuk, 30, who hails from Ukraine. Then in 2007 the AF4C bowed out as sponsor of this event.

34. THE SIXTY-FIFTH SQUARE
March 6, 2006

Gens Una Sumus—meaning "we are all one family"—was FIDE's motto since its inception in 1924. It became a mockery under the infamous regime of Florencio Campomanes (1982–1995) who moved chess away from the 64 squares into political areas where FIDE lacked jurisdiction: the 65th square.

In 1988 Austria's Kurt Jungwirth, president of the European Chess Union, summed up the feeling of many observers: "I am of the opinion that at present, under certain politicians, FIDE has become superfluous, even prejudicial to world chess."

To retain his power base, Campo pandered to the Soviets and to the Third World nations. The crowning glory came in 1989 when we reported that he had transferred FIDE's bank account in Switzerland to his own name at the Alliance and Leicester Building Society in England. When this outrage was exposed, the funds were returned to Switzerland. Nonetheless Campo was elected to two more terms until his ouster by a palace coup in 1995. Later he was convicted of embezzlement.

WRITERS UNDER SIEGE

"The greatest weapon of our enemies is that people will tire of fighting them." This quote is from Ricardo Calvo, a Spanish medical doctor and international master censured by FIDE for a letter critical of FIDE that was printed by *New in Chess*.

Once the leadership showed they could violate the rule of law with impunity, they did it to serve their own agenda. It began with FIDE's ouster of South Africa and their banning of players who went there, the boycott of the Haifa Chess Olympiad by Arabs and the Soviet bloc in 1976, the exclusion of Israel from the Olympiad at Dubai in 1986, and the censure of Dr. Calvo in 1987.

This fiasco was followed by a proposed FIDE Code of Ethics in 1988, which flopped, with severe press restrictions to muzzle critics. The code provided sanctions even if what chess journalists wrote was true! If passed, it would have enabled FIDE to bar players for up to four years because of things they wrote or said. Loyalty oaths (gag orders) were also suggested for new titleholders.

The code was drafted by David Anderton. a FIDE officer and British lawyer who patterned it on England's dubious Race Relations Act. During the debate in 1987, Anderson said FIDE did not go far enough in censuring Calvo: "I have seen many other articles written by many other people that I would put in precisely the same category...A lot of others have been equally deplorable in going over the top and bringing chess into disrepute."

But to stifle criticism is to stifle freedom. Disgusted with chess politics, Calvo turned to the study of chess history and wrote about its Persian roots. He traced the politicization of chess to the 1940s:

> "A critical turning point was the end of the second World War when FIDE became politicized in the worst sense of the word. One of the first results of this new situation was the exclusion of the reigning world champion, Alekhine, from the list of participants in the Victory Tournament in London 1946. The official reason was a couple of articles of anti-Jewish content published during the war in the "Pariser Zeitung" under Alekhine's signature.
>
> A ban against a chess player based on any political ideas is in itself an intellectual and juridical monstrosity. Canadian professor Nathan Divinsky once told me: "I would have accepted the participation of Hitler in any chess tournament." This is the real greatness of our game, a spiritual refuge far above the dirty politics of everyday life in any country."

Here is my interview with Dr. Calvo from *New in Chess* (#2 1989).

I DON'T LIKE TO BE FAMOUS IN THIS WAY

EVANS: You are the center of a storm ever since FIDE declared you persona non grata at its Seville congress in 1987. How do you feel about it?

CALVO: First of all it's a personal insult. FIDE's own statutes do not provide for such a punishment. I was never heard or given the opportunity to explain my position. They decided without giving me a chance to defend myself, which is contrary to the principles of natural justice.

EVANS: Arnold Denker in a letter to *Chess Life* of August 1988 said that you refused to appear before his committee.

CALVO: I was never asked to appear before any committee. Never. The resolution stated that I could be heard only AFTER the punishment had been inflicted. The damage was already done. I am now more or less famous. I don't like to be famous in this way.

EVANS: You were accused of "election irregularities" and racial slurs.

CALVO: Ridiculous. It's an insult and a lie. I tried to gather votes against Campomanes in South America and said in my article that a Kasparov tour of the region was possible but only under a different FIDE leadership.

EVANS: Did you ever tell anyone that if they voted for Campomanes then Kasparov would not make an appearance in that country?

CALVO: Never, never. I offered simuls to all nations I visited, regardless of whom they supported in the FIDE election. If making promises during an election campaign is a crime, then Bush and Dukakis should be also censured. Anyway, how can there be "election irregularities" in an election that never took place? Don't forget that [Lincoln] Lucena withdrew before the vote at Dubai.

EVANS: What about the charge that you traded free Kasparov simuls for votes?

CALVO: Not true at all. I told everyone Kasparov's normal fee for a simul was $5,000. El Salvador was on the brink of a civil war and had just endured a terrible earthquake. I told them a simul would be possible if the proceeds went to charity. That was the only free offer. In some other places I suggested the fee might be reduced based on ability of poor nations to pay.

EVANS: How has this FIDE censure affected your life?

CALVO: Terrible. It was a terrible insult repeated in the press, TV, radio. My family has heard it, my children know about it, my patients, my friends, officials in the Ministry of Health where I am applying for a post as a doctor. I have not been invited to any tournaments since then. Day and night I feel humiliated. I have put aside all my professional affairs to concentrate on promoting chess and acting as effectively as possible against this chess mafia. I used to be a normal physician with a life more or less in order. Now I understand those old-fashioned cowboy films when an Indian says that his soul cannot rest until his honor has been restored. I feel like that.

EVANS: What are you doing about it?

CALVO: I am suing FIDE Executive Council member Ghobash of the United Arab Emirates because he stated during the FIDE debate that I was a criminal of the worst type. [Calvo won the case but never collected a penny because Ghobash didn't set foot in Spain again.]

I also have a civil suit against FIDE in Lucerne. FIDE lawyers argue that Lucerne has no jurisdiction because Campomanes must be sued in the Philippines where he resides. This is ridiculous according to international law, but the case is moving slowly ahead.

EVANS: What do you think is the reason FIDE took this action against you?

CALVO: I think the timing was chosen in Seville as a way of putting more pressure on Kasparov, warning him what might be in store for him if he lost the match to Karpov.

EVANS: After Kasparov won the match he used you as his translator and publicly embraced you on stage, saying that just the title in his hands would kill corrupt FIDE. Is it also true that Campomanes was booed off the stage?

CALVO: That's true. After the last game.

EVANS: Why do you think Mr. Denker who is an American headed such a committee and recommended a five-year ban? In an interview Campomanes said that Denker privately was in favor of an even harsher ten-year ban against you.

CALVO: I would like to ask this question of Denker himself. How can he pretend to know better than many lawyers who have found nothing exceptional in my article? I think it is a question of psychology. In the final analysis some people have a democratic mentaltiy and some don't. Denker and many others in FIDE have a lot of vanity and arrogance. Denker's book of best games shows that he once was a big player. On the other hand I remember that Alekhine was banned from a tournament at London in 1946. Many of his enemies such as Denker refused to play if Alekhine was invited. I think they were simply jealous of his genius.

EVANS: In a debate with me over the LINC computer network our FIDE delegate Don Schultz said that he was not prepared to support Denker's ban had it come to a vote even though he voted for the persona non grata motion. Can you comment on this?

CALVO: I read your debate and I don't put any credibility in Schultz, especially since on the FIDE tape [recording] he called for "a big vote" against me. But he told you twice that he "never opened" his mouth. So I think that Schultz and Denker, or Don and Arnie, were working closely together as they always do.

EVANS: Canada's Dr. Divinsky, who led the fight against the Denker ban, told me that the next day Schultz tried to actually strengthen the minutes against you, to tighten the penalties. Did you know about that?

CALVO: Divinsky also told me this. I believe him.

EVANS: In a telex that Mr. Schultz sent to the USCF on April 12, 1987 just a few days after the vote was taken he said that you were punished for your racial attacks against South Americans. And Mr. Denker said that you insulted your hosts by calling their daughters prostitutes. Any comment?

CALVO: I think they are just trying to invent some reason to justify their actions. But the truth is obvious. My article "One Bridge Too Far" in *New in Chess* simply stated facts noted by many observers. There is child prostitution in many Third World countries. I regret it, but it is a fact. The fact that these counties have a lot of poverty is not an insult, just a description. I was tying to explain my experience in Latin America to European chess players. How can nations with civil war, dictators, drugs, corruption, pretend that an election in a chess federation is a clean thing? The Arabs sent free tickets to a group of carefully selected nations, claiming it was to help poor people. But the facts say otherwise. Portugal is a poor country opposed to Campomanes, so it got no free tickets to the Dubai Olympiad in 1986. Spain is rich but got free tickets because Toran is a friend of Campomanes. By the way, the UAE press openly stated that sheiks spent over a million dollars to get Campomanes reelected. He did them a big favor by keeping Israel out of the Dubai Olympiad.

EVANS: In view of the proposed FIDE code of ethics with its press restrictions do you still regard this action against you as a personal thing or as a broader attack against the free press?

CALVO: Of course it is an attack against free speech. Many journalists who are also active players have good reason to be worried about the way Campomanes is running things. Basically he is afraid of light and people telling the truth, what they really think and really see. The best part of the American spirit is exactly this defense of freedom. I think the behavior of Denker and Schultz was un-American and inexcusable.

EVANS: Just before you were censured, Larry Parr was fired as editor of *Chess Life*. Do you see any connection between these events?

CALVO: Yes. I think that if Parr had an independent voice it was dangerous for Campomanes, so it is clear his henchmen managed to get rid him. I feel solidarity with Parr and if I can one day join him in his battle against dictators in chess, I will. The best thing in this whole story is that I have found a lot of new friends and I am proud of many of them.

EVANS: Do you know of any other critics of FIDE who have been punished or attacked apart from yourself and Parr?

CALVO: Yes. During the Moscow title match Ratko Knezevic was punished because he published an interview with Kasparov in Belgrade that was very damaging to the FIDE leadership. They denied him a visa at the critical moment when he had to stay in Moscow. Ratko said that Campomanes was the hand behind the scene. And David Goodman of the AP has spoken ot direct threats by Campomanes. That in the Philippines they know what to do with journalists like him. It reflects very well to the reader the mentality of these FIDE people.

EVANS: What would you like to say to the reader that we haven't covered in this interview?

CALVO: I am solidly convinced of one thing: I love chess honestly and seriously and have always tried to do my best for the game all my life. Chess is important to culture. Chess deserves better leadership. I shall carry on the struggle because I believe that Kasparov and others are right. The greatest weapon of our enemies is that people will tire of fighting them.

CALVO vs. KORCHNOI
Sicilian Defense Havana Olympiad, 1966

1 e4 c5 2 Nf3 e6 3 d4 cxd4 4 Nxd4 a6 5 Bd3 Bc5 6 Nb3 Ba7 7 c4 Nc6 8 0–0 Qh4?! 9 N1d2 Nge7 10 c5 Ne5 11 Be2 b6 12 f4 N5c6 13 Nc4 bxc5 14 g3 Qh6 15 f5 Qf6 16 fxe6 Qxe6 17 Nd6+ Kf8 18 Bc4 **Black Resigns**

ONE BRIDGE TOO FAR
By Dr. Ricardo Calvo (from *New in Chess*, 1986, No. 8)

To summarize the fight between Lucena and Campomanes for the presidency of FIDE I cannot avoid remembering a well known film: In the second World War allied troops tried to conquer three consecutive bridges. Exactly the same as in this episode, the Kasparov forces were sufficient to conquer brilliantly the first bridge, which was the World Chess Championship. They did it however out of schedule, and the delay proved to be a decisive factor in the next two objectives. The second bridge was the Soviet Chess Federation. Here, the enemy forces have seen Kasparov approach, and even if they lost the Bridge (Sebastianov and some of his aids were substituted), they managed to build up some resistance, and several minor fortresses of this system could not be taken and kept the invaders under continuous fire. Krogius and the people in the Sports Committee have not yet (and possibly never will) surrender to Kasparov's offensive.

The third bridge (in the film the one at Arnhem) was FIDE and its captain Campomanes. Here the defenders have had a lot of time to prepare, hold a superior strategic position, their troops were well trained and equipped, with no logistical difficulties for fresh supplies. The result of this third battle is known: The bridge remained in tact in the hands of the enemy, due to the decisive support at the critical moment of the battle by a division of tanks coming from the second bridge. Lucena capitulated, to avoid a massacre.

Since I have participated actively in the third battle, as a direct adviser of Lucena, I can give a personal view of what happened. I have no pretensions of objectivity. Historical reports have always been a puzzle of thousands and thousands of irregular pieces, somehow interrelated but to obtain the whole picture you need time, distance and above all luck.

The story began in London, in August, during the first part of the third Karpov-Kasparov clash. Under the (questionable) assumption that Kasparov represented the Truth, and the (even more questionable) that Truth always triumphs, a worldwide campaign was quickly designed. The funds were provided by private means, and Lincoln Lucena started vaccinating himself against all tropical diseases and applying for visas to many countries in Africa, the Caribbean, Central America, Asia, Australia, and Oceana, carefully selected before his landing in Dubai the 14th of November. Ray Keene was to visit the Caribbean part of the British Empire, the flying Dutchman Timman several obscure federations in Africa, and I was sent to Latin America. My only weapon was a letter by Garry Kasparov giving me full powers to arrange a tour of simuls, exhibitions and lectures to most Latin American countries. It opened me, as expected, even the iron doors of the most reluctant pro-Campomanes federations, and so I had at least the opportunity to talk.

I started at the 21st of September (that is, before the first bridge was taken) in an overbooked flight Madrid-Rio de Janeiro and the total picture of surprises, incidents, accidents and experiences is impossible to summarize. A few sentences for each country: In Brazil I had to perform a painful surgical correction. The FIDE delegate was intending to apply for the post of Deputy President, and I had to talk him out of linking his aspirations with our support, because two members of the same federation would be too much, even under Campomanes rules.

Paraguay's chess federation has been for many, many years, in the conservative hands of a group of Strossner supporters, with the brilliant results the world knows. The best player, Zanon Franco, has been practically expelled from the country. Several times chess events have been arranged by a rival chess group, but even if its leader was married with the daughter of President Strossner, he was unable to obtain the approval of his father in law in order to represent Paraguayan chess in Dubai. The officials in charge, needless to say, had tickets paid by the Arabs and were enthusiastic supporters of Campomanes.

Uruguay was a pleasant surprise, with a democratic federation in which chess players actively participate. Obviously, they were natural supporters of the Kasparov-Lucena flag. They were a helping hand even in Dubai. Argentina did not cry for us, but if so, she would have plenty of reasons. The chess federation is run by a small group of persons in the best 'Mafia' style, and even the calming chorus of voices from Najdorf, Quinteros, Larsen and a large etc. is helpless. An official, Giannotti, was already appointed arbiter at the Olympiad (and he is not an international arbiter of course), and Noguues has been nominated after the elections in Dubai for the Executive Council of FIDE.

Before entering Pinochet's Chile I put Kasparov's letter well hidden in the bottom of my case, but it didn't help in my talks with the president of the chess federation. After a long and disgusting discussion, it became clear to me that when nature put an ocean and a big chain of mountains between us two it was a wise decision to which I am extremely grateful.

The legitimate Bolivian chess federation was in the city of Cochabamba for the period 1985-1987, according to an official statement by the Ministry of Sports. But a pro-Campo group engineered a coup, and obtained at the end the tickets and a 'de facto' representation. The president in Cochabamba foresaw this, and gave me a proxy with full powers. It caused an open conflict in the General Assembly in Dubai, irrelevant to the result.

Peru, Ecuador and Colombia suffer from the same evils. There is a lot of possibilities of chess events, talented players, active circles. But internal fighting and official ineptitude paralyze everything. Sometimes it seemed to me that in the whole country there was only one single person favoring Campomanes, but in each case, this person was in charge of the delegation and with the tickets in his hands. Prestigious FIDE delegates were helpless for various reasons: In Peru, Aaron Goldenberg declined to come to Dubai, needless to say why. In Ecuador Paul Klein was very ill, and it took me a trip to the other end of the hemisphere to learn with horror that the man in charge had spent in Guayaquil three days and three nights with Campomanes, the year before, a chess directive in Ecuador still keeps in his safe a written confession of his sins signed by the man, the one who was going to vote for Campomanes. Sometimes, in Dubai, I was tempted to use this, but in general I intended in this campaign to behave properly, though it was extremely difficult at certain moments. About Colombia, I prefer not to talk.

Venezuela had a new chess president, a delightful old woman called Adalgisa de Briceno. She was physically beaten during her campaign by her rival, a pro Campomanes man. In Dubai, she wore an orthopedic collar around her neck, because of vertebral injuries. Chess is not a pacific game any more.

Panama has no official chess federation, but there is a man accepted as representative by FIDE. He runs a club for Chess and Back-Gammon and intends with a certain touch of desperation, to make it profitable. He was a Campo man. On the contrary, Costa Rica, where Lincoln Lucena and I met, fell completely into our arms. We jumped then to Guatemala, where the Juarez clan (four brothers in the Olympic team and a Juarez as president of the chess federation) was so interested in a simul with Kasparov that they agreed to vote for Lucena in principle. This was extremely important at this point, because six Central American countries had decided to vote together, and we therefore had two out of three. We got also a very positive impression after our visit to Republica Dominicana and Haiti, so that when we arrived at Havana to meet Jiminez, a well known pro Campomanes man, we were able to make him clear that he could not underestimate our chances, and we enjoyed asking him the tricky question whether he was or was not in favor of Kasparov. In Mexico, a simul by Kasparov would give us the vote. Lucena and I separated here, and I went alone to Honduras where the talks were inconclusive. El Salvador supported us because I promised that in case of victory Kasparov would give a simul, free of charge, to the victims of the recent earthquake. For the man in charge of the federation of Nicaragua, (his name is Hamlet Danilo) the question was to be or not to be in good terms with his neighbors, also in chess, so he would accept the majority opinion of the Central American group, at this point already tilted to us in spite of Campomanes previous efforts. This quick campaign (I was only two days in each country) convinced us that in the Latin American board we had at least a draw, so our chances of fighting the elections successfully became more and more real.

DUBAI 1986
When Keene, Levy, Lucena and I met for the first time, we had first of all to overcome shock. The Arabs had sent free tickets to almost 70 carefully selected countries. The excuse of helping poor people was untenable. For instance, Spain received free tickets, but Portugal did not.

We went on with the campaign, talking with the delegates, arranging meetings, writing statements or translating documents. By far, the most effective weapon was Kasparov himself. He met every day with a group of selected delegates in an open discussion lasting till 2 or 3 a.m. He was terrific, brilliant, extremely convincing. I firmly believed that he alone could have won the election, regardless of the Soviet vote if he had time to talk continuously to the delegates.

But unfortunately he had to play chess as well, and prepare carefully the game with the Soviet team, which was very insecure from the beginning. The talks exhausted him and meanwhile the Soviet chess federation, (the second bridge) had not yet supported his position openly. So his attempt to make an arrangement with Campomanes was understandable, even if it interrupted the campaign for several days.

The loss of a game against Seirawan aggravated the situation. At this moment the battle was still uncertain. Some 20 votes were undefined, including the Soviet one. Each side had more or less 50 votes, with a small number fluctuating from day to day, because the intention to vote is a fluid state of mind in most of the cases. So, it was clear that the Soviet vote would decide. This was day 3. The Soviet delegation announced officially its support to Campomanes only hours before the new president, Alexander Chikvaitze, landed in Dubai. From this moment on, a snowball of heroic voters who wanted to help the winner grew and grew, so that the day before the election no one dared during a big dinner, to sit at the table where Lucena and I were seated. It was an elegant gesture from Mr. Littorin, president of the European Chess Union, to cross the big Saal and to invite us to join the European delegates.

The rest is known. I have tried to understand why. I have seen that many countries have so many problems that to speak about purity in elections of a chess federation seems almost a joke. There is an atrocious civil war in many of these countries, and most Europeans simply do not realize how cruel this can be. There are also open veins in the economy of these regions, where a girl must become a prostitute from 14 years on, or a boy must become a policeman or a soldier of the dictator if they want to survive. In these situations, chess delegates are delighted with a small piece of the big cake of money, or power, or traveling away from their unhappy surroundings. They are grateful for a free ticket, or a good meal, or oh my God, the possibility of a post in FIDE with a beautiful flag over an international table. I believe that this is the kind of people who have supported Campomanes.

But I have seen, in remote towns, chess players meeting for a lecture, with shining eyes when they discover the second idea of a study by Liburkin. In many chess circles the daily work of the enthusiastic teachers has impressed me, and one is touched when the parents come with a seven year old boy with an Indian face, dressed with his best shirt, to ask to play a game against the boy, because he is talented, and not many masters have visited the town. As an emanation of these people, appear to me many Latin American delegates, clever, resourceful, trying to help Lucena and his campaign even if they must do it in a hidden manner. Because of these people, I believe that the battle is not over, and that the third bridge can be taken one day.

Ricardo Calvo
Madrid, Spain

35. BEHIND CLOSED DOORS
March 13, 2006

Someone once quipped that if Russian and American chess officials changed places, nobody would notice the difference. Have you ever wondered about how policy is made or what goes on behind closed doors of the United States Chess Federation?

Lev Alburt, now 60, was the first grandmaster elected to the seven-member USCF board of directors and soon became the odd man out. In this exclusive interview he pierces the veil of secrecy and begins naming names.

After defecting from the USSR in 1979 he settled in Manhattan, married, and quickly became a fixture in American chess. After capturing our nation's highest title three times, he retired from tournaments to write books and give lessons. Is what he had to say in 1989 after completing a three-year stint on a dysfunctional policy board still pertinent today?

INTERVIEW WITH GM LEV ALBURT

EVANS: You are the first grandmaster ever elected, yet on most major issues you were outvoted 6-1. How would you sum up the experience?

ALBURT: Disappointing. At the Delegates meeting I said I was leaving without any great sense of accomplishment but with a great sense of relief. This sentiment was probably shared by most of my colleagues on the board who joined in the general laughter.

EVANS: What were some of your objectives when you ran for office?

ALBURT: I wanted to reverse our FIDE policy and condemn such extravaganzas as the Soviet blacklist that our leadership accepted in the hope of launching a USA-USSR Summit Match in 1986. But my main goal was to work with the board to pursue what I thought was our common interest: to promote chess in this country, to help our federation grow towards the 100,000 mark. This certainly shouldn't be a big task since all polls indicate that tens of millions of Americans know how to play chess.

EVANS: Did you start with high hopes?

ALBURT: Yes and no. Some of my friends who were familiar with USCF politics told me: "Look, Lev, don't count on making any significant changes. Those guys really don't want the USCF to grow because if it stays small they can control it. But if it grows and attracts real money, then high-powered executives might start running things properly."

NO-GROWTH POLITICIANS

EVANS: Lev, it's hard to believe that people who are supposed to promote chess in America are actually holding back its growth.

ALBURT: I couldn't believe it myself. But I learned that everyone in the business office and above all members of the board were interested primarily in doing almost nothing. Nothing real. Nothing to promote chess. When I get together with Allen Kaufman or Jimmy Sherwin of the American Chess Foundation we usually discuss ways to promote growth and emulate the success of England, which sprang from nowhere to one of the top nations.

EVANS: Didn't the board discuss these things?

ALBURT: No. I was extremely surprised that such topics were never addressed. Never, ever.

EVANS: What was their goal?

ALBURT: Let me continue. Even when we went to a restaurant I always expected them to bring up the subject of what can be done to make chess grow. But always the topics during our sessions was who should run for the board next year, who should be awarded national tournaments, or how to avoid being attacked by critics.

EVANS: Well, what did they get out of serving on the board?

ALBURT: Perks, of course. Free trips, and so forth. Some old timers look upon the federation as their toy, their plaything. They hang around people they chummed with for years. They love to give each other awards. When I left they offered me a Certificate of Service, but I said I wasn't interested in such things.

SECRECY AND CLOSED SESSIONS

EVANS: Let me ask you about some of your frustrations. For example, during president Steven Doyle's administration you were denied access to certain documents when you tried to procure expense records or phone bills of fellow board members.

ALBURT: It is part of this overall hysteria over secrecy. They try to keep a tight lid on things while pretending everything is open and above board. They feel insecure when people criticize their policies. Before the Renaissance Group there were no real critics, just different cliques like themselves fighting for power. But nobody ever challenged the system the way the Friends of the USCF did by pushing for one-member-one-vote. In the past chess politicians attacked each other for trivial things, not fundamental changes. The board senses that they lack real legitimacy because the 350 or so voters are to a great extent handpicked by their cronies in various states. [Today regular members can vote for candidates who run for office and publish statements in *Chess Life*.]

EVANS: But isn't such secrecy extraordinary in a not-for-profit, tax-exempt organization charged with promoting chess in America?

ALBURT: The board certainly keeps a lot of things secret that they shouldn't. I was denied access to many documents. And when president Harold Winston came in, he tightened the secrecy despite his pledge to run an open administration. He regarded critics as enemies and tried to hide things from them.

EVANS: The board voted to ban tape recorders from open sessions but had to back down when Friends of the USCF blasted them in its newsletter. Isn't the board spending more and more time in closed session anyway?

ALBURT: They discuss a lot of things in private which to my mind don't belong in closed session. They often use these sessions as an excuse to say nasty things they would not dare to repeat in public. Sometimes they knock people I respect and I challenge them to produce evidence or shut up.

EVANS: So didn't they become more careful around you?

ALBURT: To some extent I think I spoiled the good feeling they shared together—the feeling that the less anyone outside knows, the better. When someone new was elected to the board, they immediately closed ranks and developed a bond. Even reform candidates wanted to become one of the boys as soon as they were elected.

EVANS: Can you give an example?

ALBURT: The change in David Saponara was dramatic. At first he strongly opposed the board's austerity budget. But after they talked to him in Boston [1988] he did an abrupt about face. What the board did was, in my opinion, technically wrong. They called an unofficial session from which I was excluded where they made deals and persuaded Saponara to change his mind.

EVANS: There's an old saying in politics that to get along you have to go along. Weren't you tempted to do this?

ALBURT: I felt a great temptation to be more conciliatory. You see, after all, they are not evil people. Personally many of them are very nice. When you're in the same room and spend a lot of time together, exchange jokes and try to solve problems, you develop a sort of camaraderie. It's natural. But I had to remind myself that although we were friendly, the things they were doing in secret were plainly wrong. The system which existed, a system of secrecy, could be easily abused. It certainly invited corruption.

EVANS: Board member Harry Sabine said all that the reformers would accomplish by trying to open things up is to force the board into doing more things behind closed doors.

ALBURT: Okay. It just shows their type of mentality. A siege mentality.

EVANS: I was under the impression that the board only had the right to go into closed session to discuss things like sealed bids or legal and personnel matters.

ALBURT: They do many other things that should be discussed openly. For instance, they went into closed session to discuss candidates to replace Don Schultz as FIDE delegate. They argued it was necessary because otherwise they could not say nasty things about other candidates in public, like so-and-so is a drunk. My position was that if someone wanted to say something derogatory, they could stop briefly to go into closed session.

EVANS: But doesn't much of this information get out anyway?

ALBURT: Of course. They leak information all the time to their friends. For instance, when executive director Gerard Dullea was given authority to fire Larry Parr as editor in closed session, it was supposed to be a deep dark secret. But when I came out of the meeting I was met by Jerry Hanken who told me how sorry he was, that if only he had been elected instead of Sabine such a dreadful thing never would have happened. Probably some board member broke the news to him on the way to the bathroom.

EVANS: Why should there be such a need to classify information? Chess is not the Pentagon.

ALBURT: The board is playing with its power. I can hardly ever recall when any justification was given for going into closed session. Often they just wanted to bad-mouth people not being considered for jobs. Especially people who were my friends, but even some I didn't know. When I challenged them and asked for proof, they said they were merely speaking their piece and giving their opinion.

EVANS: But, Lev, you say these are decent people. Decent people don't do these things.

ALBURT: I agree. But people are not all black and white. I think the problem is they created an artificial environment. It creates a bankrupt mentality. It creates a sense of belonging to an exclusive club. They feel they can do almost anything, and that others are beneath them—even grandmasters. But when Ed Labate sued them, they immediately retreated. So what I am saying is that they are not evil people, they are not bad people. But the system is so bad that even normal people are encouraged to act wrongly.

THE USCF AND FIDE

EVANS: What is their attitude towards FIDE?

ALBURT: They strongly identify with FIDE, but they are still Americans and don't feel comfortable with everything FIDE does. Some of them have a total attachment to FIDE, some have reservations, but they all admire FIDE as an institution. They feel that FIDE is their home. They feel that FIDE gives them more legitimacy. They may pay lip service to grandmasters organizing but really don't like the idea of them deciding their own affairs.

EVANS: Why not?

ALBURT: Because it makes FIDE and their own political structure irrelevant. On the whole the board is happy that top players in America are basically disunited. The fact that most grandmasters are not rich gives the board more control over them. They use whichever grandmaster who says something they like at the moment to create the impression it represents grandmaster opinion. If one grandmaster does not say what they want, they will quote another grandmaster who does say what they want.

36. INTERVIEW WITH AVERBAKH

March 29, 2004

"I was afraid of losing to a Russian grandmaster and he was afraid of losing to a kid."

—Bobby Fischer

Position after 20 Kf1. Who stands better?
Averbakh vs. Fischer, Portoroz 1958

In 1990, when GM Yuri Averbakh was 68, I interviewed him for the December issue of *Chess Life*. It won an award from the Chess Journalists of America and took place in New York after the fall of the Berlin Wall when he could speak freely.

Averbakh first won the USSR Championship in 1954. He served as president of the Soviet Chess Federation and was their FIDE delegate for many years. In 1993 he was arbiter of the Kasparov vs. Short PCA title match in London, a testimony to the high esteem in which he was held outside the Iron Curtain. Perhaps best known for his series of endgame treatises, he spoke candidly about the sweeping changes he witnessed in a long and distinguished chess career.

EVANS: What is the difference between the chess of today and yesterday?

AVERBAKH: Now much more information is available to everyone. As editor of "Shakmaty v SSSR" I got a lot of letters from readers and recall one in particular from a boy who wanted to know about a game we had printed in the Marshall Attack with a 28th move he had not seen before. I was amazed at the depth of his knowledge.

EVANS: Despite all the advances, if you were to take the ten best players in the world today and match them against, say, the ten best of 1958, who would win?

AVERBAKH: Well, let's take a piece of paper and compare. [Writes] Botvinnik, Smyslov, Bronstein, Keres, Tal, Petrosian, Geller, Reshevsky, Gligoric, Najdorf, Spassky, Korchnoi, Larsen, Portisch. How many is that? Oops! I almost forgot Fischer. And in 1990: Kasparov, Karpov, Timman, Short, Kamsky, Ivanchuk, Gelfand, Speelman, Nunn, Beliavsky. [Stops writing] Doesn't sound nearly so impressive today, does it?

EVANS: Can you tell us more about your great generation of Soviet masters?

AVERBAKH: I believe we had a team that we never had before and will never have again. It was our golden age. Botvinnik was World Champion but Smyslov, Keres and Bronstein were on the same level. Petrosian, Geller, me, Taimanov and Boleslavsky were coming on strong. What I liked above all is that they were strong individuals with unique personalities. Then Tal, Spassky and Korchnoi rose in the sixties.

EVANS: Korchnoi said that chess was one of the few ways a bright young man could make his way up the ladder of Soviet society.

AVERBAKH: Yes, but there was a great rush in science too. Actually we had a big gap in the development of young players between the age of Spassky and Karpov. I analyzed the reason: the generation born during WWII did not produce many great players anywhere with the exception of Fischer, who was born in 1943.

EVANS: Do you remember how you felt in 1958 when Bobby won the U.S. Championship at age 14?

AVERBAKH: Actually, the first time I heard of him was in 1954. I played against him once at Portoroz in 1958 [see game below] but he was not yet developed. He became a threat years later, around 1962 in Curacao.

EVANS: What were the fifties like for you in Russia?

AVERBAKH: In 1950 I had a very good position in science and was preparing for my doctorate, then wondered if I should try to become a

135

grandmaster. It was impossible to combine the two activities, so I was given a two-year leave of absence. It was a long road to the Interzonal. First you had to qualify from the semifinals of the Soviet Championship, which Petrosian won. Geller was second, and I tied with Boleslavsky for third to advance to the finals. Keres won the title in 1951 followed by Geller and Petrosian, and I tied with Taimanov to advance to the Interzonal at Saltjosbaden in 1951. So I became a GM and abandoned engineering. For the next ten years I was a chess pro, but decided I couldn't go much farther after reaching 40. So I switched to chess administration, journalism and my endgame books, where the scientific aspect appealed to me.

EVANS: What was the most difficult period for you back then?

AVERBAKH: In 1954 I won the Soviet title outright. But in 1955 I was thrown off our team for a year for "unsporting conduct." It was the result of an incident when our team played against the United States at New York in 1954, when you won your match against Taimanov. I was disciplined not because I lost my match with Donald Byrne, but for refusing to help Alexander Kotov analyze an adjournment against Robert Byrne. A half hour before my last game I had heated words with Postnikov, the chief of our delegation, who accused me of disobeying his orders. He didn't care that I was getting ready for a game, only that he was the boss and I had refused to help a fellow team member. My hands were trembling when I sat down at the board. As you know, I lost a completely won position against Donald in that fourth game.

EVANS: Why didn't you help analyze Kotov's ending?

AVERBAKH: I was just tired. I had lost my third game to Donald on time and was feeling rotten. We had Bondarevsky, Tolush, many coaches who could help analyze the adjournment. I wasn't really needed, but I believe it was just an excuse so that Kotov could replace me on future teams. Even though I was the national champion, I was barred from playing at the Olympiad in Amsterdam later that year. Then everything seemed to go wrong at once: my father died and I was drafted. My luck returned after I got a telegram from Moscow giving me a choice between military service or accompanying Spassky to the 1955 World Junior Championship. Maybe Postnikov regretted his rudeness to me.

EVANS: What was the worst thing about being a grandmaster in the fifties?

AVERBAKH: There were so few international tournaments. In the course of two years I played outside of Russia only once.

EVANS: How did they determine who would represent the Soviet Union abroad? Was it on a political basis or strictly on chess strength?

AVERBAKH: Kotov could go to play anywhere he pleased.

EVANS: Kotov was reliable?

AVERBAKH: [Laughs] No, it was not a political question. It was a question of generation. The people on the sports committee were of the same generation as Kotov. They thought my generation was still young and had plenty of time.

EVANS: Was there something especially good about the feeling of the 1950s for you in chess?

AVERBAKH: At that time, chess was far more developed in our country than anywhere else. We could expect to win when we went abroad. We were almost invincible.

EVANS: Kavalek said not too long ago that there are more games being played now than ever before, but he's not sure they're better games. What do you think?

AVERBAKH: It's hard to compare. Each generation defends itself. May I say I believe that with these fast time limits the level of chess is not so high as it was in the fifties? And the six-hour session hurts endgame play.

EVANS: Botvinnik said that he considered Capablanca the supreme chess genius. Who would you place in that category?

AVERBAKH: I have seen two geniuses in my time. One was Tal. The other was Fischer. Maybe Kasparov also. In chess you cannot be a genius forever, only for a short burst. Fischer's highest level was after the Candidates matches in 1970 where he beat Larsen and Taimanov 6-0 and then crushed Petrosian and Spassky. Fischer was very strong with Black. With White everybody can win, but the main problem is how to win with Black.

EVANS: Was chess bigger in the Soviet Union back in the fifties than it is now?

AVERBAKH: I can't say that popularity is going down, but there is different chess now. Different chess.

EVANS: What was your reaction when Karpov didn't play Fischer in 1975?

AVERBAKH: You know, I was a very good friend of Fischer's manager Ed Edmondson. May I say we were on extremely friendly terms? He told me honestly before the FIDE congress in 1975 that we would no longer be on such good terms when the congress was over. He lashed the Soviet Chess Federation for opposing Fischer's match conditions. In my opinion, he knew in his heart that Fischer couldn't play this match but wanted us to take the blame.

EVANS: Campomanes told me that he knew Fischer's conditions were doomed when FIDE split it into two votes. Did it make sense for FIDE to vote for a 10-win match and then limit it to 36 games?

AVERBAKH: It was illogical. But ten wins was ridiculous.

EVANS: Many people think that Fischer would have beaten Karpov very badly.

AVERBAKH: I agree. But I believe that Fischer just couldn't play. I just don't know why.

EVANS: In other words, it wasn't a case of Fischer being afraid of Karpov so much as Fischer being afraid of himself?

AVERBAKH: Only.

EVANS: If Fischer had asked for a return match clause instead of ten wins, do you think FIDE would have given it to him?

AVERBAKH: Of course. Of course.

EVANS: How did you feel years later when FIDE restored the rematch clause for Karpov after having taken it away from Botvinnik in 1963?

AVERBAKH: It was top secret, but Ed Edmondson was the one who organized this return match clause for Karpov! I was present during the negotiations for the Karpov-Korchnoi match. Our federation wanted to have 24 games or a maximum of 30, and Edmondson pressed for six wins. At the FIDE congress in Caracas in 1977 Karpov demanded a rematch clause for accepting six wins. Edmondson helped him get it.

EVANS: But this clause was a bigger mathematical advantage than the one FIDE had denied Fischer. What was Ed's motive?

AVERBAKH: Probably to make up for some of the nasty things he wrote about Karpov, such as "this mouse who roars like a lion." Fischer was out of the picture already and had dismissed Edmondson, so perhaps Ed wanted to improve his relations with Karpov. Really he organized everything.

EVANS: Do you think Karpov was happy to get the title without playing Fischer?

AVERBAKH: Of course. Karpov was afraid of Fischer in 1975. Who wouldn't like to get the title by default?

EVANS: Do you think that's the main reason why Karpov was so active after that: to prove he was really worthy of the title?

AVERBAKH: For Karpov, you know, money is very important. This is his main stimulus. He may lose to Kasparov, but he is always well compensated for it.

EVANS: Why do you think the first K-K match was stopped in 1985?

AVERBAKH: For me it's completely clear. Because Karpov couldn't continue at all.

EVANS: Was he suffering from nervous exhaustion?

AVERBAKH: The chief of his delegation Baturinsky told me that he tried his best to convince Karpov to play on, but that Karpov simply couldn't play despite his two-game lead. He needed a postponement.

EVANS: Who were the best human beings among the Soviet grandmasters?

AVERBAKH: I can give you one example about Geller. I told you we played in the semi-finals of the Russian championship. We were fighting for the lead with Boleslavsky, but the three of us had already qualified mathematically. Geller asked me if I wanted to win, and I said that I only wanted to qualify. Geller said it was extremely important for Petrosian to win, so that he could move to Moscow. I was really astonished, because I had never seen such self sacrifice on the part of a professional. Later they were not so friendly, but at the time he helped Petrosian win the event.

EVANS: What was the circulation of your magazine when you first started and what is it now?

AVERBAKH: It rose from 30,000 to 70,000 in the mid-seventies. But after a second magazine *64* started, we dropped to about 50,000.

EVANS: If you had more paper, could you sell more copies?

AVERBAKH: No. Because, you know, we have at least seven separate chess magazines on the market with a total circulation of around 250,000.

EVANS: Do you find the changes taking place in your country to be pleasant, and are you happy with the direction the Soviet Union is taking?

AVERBAKH: I am happy about everything. But there is one big question: Nobody can say what will happen tomorrow. It will be okay if the economic situation can be stabilized. If not, it will be very bad. The shops are empty. It's impossible to buy anything. This is the main problem, not politics.

EVANS: Kasparov is striving to turn chess into a fully professional sport where amateurs will no longer have any control over grandmasters. Since you are running for FIDE office, what about relations between FIDE and the GMA?

AVERBAKH: Let grandmasters run grandmaster chess and let FIDE run FIDE. I see no contradiction. I see only personal problems between Kasparov and Campomanes.

EVANS: Who do you think will win the Karpov-Kasparov match [in 1990]?

AVERBAKH: I think Kasparov will score 60 percent. [Actually Kasparov scored about 52 percent by 12½-11½]

EVANS: What about the quality of the games?

AVERBAKH: You know, when you are playing for the title the main goal is to win the match and not to create brilliant masterpieces.

EVANS: Thank you, Yuri.

AVERBAKH vs. FISCHER
King's Indian Defense, 1958

1 d4 Nf6 2 c4 g6 3 Nc3 Bg7 4 e4 d6 5 Be2 0–0 6 Bg5 h6 7 Be3 c5 8 d5 e6 9 h3 exd5 10 exd5 Re8 11 Nf3 Bf5 12 g4 Be4 13 Rg1 Nbd7 14 Nd2 a6!? 15 h4 b5 16 g5 b4 17 gxf6 bxc3 18 Nxe4 Rxe4 19 fxg7 Qxh4 20 Kf1 cxb2 21 Rb1 **Draw agreed!?**

The Interzonal in Portoroz, Yugoslavia, was Fischer's first international outing. In a tough field of 21 he scored a respectable 12-8, trailing victor Mikhail Tal by 1½ points. In round 7, facing Averbakh for the first and last time, Fischer embarked on a risky piece sacrifice instead of settling for 14... g5 (or Qb6) 15 h4 gxh4 16 g5 hxg5 17 Bxg5 Bg6. At the end, he offered a draw in an unclear setting.

37. RED SQUARES
October 14. 2002

"Russia is good for chess and ballet, but that's it!" says Sergei Dovlatov in his book *Ours: A Russian Family Album.*

The Bolsheviks pushed chess for the masses in the 1920s after Lenin dubbed it "the gymnasium of the mind." Chess was a cheap way to fill long winter nights, and everyone learned it in school.

"When we have worries, we play chess to forget our worries. When we have no worries, we play chess because there is nothing else to do," they joked.

"Chess is a true weapon against religious delusions," ran a slogan by Nikolai Krylenko, architect of the successful chess program, later became a prosecutor and Commissar for Justice. In 1938 he perished in one of Stalin's purges.

In 1948 Krylenko's protegé Mikhail Botvinnik, who survived the terror, was at the forefront of a stable of pampered stars subsidized by the state. Chess supremacy was touted as a triumph of Communism—until a kid from Brooklyn named Bobby Fischer dethroned Boris Spassky in 1972.

In 1993 when Nigel Short faced Garry Kasparov at a title match in London, the BBC aired a remarkable half-hour TV documentary about the Soviet domination of chess. *Red Squares* featured chess sets carved by inmates of the gulags and some interviews with chess notables.

Botvinnik, a fit-looking 82, was still proud of a mission that made chess into a game of the people. And Victor Baturinsky recalled his amazement when arriving in Moscow at the height of World War II to find the USSR Chess Championship underway despite the proximity of the German army.

During the 1930s Baturinsky was in a troika that tried and executed hordes of innocent people. In the postwar era he was the handler of Anatoly Karpov, who wielded more power than any other world champ. After taking the title by default from Bobby Fischer in 1975, Karpov held it for ten years and decided which Soviet players could compete abroad for hard currency.

The great Mikhail Tal was often forbidden to play in other countries before he was married, because he left behind no "hostage" to insure his return. Grandmaster Yuri Averbakh, a chess official, said the KGB routinely shadowed players outside of Russia. When Spassky expressed contempt for the regime to their ambassador in Amsterdam, Averbakh was told that Spassky's behavior was intolerable.

Melik-Karamov, a journalist, cited secret KGB files about Karpov's attempts to bribe Kasparov's aides. In 1985 after Karpov lost two games in a row, their first title match was aborted by FIDE president Florencio Campomanes. "Purely in the interests of chess," he told the BBC. "I'm convinced I wasn't wrong."

The program revealed that in reality Politburo member Pavel Demichev gave the order to kill the match and rescue Karpov, whose nerves were shot. Averbakh said the Kremlin repaid the favor by backing Campomanes for reelection in 1986 despite an outcry from Kasparov and many others.

"Had the umpire in any other sport stepped in, as FIDE President Florencio Campomanes did in 1985, to halt a championship final 'without result' at its most interesting and climactic stage, that unfortunate official would undoubtedly have been lynched by a raging mob of frustrated fans!" noted Ray Keene, chess editor of *The Times of London*. "Somehow, FIDE got away with this act of dubious prestigidation, but inevitably there were consequences."

Red Squares paints a dark picture of days gone by. Color it blood red.

38. SANDBAGGING
September 26, 2005

"What's your rating?" is a mantra that's frequently heard wherever players gather. The rating system devised 50 years ago by Arpad Elo is still remarkably accurate.

It ranks players internationally, predicts results, and can even compare champions from different eras. It also assigns contestants to sections compatible with their level of skill in big weekend tournaments.

Most players strive to raise their rating a notch, perhaps to reach a master level of 2,200 points. Yet, believe it or not, some players actually try to lower their rating by losing games on purpose. This devious practice is called sandbagging.

The idea is to remain eligible in the future for high-class prizes that such players would normally be too good for. Cash prizes are usually based on entry fees and many people simply won't come if they have no chance to win something. So most of the money is distributed to the lower sections.

The USCF installed rating floors to combat sandbagging. Once your rating hits its peak, this determines your section even if your play got worse. Critics argue that floors artificially keep ratings high and fail to catch cheaters.

"As long as we have the goofy system of paying large class prizes we will have sandbagging. Reward excellence and just maybe there will be more of it," said an idealistic official, a voice in the wilderness.

Last May the inaugural HB Global Chess Challenge in Minneapolis adopted a stringent anti-sandbagging policy. "The organizers are well aware there is a small minority who do not put a premium on fair play. Because of this unfortunate reality, the tournament will use each players' highest published rating between October 1, 2004 and April 2005."

This was deemed necessary because the $500,000 purse was the highest ever guaranteed for an open tournament. Only $100,000 went to the top where 50 grandmasters vied for a $50,000 first prize. The other $400,000 went for 300 cash prizes to 1,500 players in lower sections who each paid nearly $400 to enter.

In the old days entry fees and prizes were small and everyone played in the same section. Since then running tournaments has become a business. Organizers must attract a large turnout to make it profitable and sections appear to be the solution.

Perhaps the absence of big money once enabled chess to retain its innocence. Today the rating system coupled with lavish class prizes has created a new breed: sandbaggers.

39. CHEATERS
July 29, 2002

A reader wonders how we can uphold the integrity of competition now that Pocket Fritz is out. "What stops anyone from using it on a bathroom break while the other guy sweats it out at the board?" he writes.

"What can we do about it? Install cameras in the stalls? Seal off the room and not allow anyone in or out? Place a metal detector at the door? And there are a thousand other ways to cheat that nobody has dreamed of yet!" he continued.

Tough questions.

Maybe players must be sealed in glass booths. Bridge is dealing with many of these same issues. Players in duplicate tournaments no longer can call out their bid because of inflections in the voice that could convey vital information about their hand. Bidding boxes have been used for years, and in advanced bridge circles, screens prevent you from seeing your partner's facial expressions.

Paranoia is rampant. This year, the *New Zealand Herald* reported that a player in the 109th National Chess Congress was accused of sneaking off to consult a computer during a coffee break.

The incident made the evening news on television. The claim was investigated. The suspect had an alibi because three people testified they were with him the whole time.

His accuser not only lost the game but was also warned he would be expelled from the tournament unless he apologized.

He apologized.

These tempests in a teapot are bound to happen again. The only question is when a real scandal will hit the headlines.

Expect it to come when someone is banned who violated a drug code by drinking too much coffee or using an over-the-counter cough remedy. Bridge and chess officials are still pushing mandatory random tests in the crazed hope that someday these games will get into the regular Olympiad—even though the U.S. Olympic Committee flatly rejected the idea of chess as a sport.

"If chess were a sport, my 83-year-old grandmother would be unable to play it. She cannot snook, she cannot dart, she cannot curl, but she plays it quite well and still manages to push a pawn," sneered a British player.

"If a computer can do it, it's not a sport," quipped one grandmaster.

40. ABSTRACT PROBLEMS
May 12, 2003

"In 1927 the renowned artist Marcel Duchamp spent most of the one week they lived together [with his wife] studying chess problems and his bride got up one night when he was asleep and, in desperate retaliation, glued the chess pieces to the board. They were divorced three weeks later."

—*The Oxford Companion To Chess*

This reminded me of an article by Carl Schreck in the *Moscow Times* about how politics even affected chess composers in the old USSR. "It's difficult to imagine an activity more benign than composing chess problems. What harm, after all, could come from creating a position on the board that requires the observer to find the correct move?" he asked.

Yet in 1936 the magazine *Chess in the USSR* ran "Confusion in Composition" by future world champion Mikhail Botvinnik who claimed that "the basis of chess is practical play." He advocated a "merciless" fight against abstract composition which coincided with a crusade for Soviet realism in art.

He favored endgame studies that might arise from real games while condemning abstractionists who preferred unusual themes (like our mate in 2) without restricting their art to practical positions.

"Things like chess composition which were so far from anything relating to everyday life started to become the center of political discussion," said grandmaster Yuri Averbach.

During Soviet purges in the late 1930s Rostislav Alexandrov and Alexander Rotinyan were expelled from the Soviet chess federation because some of their problems were published in Nazi Germany. After that, all such work had to be approved by the proper authorities before being submitted abroad.

After World War II when world champion Alexander Alekhine was accused of collaborating with the Nazis, an opening called Alekhine's

Defense was changed to the Moscow Defense in the USSR. His death in 1946 ended negotiations for a title match with Botvinnik.

Alekhine, born in Russia, is now rehabilitated there. A book praising him, written by Kotov, was allowed to be published in England in 1975 (See "Alekhine's Last Meal").

41. RIGGING RATINGS
December 15, 2003

At the Dubai Olympiad in 1986, FIDE voted to give every woman in the world 100 free ratings points—except Hungarian prodigy Susan Polgar. In one of this intrepid reporter's forays into the arcane realm of investigative chess journalism, we revealed how she was bumped from the top spot to number two behind a Soviet titleholder on the women's ranking list.

This scandal occurred during a hotly contested presidential campaign where the Soviets, despite dogged opposition from their own world champion Garry Kasparov, threw last-minute support behind the reelection of Florencio Campomanes, who in 2003 was convicted of embezzling funds in a Philippine court.

Back in 1987 Mr. Abundo decried what he called my "imaginative allegations on the rigging of the FIDE rating list. In the interest of fair play, no doubt a trait dear to Americans like you," he defied me to publish this letter from Arpad Elo, an American who devised the rating system. Here is Prof. Elo's explanation of what happened at Dubai followed by my reply.

ELO TO EVANS ON FEBRUARY 18, 1987
"The charge is advanced that President Campomanes and the Soviet Chess Federation somehow conspired to elevate the ratings of women players by 100 points so that their world champion Maya Chiburdanidze could become the highest rated women player. Nothing could be further from the truth. To stem the anti-Soviet hysteria it could fuel, I wish to set the record straight. I take full responsibility for the change. It had become obvious over the years that an unconformity developed or existed between the FIDE rating lists for men and women which had to be corrected."

EVANS TO ELO ON FEBRUARY 21, 1987
"It was nice chatting with you again on the phone today. You confirmed that Susan Polgar would have been number one if the ratings had not been changed. You also suggested that all women be raised 100 points with only

four exceptions. Yet only Polgar remained frozen while your other three recommendations were ignored. You apparently still see no hanky panky, presumably because you are accustomed to dealing with honorable people. I fear your mathematical labor was exploited by some unscrupulous FIDE politicians."

THE AFTERMATH

A few journalists who were in Dubai also expressed outrage at FIDE's shenanigans. Newsflash, a defunct organ of the British Chess Federation, noted: "Whether or not this has some sinister motive behind it is anybody's guess."

Susan's mother said, "We regret this unprecedented manipulation of ratings but realize we can do nothing about it. Susan understands the facts which motivated it, but she also is young and knows time is on her side."

Susan Polgar won the women's world championship in 1996 at age 26 by dethroning China's Zie Jun. But FIDE stripped her of the title by refusing to grant a reasonable request to delay her next match for a short while after she had a baby. She sued FIDE and won $25,000. Today she teaches chess at her club in Queens, New York.

At her website, www.susanpolgar.com, she wrote an interesting account about meeting Bobby Fischer in Budapest after he beat Boris Spassky in a 1992 rematch.

"If you randomly ask someone on the street to name one chess player, chances are the name Bobby Fischer will come up. Some consider him the greatest world champion ever. Some consider him the most eccentric. People may disagree with his views on various issues. However, no one can ever dispute what he has done for chess. No one can doubt his love and passion for the game and definitely no one can question his skills in chess. Bobby Fischer is a chess genius. He is a chess legend. He raised chess to another level.

One of my memorable moments in chess was meeting him. He visited my family and me in Hungary and stayed in our summer home. Even though it was supposed to be a secret, he could not escape the media frenzy. When Bobby did not talk about issues that were very dear to his heart or chess, he was a very friendly, funny, and definitely 'normal' person. When he talked about issues he feels strongly about, he became very 'passionate.' Whether I agree with his views or not is irrelevant. It does not change my respect and admiration for his abilities, knowledge and accomplishments in chess. He is simply one of best ever. And he is definitely one of the most colorful and one of the most recognized world champions ever.

It was such a unique experience for me to be able to play Fischer Random Chess against Bobby. Some of the games were blitz at home. Others were played while we were in restaurants. We also analyzed some positions. Everyone knew what Bobby used to think about women's chess. After our many games, even though I was not able to change his mind about many other topics, I am sure I changed his mind about women's chess. I had very good results against Bobby. But the final score is something I would never reveal unless Bobby consents. Trust is something that is very important to him.

He did not play either of my sisters. Bobby is a charming person if he did not talk about those few topics we all know about. For the most part, we stayed away from those topics."

In 2007 Texas Tech in Lubbock established the Susan Polgar Institute for Chess Excellence and she delivered the commencement address.

42. KILLER INSTINCT
June 6, 2005

Chess, vampires, and sex—who could ask for anything more? It's the plot of *Under the Black Sun* (1995) an obscure first novel by Eric Woro. His next book *Stalin's Dacha* is about a poor working stiff who kills to finance the immigration of his mail-order bride to America.

Under the Black Sun uses real games. His hero works for a small chess magazine, as the author once did, before seeking revenge for getting fired. Readers familiar with the staff at *Inside Chess* might recognize some of the people he describes.

"I lament the deplorable scarcity of fiction in the chess world. My title is taken from *The Divided Self*, Laing's classic study on schizophrenia. I will merely point to Bobby Fischer's comeback in 1992 and suggest that his spirit informs my novel," explained Woro.

This reminded me of something Bobby once told me. "Winning feels like you're sucking blood from the other guy's neck!" As if sharing a ghoulish secret, he asked if I felt the same way. I said no.

Come to think of it, vampires should excel at chess thanks to their killer instinct. Not to mention long life.

"I have little interest in reading a chess novel about a geeky prodigy or even much of a desire to read about vampires," opined one critic. "Like a cult movie, panned by the critics and ignored at the box office yet worshiped by a select few, this book is so bad that it's actually quite good," said another. A third critic also found it entertaining:

> "The main character Martin Fairchild has an incredible talent for chess, a deeply hidden family secret, and an almost unbelievable naiveté. His life is touched by kind, golden gods who present him with all he could ask for: the means and ability to develop his passion for chess and a loving girlfriend. But then he is thrown out of college, betrayed by his employers, and a foolish fling costs him his girlfriend. All seems lost."

Enter the vampire Monique. She leaves a trail of corpses on California beaches and vows to make Martin her demon lover. Will she claim his soul?

Martin struggles to discover who he is and what he wants. Only his passion for chess has the power to redeem him, but does it?

43. COMING TO AMERICA
Monday. June 13. 2005

For centuries troubadours sang the praises of chess far and wide. The game vaults all barriers and national boundaries. Many strong, unknown players finally could travel freely in search of a better life after the fall of the Berlin Wall and the demise of the Soviet empire. There's not much prize money, but these newcomers won so many events that wary rivals viewed them as poachers on their turf.

Patrick Wolff was introduced as the reigning champion at the 1993 USA Championship. "Well, yes, for another three or four hours," he said ruefully as he was about to be displaced by Alex Shabalov and Alex Yermolinsky, two Russians.

"Like it or not, American born players hold a grudge against Russian grandmaster immigrants," wrote the new co-champs in *New in Chess*. Responding to jibes from jealous rivals, they argue that competition is healthy and America can only benefit in the long run from a keen challenge.

Ironically, these transplants now preach the gospel of free enterprise. They are mostly rejects from the Russian school of chess whose careers blossomed only after coming to America.

"I really get upset when locals complain about how foreigners are spoiling things for them," said Alexander Khalifman, a Russian grandmaster who plays in Germany. "They gripe because their $500 starting fee for a tournament doesn't even cover a month's rent, but the fact we can exist for a long time on $500 back home is not a blessing. It's a tragedy."

Russia is so bleak and crime is so rampant that chess stars often fear returning after playing abroad. Artur Yusupov moved to Germany after being shot in the stomach when he startled burglars in his Moscow apartment.

Garry Kasparov is wealthy and travels with bodyguards and a gun. "You must have it these days in Moscow," he said. His ex-wife Maria worried about a plot to kidnap her daughter. "I want to tell the Mafia that I'm not rich. No one will pay a ransom for us," she said before moving to America.

"Only a Russian can understand another Russian," said Vladimir Kramnik, who at age 25 in 2000, finally dethroned Kasparov.

44. A LIFE IN CHESS
May 29, 2006

Of all the grandmasters that came to the United States after the fall of the Soviet Union, none was more colorful than Eduard Gufeld (1936–2002). "I am the world's greatest chess coach!" he boasted, and not without reason.

Gufeld trained a string of female titleholders in Soviet Georgia as well as various Olympic teams in India, Malaysia, Philippines, and Russia. While circling the globe he found time to write more than 50 chess books.

This affable ambassador of the royal game delighted audiences with a cornucopia of chess tales. Many of them along with 217 of his games are contained in his autobiography *My Life in Chess: The Search for La Giacondo* (1994). Wit shines in each page. "This story happened a long time ago and I have my own system of counting time. It happened 40 kilograms ago," wrote the portly author.

"I was jubilant when a famous chess magazine awarded one of my moves four stars. I wanted to go out and buy a bottle of cognac with the same number of stars," he recalls.

In a serious vein, he notes: "Peace is indispensable for human society but totally unacceptable in chess. Once you sit down at the board, the struggle is inevitable."

In an obituary, British GM William Hartston observed:

> "In the pantheon of great Russian players, Gufeld was never destined to gain a prominent place. Yet he was, for over 30 years, one of the most prolific grandmasters from the old Soviet Union. Why him when so many stronger players longed for international travel? Since no Soviet delegation in that era was permitted to travel without someone monitoring their behavior and reporting back, a persistent rumour grew that he was in the pay of the KGB. His ebullient spirit and generosity, however, made it easy to forgive him. After all, someone had to do the job and perhaps it was better to have someone with a genuine love for the beauty of chess."

Former world champion Garry Kasparov had this to say of his colleague: "Behind all the oddities, interspersed with humor and gags, lies a limitless devotion to our noble game, a sacred faith in its inexhaustibility, and a permanent striving for beauty and harmony in his games."

The great Mikhail Tal added: "Gufeld can beat anybody. He can also lose with equal ease to anybody."

Gufeld once told me that Bobby Fischer, who despised most Soviet players, and Mikhail Botvinnik, the icon of Soviet supremacy, were both alike in some ways. Puzzled, I asked him to explain. He said, "They were both legends, you see, who set out to destroy chess after they lost the crown. Look what happened when they were past their prime. Botvinnik ended his days working on a machine to smash young rivals. And Fischer stopped playing unless each game starts from a different position with a random setup of pieces on the back row."

A chapter on Fischer, whom Gufeld greatly admired, recalls their first meeting at Tunisia in 1967: "Oh, Gufeld! I know you! I saw your victory against Smyslov," said Bobby.

This is probably Gufeld's most famous game. He employs his favorite bishop fianchetto on g7 as Black and embarks on bold sacrifices in the opening that Smyslov failed to refute.

SMYSLOV vs. GUFELD
King's Indian Defense, USSR Championship, 1967

1 c4 Nf6 2 Nf3 g6 3 b4 Bg7 4 Bb2 0–0 5 e3 b6 6 d4 c5 7 dxc5 bxc5 8 b5 a6 9 a4 Ne4 10 Bxg7 Kxg7 11 Qd5 Qa5+ 12 Ke2 Bb7 13 Qxb7 Nc6 14 Nfd2 Ra7 15 bxc6 Rxb7 16 cxb7 Qb4 17 Nxe4 Qb2+ 18 Nbd2 Qxa1 19 Nxc5 Rb8 20 g3 Qa3 21 Nxd7 Rxb7 22 Bh3 Qd6 23 c5 Qd5 24 f3 Rb2 25 Rd1 e6 26 c6 Qc4+ 27 Ke1 Qd3 28 Bf1 Qxe3+ 29 Be2 a5 30 f4 f6 31 c7 Rc2 32 Kf1 Rxc7 33 Nc4 Rxc4 34 Bxc4 Qf3+ 35 Ke1 Qc3+
White Resigns

---

45. THE SPEED LIMIT
August 12, 2002

How fast can we play and still have quality chess? The outcome of this debate will shape the future of serious chess.

The chess clock didn't exist at the first international tournament in London 1851. Howard Staunton, England's premier player, groused that patience ceased to be a virtue when his opponents took forever thinking about each move.

A year later, a time limit of 29 minutes per move (!) was adopted at a match between Harrwitz and Lowenthal, who promptly blamed his defeat on the lack of necessary time to think. At the Anderssen vs. Kolisch match in 1862, an hour glass was used to give each side 2 hours for 24 moves.

The now familiar double chess clock made its debut at London in 1883. Each side had an hour for 15 moves, and the clock soon became a fixture. The penalty for breaking the speed limit used to be a fine, but now you forfeit the game.

Time limits got tighter and tighter until today, when we have a bewildering array of fast and slow controls. Most serious events require 40 moves in 2 hours followed by 20 moves an hour and 1/2 hour of sudden death beyond move 60. Thus no game can last more than seven hours. This compromise is considered the best way to preserve quality and still complete all games in a single session.

Although the clock forces error, pressure is mounting to make chess possibly more telegenic by speeding it up. World champion Mikhail Botvinnik once called this "a lightweight approach that panders to cheap pragmatism and erases the line between serious chess and blitz."

CHESS LITE

Apparently there is no line that FIDE president Kirsan Ilyumzhinov is unwilling to cross. His motive is purely mercenary as he and his cohorts in FIDE Commerce slowly but surely tighten their grip and strangle the life out of world chess. His outrageous proposal to limit all rated games to an hour per side, including the world championship, has met with stiff resistance from players and organizers.

Most grandmasters know that speed kills, but they hope their income will improve if sessions are shorter. "Games can still be played on an extremely high level," argues GM Alexei Shirov.

If the royal game is to become more than an arcane pursuit, it must meet the demands of the modern world. But at what price?

Must quality be sacrificed for quantity? Clearly seven hours is too long and two hours is too short for a real tournament game. Lest we destroy chess to save it, we should go slowly before moving too fast.

46. HAPPY TALK IS HERE AGAIN
June 12, 2006

This June, new editor Daniel Lucas undertook a makeover of *Chess Life*, a house organ of the U.S. Chess Federation. Although the USCF is expected to end this fiscal year in the red, the redesign was implemented by a consultant who was awarded the $50,000 job without any open bidding.

The first order of business for consultant Paul Hoffman, former editor-in-chief of *Discover* magazine, was to fire three popular grandmasters with long-running monthly columns in *Chess Life*, including this writer. Some readers called the new issue fabulous. Others said it sucked and that their favorite columns were absent.

The new editor, interviewed in *The Chess Journalist*, said that cutting several regular monthly columnists will free up space for more features. Like what? He cited an article on "women in correspondence chess" as his vision of what might interest readers.

Hoffman, who calls himself a "mainstream journalist," was paid $10,000 in advance without submitting a written report. It must be nice to have friends on the board. Dodging all questions about how he reached his conclusions or if he consulted past reader surveys, he issued this statement:

> "I'm just a consultant. I give the USCF advice and implement ideas they want me to implement. I have prepared no written reports. I am not going to discuss personnel matters like who writes for the magazine and who doesn't because that it not an appropriate subject for a public forum. I'm trying to use my 25-year experience in magazines to help the USCF publish a more engaging magazine that will attract new members and better retain existing ones. And I'm trying to avoid being embroiled in the ugly petty politics of chess that have doomed many well-intentioned efforts in the past."

As a matter of fact the USCF has earned a reputation for secrecy, sweetheart deals, and censorship. In 1961, for example, an outstanding editor named Frank Brady (author of Bobby Fischer's biography, *Profile of a Prodigy*) was fired for printing letters from readers who were outraged when a brash young Fischer forfeited an unfinished tied match against veteran Samuel Reshevsky in California. A small clique of politicians who controlled *Chess Life*, not daring to offend the wealthy match sponsor, tried to conceal how the kid got a raw deal. This incident contributed to his feelings of persecution and so embittered Bobby that he later dubbed the magazine "Chess Lies."

Some editors waged lonely struggles on behalf of readers kept in the dark as various USCF regimes buried mistakes and misdeeds in the pages of what they regarded as their magazine. Too often editors were caught in the middle, lacking support and independence, serving at the pleasure of petty bureaucrats with agendas of their own.

A good example is what happened after Yasser Seirawan won the U.S. Championship in 1986 and decided to run for USCF president. Editor Larry Parr was ordered to remove Yasser's picture from the cover of *Chess Life*. Parr told them to put the order in writing. They refused. Parr ran the cover in February 1987, as planned. He was axed about a year later but extracted a large settlement.

The job is a minefield. A remarkable 10-page letter from Frank Elley summed up his watch as editor before Parr from 1982 to 1985. His testament was solicited but predictably omitted from a comprehensive review of *Chess Life* in 1987 by a board member. Here's an excerpt from Elley's suppressed report:

THE HAPPY TALK COMMANDMENT

"I have many times stated that *Chess Life* is not the *Time* magazine of the chess world. I was wrong. Whether we in positions of influence like to admit it or not, we do not have the right to take someone's dues money and then feed him only what we think he needs to know. His money pays our salaries. His votes put us in office.

You may think I'm barking at shadows, but we've already cast our fear of information into stone for all to see. I call it The Happy Talk Commandment—thou shalt not speak unkindly of chess. A true embarrassment. I'm certainly glad not to have been editor for the past two years. World champion Garry Kasparov called a press conference and labeled the FIDE president a Mafiosa. We sent a team to an Olympiad at Dubai in 1986 that barred Israel. And so it goes."

The respected British magazine, *Chess*, reported that the American team should have walked out in protest at Dubai, as mandated by USCF delegates, when our officials failed to strike a FIDE statute allowing such boycotts to happen all over again. Instead these worthies just declared victory and stayed.

The USCF spent $10,000 (it took months to pry this figure loose) to send four officials to the United Arab Emirates while funds were said to be lacking for the customary team coach. A coach might have made a vital difference because our team narrowly missed the gold in a field of 108 men's teams after defeating Russia in our individual match. The USA took the bronze behind Russia and England. Several countries, but not many, boycotted this team championship because Israel was excluded.

Instead, a cargo of four chess politicians enjoyed a pleasant junket to the FIDE congress in Dubai, all expenses paid courtesy of the USCF. But the only way fans could find this out was in a British journal—not in *Chess Life*.

THE MOST RECENT SCANDAL

It's hard to think of an international organization more corrupt than the United Nations; but FIDE, the world chess body, comes close. American officials returned from the June election in Turin, Italy, where the 37th Chess Olympiad was held featuring a record 150 men's teams.

Kirsan Ilyumzhinov won another term as president by a margin of 96-54. It was a secret ballot, but why votes aren't recorded openly on the floor of the General Assembly escapes me. At any rate, Parr reported how Kirsan rigged the election:

> "Votes for Kirsan routinely cost about two to three thousand dollars each. Payments were made half in cash beforehand and half in cash after voting. Members of Bessel Kok's team searched the ballot booths very carefully in advance looking for cameras. They found none. THE TRICK: Those who cast votes and received payment were required to take a handphone with miniature camera capability into the booth and click a picture of the ballot showing for whom they voted. These photos were checked by Kirsan's team, led by Giorgios Makropoulos, and the bribetakers received the second half of their stipend. Members of our FIDE "team" did not feel that we should know this, and they failed to mention such inconvenient details of international chess governance. Corrupt in warp, corrupt in woof.
> There are no denials from our FIDE team. Instead we are

told that America must go along to get along. There is basically nothing that the FIDE leadership might do—murder, theft, bribery—that will prompt our representatives to support Europe in the creation of a new international chess organization."

One figures that the current crew will sanitize it all. The editor will follow orders right down the groove, no matter how Sovietized or sanitized the reporting that is required.

If the editor deviates, he's gone. The classic line of our FIDE team over the years has been that there are lots of fine people in FIDE with just a few bad apples. Nonsense. This last election featured open paying of bribes, arrogant and arrant, smiles and open taking of money.

Dutch GM Jan Timman added: "Intimidation and bribery went much farther then we had expected. People actually saw banknotes changing hands, but how to prove what the money was for? Bessel Kok will drop out after this adventure, this is sure."

In an interview that took place in June 2007 British GM Nigel Short opined:

"As to chess politics: it is well known that I supported the Right Move campaign of Bessel Kok in the last FIDE Presidential election. I have come to the conclusion that FIDE is unreformable in its current state and that corruption and incompetence are deeply entrenched. Due to the manner with which this election was won, with cash-stuffed envelopes being handed out to the more flexible delegates, I cannot see myself wishing to get involved again in such an ugly process for many years to come. I will confine myself to rather more modest attempts to promote chess throughout the Commonwealth."

The chess Olympics is held every two years in a different city where players compete and fraternize despite their nations' conflicts and squabbles. Computers that make the pairings are even programmed to avoid matching antagonistic nations whenever possible.

Mark Crowther in *The Week in Chess* lamented:

"At only 44 it's possible we may have another 30 years of Kirsan's rule. Originally he was only supposed to rule for two terms in Kalmykia, it now seems there is no end in sight there either. My overwhelming feeling is that FIDE has been bought and paid for by a maverick who has no place being in charge of anything."

FIDE president for life?

BACK ON THE HOME FRONT

The good news is that the USA captured the bronze behind Armenia and China in a record field of 150 men's teams. Unlike the days of yore, not one single member of our six-man squad was born in America. Russia (ranked #1) tied for sixth; another upset was India (ranked #2) finishing thirtieth.

Thanks to the Internet, it is no longer easy to keep information from the public. How will news about the rigged election be reported in *Chess Life*?

If you want the truth about this tyrant whose autobiography contains a chapter heading like "It Only Takes Two Weeks to Have a Man Killed," check out Planet Kirsan in the *New Yorker* (April 24, 2006). Kirsan claims to have the ability to communicate with aliens after having been aboard a U.F.O. and he is still a great admirer of Saddam Hussein.

Kalev Pehme, the previous editor who lasted a year, recently posted an open letter on the Net summing up his frustration with FIDE and USCF officials:

> "I frankly have found my run with the USCF to have done one thing which I cannot forgive. I have come to despise chess even though, throughout my entire life, I have loved the game. Part of the reason that I learned to love the game were the books and articles written by Larry Evans, which I read as a young teen when I was president of my school's chess club and when we played against other schools. My experience with USCF politicians have made me feel pain every time I look at a chess board when I should be feeling the joy that I felt when I first read Evans' books. For that, I can't forgive the USCF."

The "new" June issue contains neither letters to the editor nor a whiff of controversy, though President Bill Goichberg concedes: "The Federation has been losing adult members since 1995. This issue introduces a redesigned *Chess Life* under Editor Daniel Lucas; I trust you will find it more attractive and readable."

We'll see.

47. USA VS. USSR 1955
March 15, 2004

At the height of the Cold War, I played on an American team that went to Moscow and wrote about it for *Newsday*, a Long Island newspaper. Travel with me down memory lane, behind the Iron Curtain.

THE CHESS MATCH

This 8-board match was held in the Hall of Columns where the infamous purge trials took place and where the bodies of Lenin and Stalin lie in state. Each day capacity audiences flooded the building and, after the games, autograph hunters rushed onstage to seek us out.

In the USSR chess is the national game. It is taught in school and looked upon as an art form rather than as mere recreation. Chess masters are subsidized by the state to the extent of 2,000 roubles ($100) a month while grandmasters receive 2,500 roubles ($125) a month for doing nothing but studying chess. In addition, these players accumulate the equivalent of a small fortune by giving lectures and exhibitions, writing articles and winning prize money in international competition.

We lost by a final score of 25-7, while last year in New York we lost 20-12 and we have no excuse to offer other than Soviet grandmasters are the finest players in the world. Our players receive no governmental assistance and compete during our leisure time or at the expense of our jobs. Probably the reason for our poor showing is the lack of first-class competition in the United States and the fact that most of our players are not professionals.

The Soviets use chess as a weapon to demonstrate the superiority of their culture, hence the great pains taken to develop and maintain talented players. For propaganda purposes, they try to prove the thesis that our commercial economy has no place for non-commercial artists. I can appreciate this argument to some degree. Of course, I feel there are equally cogent arguments against state-supported art where artists must toe the mark or be purged. The Soviets themselves are very touchy on this point. They go out of their way to avoid admitting that their team consists almost entirely of professional chess masters. World champion Mikhail Botvinnik is an electrical engineer and several other players on their team also claim outside professions.

Some of the American players who had been to Moscow to compete in 1946 observed that chess seemed to have diminished somewhat in popularity. They suggested that the return to postwar normalcy may be responsible. Chess, you see, is not only a game. It's a narcotic, cheap to play and takes one's mind off politics and social questions. When I was in Yugoslavia in 1950 a joke circulated that people played chess to forget their worries; and when they had no worries, they played chess because there was nothing else to do. In America the depression produced our finest players, and this is demonstrated by the age gap between our five young players (in their 20's) and our five veterans (in their 40's).

The Soviets spared nothing to facilitate spectator interest. On stage giant wallboards manned by young master candidates illustrated the position after each move as well as the time consumed by each player. My own four games with David Bronstein, who drew a world title match with Botvinnik in 1951, were tense and exciting. We drew the first, he won the second, we drew the third and he escaped with a draw during a wild time scramble in the last one.

THE RED CARPET

Our team was put up at the Hotel National where several delegations from Communist China were also being housed. Each morning a bus was sent to conduct us on a different tour— to the Kremlin Museum, the Agricultural Fair, the Dynamo Stadium and the Bolshoi Theater.

Two interpreters were assigned to our group, but I never experienced the feeling of being watched or followed. There was, however, an atmosphere of regimentation and monotony that hung heavily in the air. It was not until I reached sunny Stockholm to play against a Swedish team that I realized how profound my depression had been.

Our interpreters were always dressed in the same suits; our

meals always the same. The food was good; in Russian eyes, delicacies. There was sturgeon, ham, fried chicken, fish, caviar, cider, milk and mineral water. Delicious, but always the same.

The Soviet mind seems to function in a set pattern, according to protocol. This sameness was particularly evident in the many speeches we heard, each extolling the value of the match in terms of international peace and the strengthening of cultural ties. Often the very phraseology was identical in different speeches, probably to prevent speakers from deviating from the party line. When our team manager Rosser Reeves said on the first day that he hoped the Soviets and Americans would meet in no greater combat than chess in the next 10,000 years, he got a resounding ovation.

The hospitality of our hosts was incomparable. They did everything possible to make our stay pleasant, including front and center seats to the opera and ballet. We received the full red carpet treatment and they even gave each of us 120 roubles for spending money.

ROUBLES VS. DOLLARS

The entire subject of money and buying power is very complex. This is because the official rate of exchange is four roubles to the dollar—a fantastically unrealistic rate. I understand that on the Tel Aviv free market roubles are selling for 20 to the dollar, a much more reasonable yardstick.

At the black market rate of a nickle a rouble, oranges cost $1.40 apiece, a dish of caviar 60 cents, a cup of tea 15 cents, a striped shirt $6, a Mickey Mouse-type watch or women's high-heeled shoes $19.25 and a motorcycle $119.50. While these prices are not fantastically out of line with those in the United States, it is most important to realize that the average monthly salary in the USSR for a six-day, 48-hour week is $40—less than $10 a week.

For most Russians, however, this income does not imply the same poverty-stricken conditions that it would in the United States. Most necessities are far cheaper than anything Americans know. For example, it is possible to obtain living quarters for as little as 50 cents a month. Medicine, too, is very inexpensive. I saw eyeglasses for 30 cents being fitted by trial and error in a drug store. And prescriptions can be filled for less than a rouble.

Many items regarded as necessities by Americans—such

as several changes of clothing—are considered luxuries by the Russians. The most familiar dresses are flower-print cottons. These sharply contrast with the men's dark, durable, regimented patterns. I learned that light colors, because they stain so easily, are the distinguishing marks of important people.

Automobiles are rare and—since the rural roads are so poor—confined almost exclusively to the cities. In Moscow most of the vehicles were Soviet-made cars resembling 1952 Packards. Occasionally a chauffeur-driven official Cadillac or Chevrolet passed with drawn green curtains.

It is almost impossible to compare purchasing power in the United States and USSR. In addition to the problem of determining true costs, those not twisted out of proportion by supply and demand, Soviet favoritism further complicates the picture. In many cases talented individuals like ballet dancers may obtain a sumptuous apartment for the same rent that a sanitation worker pays for a hovel.

Privacy as we know it is virtually nonexistent. An American reporter told me that the average living space was 6½ yards a person. Thus, a four-room apartment might house about 20 people.

BOOKS ARE CHEAP

I was struck by the fact that the entire Soviet economy is governed by political expediency. This was most apparent in the case of books and printed matter. This material, through which the state can best propagandize, is devilishly cheap.

Despite this, however, the people themselves are quite outspoken, not half so petrified of the secret police as we assume. For the most part the Russians were not only curious but quite friendly. When I asked an injudicious question—through my interpreter—I received only a tolerant smile. In fact, one thing impressed me above all: the Russia-hate in our country vastly exceeds any America-hate in the USSR.

I found that the contact between Russians and foreigners was very limited and that few Russians have ever been outside their own borders. In this light some of their distortions fed via a one-party press are understandable to an American, if not totally amusing. They think, for example, that bail is a means by which a rich man can buy himself out of a prison term. I tried to explain that he can only buy freedom while awaiting trial, because we think a man is innocent until adjudged guilty.

They think that discrimination and segregation are widespread national practices. They are violently aroused by tales of Negro-baiting and lynching. A book by Howard Fast entitled *Peekskill, U.S.A.*—which is highly inflammable propaganda—is available in every bookstore.

The Russian people I spoke with thought of the typical American as self-centered, money-loving and culturally materialistic. They viewed the United States as the cold war aggressor. For instance, several of them pointed to the Marshall Plan, the re-arming of Germany and a ring of U.S. bases in Europe as evidence of active hostility.

HOW THEY SEE AMERICA

I gathered it is their view that the people of America essentially want peace, but there are certain warmongering circles provoking war. All believe that both the Republican and Democratic parties are parties of "the upper classes." When I said that Lenin himself had written that communism and capitalism cannot exist side by side, they replied that these words had been written about 1921 and time had changed their meaning. They told me they felt a war to defeat capitalism would be unnecessary—that capitalism is a rotten apple that will fall even if the tree is not shaken.

The Russian man-on-the-street convinced me that he wants disarmament. When I said the USSR had rejected the Baruch Plan for nuclear disarmament, they said they read that the United States had turned down a similar Soviet proposal.

I discovered that the Russian people have implicit faith in their press. Every word printed in Pravda is regarded as The Truth. They think of themselves as democratic and free, and it was impossible for me to convince them that a multi-party system with choice of candidates in an election is superior to their one-party system. Their setup functions very much like a Democratic primary in the South where the candidate who is nominated invariably wins. The fight takes place within the party—at least in theory.

The Russians were impressed only when I spoke of the material goods possessed by the average American worker. They were agog when I said that a man can pack up and quit whenever he wants and travel from New York to California without permission. Freedom of movement is unknown here. Each citizen carries a "permit to live" and must receive official sanction before leaving his city. Even this is not viewed as an infringement of their liberty. "Your life is planned," they say. "Each worker is important in place."

Never having had freedom as we know it, they don't miss its blessings. I feel the essential difference in our ways of thinking concern the relation of the individual to society. The Soviets cannot conceive of individualism, and the pursuit of pleasure is viewed as egoism and license rather than liberty. They hold that an individual finds his greatest fulfillment when subordinated to the mass or state.

When I asked why criticism of their government was forbidden to them, they replied that their solidarity was their strength. It is difficult for one schooled in the liberal tradition to understand these sentiments. They believe that their leaders are genuinely working for the good of the Soviet people and are trying to better social conditions.

Any talk of the Russians rising in revolt against their masters is sheer gobbledegook. They seemed overwhelmingly patriotic and loyal. Their feelings toward their leaders go far beyond anything that we experience. Their party chieftains assume the proportions of demigods and death does not destroy the images. If anything, the adoration of Lenin and Stalin has increased since their passing. Photographs of the two appear everywhere. Lines three blocks long are queued up in front of their mausoleum, and the worship of them is almost supernatural.

I questioned people about their favorite American authors and films. The most popular writers are Jack London, Theodore Dreiser, Howard Fast, Ernest Hemingway and Langston Hughes. Several people were bitter about the imprisonment of Fast and interpreted it as a lack of political freedom in America. They did not believe me when I told them a Communist could preach on Times Square and hand out propaganda.

Generally, Hollywood films are liked. *Snow White and the Seven Dwarfs* was playing to good audiences. I even met one girl who was crazy about Robert Taylor. The most popular American films seem to be prewar Charlie Chaplins. One of the chess players who had been to New York in 1954 had seen *Three Coins in the Fountain*. I asked his opinion of it, and he said he preferred films with more substance that left him with something to ponder.

INDEPENDENCE DAY

For me, the greatest surprise and most interesting experience of our visit came July 4 at an Independence Day party in the American Embassy. It had just begun when Communist Party boss Khrushchev, Premier Bulganin, Deputy Premier Malenkov and a half-dozen lesser figures filed into Spaso House—the Embassy headquarters. It was the first time in history they had ever visited there and photographers, unprepared for the occasion, scrambled frantically for pictures. The gathering was a scene of utter confusion.

The first person Khrushchev asked to meet was Samuel Reshevsky, our No. 1 player, who had defeated world champion Botvinnik. Then Khrushchev, Bulganin and Malenkov posed with the American team. One of our tourists took and developed a group photo within one minute on his Polaroid camera. Bulganin was so impressed that he exclaimed in English, "Must be American invention. You Americans always first with new things."

RUSSIANS ARE DECENT, TOO

Then Bulganin tried to pocket the picture in jest. A newsman asked if he always took things he was fond of, and he surrendered the photo instantly. Khrushchev, looking on, added defensively, "We Russians are as decent as you Americans."

The Soviet leaders struck me as being warm and human and trying very hard to convince us they were democratic as well. Of the group, Bulganin was the most dignified and reserved. He hovered watchfully and silently as Khrushchev delivered a prepared statement to our acting ambassador to the effect that the United States should not mistake recent Russian concessions as coming from weakness rather than strength. It became apparent that these men were very sensitive to the free press, because at one point Krushchev said reports in America that Soviet agriculture was lagging were untrue, that their economy was stronger than ever.

Then a reporter asked Khrushchev and Bulganin who would be accompanying them to the summit talks at Geneva and whether the unification of Germany and the status of Formosa were going to be discussed. Both men smiled and said firmly that everything would be announced "at the appropriate time."

"Everything in its time and in its place," they kept replying to all questions. The Russian dialectic is not yes or no but rather "it is possible" or "it is not altogether impossible." It was obvious they were not accustomed to American-style press conferences. Throughout the "conference" I was wedged between Khrushchev and Bulganin. Finally, through an interpreter, I asked Khrushchev whether he thought an annual chess match between the USA and the USSR would help strengthen cultural ties. He said "of course" but added that no Soviet team would journey to America as long as they had to be fingerprinted like criminals. He held out a thumb to emphasize his words.

"Remove your Iron Curtain and he will come," he said. I replied, "If there are two Iron Curtains, why doesn't the Soviet Union also remove hers?" To this he concluded, "Then remove your dollar curtain."

At that moment, my admiration and sympathy for American diplomats who have dealt with the Soviets was inestimable.

Life magazine ran a photo of the red leaders posing with our entire team during a Fourth of July party at the U.S. Embassy. It was reprinted in the *American Chess Quarterly* 1962, Volume 1, Number 4.

In my fourth game with Bronstein my last chance to win was 41...h5! 42 gxh5 Rh3.

BRONSTEIN vs. EVANS
Slav Defense, Moscow, 1955

1 d4 Nf6 2 c4 e6 3 Nf3 d5 4 Nc3 c6 5 e3 Nbd7 6 Bd3 Bb4 7 a3 Ba5 8 Qc2 0–0 9 0–0 Bc7 10 Bd2 dxc4 11 Bxc4 e5 12 Ba2 h6 13 Rae1 Re8 14 dxe5 Nxe5 15 Nxe5 Rxe5 16 f4 Bf5 17 e4 Bb6+ 18 Kh1 Rxe4 19 Nxe4 Nxe4 20 Rxe4 Bxe4 21 Qxe4 Qxd2 22 Bb1 Rd8 23 Bc2 Kf8 24 Re1 Bc5 25 h3 g6 26 Rd1 Qa5 27 Rf1 Re8 28 Qc4 Qb5 29 Qxb5 cxb5 30 f5 g5 31 Bd3 a6 32 Rc1 Bd4 33 b3 Bb2 34 Rd1 Bxa3 35 g4 Re3 36 Kg2 Bb2 37 Kf2 Rxh3 38 Be4 Rxb3 39 Bxb7 a5 40 Rd7 f6 41 Bc6 a4? 42 Rd8+ Ke7 43 Rd7+ **Draw**

48. A LIVING LEGEND
July 5, 2004

Why won't Viktor Korchnoi, 73, act his age? He is the oldest player on the pro circuit and arguably the strongest player who never became world champion.

In 1976 he defected from the USSR to Switzerland. "If it looked as if I might win my match against Karpov in 1974 I had a feeling something might happen to me, like an accident in the street," he said. "That may sound paranoid, but in Soviet Russia there is no clear difference between paranoia and real fear. Now they cannot force me to lose anymore."

But he was wrong. His family was finally released from the USSR only after he lost two title matches to Anatoly Karpov in 1978 and 1981, one of the greatest scandals in the history of FIDE, a "neutral" world chess body.

Korchnoi never again was a real threat to Soviet supremacy and the Kremlin ended a boycott by permitting its stars to compete against him in international events, but this living legend still continues his winning ways in an era of 12-year-old grandmasters. He dominated a field of six at the 2nd György Marx Memorial held in honor of a Hungarian physicist, a full point ahead of Ferenc Berkes, 18, in this grueling double round robin tournament.

A SPOT OF LUCK
Korchnoi won 6, drew 3, and lost once to Alexander Beliavsky, 50, who also had him on the ropes in their second game after Black rejected 16...cxb4 17 Nd4 Qb6 18 Bd2 bxa3 19 Rdb1 Qd8 20 Bxa5 Qxa5 21 Rxb7 Ne5 22 Rb3 with equal chances. Later White missed 30 cxb6! axb6 31 Qa1 keeping an extra pawn. At the end Beliavsky lost a knight in a bizarre way when he spurned a draw by repetition with 38 Qf1.

BELIAVSKY vs. KORCHNOI
Nimzo Indian Defense, 2004

1 d4 Nf6 2 c4 e6 3 Nc3 Bb4 4 e3 d5 5 Nf3 0–0 6 Bd3 c5 7 0–0 dxc4 8 Bxc4 Bd7 9 Qe2 Bc6 10 Rd1 Nbd7 11 d5 exd5 12 Nxd5 Nxd5 13 Bxd5 Qc7 14 Bxc6 Qxc6 15 a3 Ba5 16 b4 Bc7 17 Bb2 Rad8 18 Rac1 b6 19 Qc4 Rfe8 20 Rd5 Qe6 21 Ng5 Qg6 22 h4 h6 23 Nf3 Qe6 24 Rcd1 Nf6 25 Bxf6 Qxf6 26.Rxd8 Rxd8 27.Rxd8 Qxd8 28.bxc5 Qd1 29 Qf1 Qb3 30 Qc1 bxc5 31 Nd2 Qd3 32 g3 Ba5 33 Nc4 Bc3 34 Qf1 Qc2 35 Qg2 Qd1 36 Qf1 Qc2 37 Qg2 Qd1 38 Kh2?? Qd3! 39 Qa8 Kh7 **White Resigns**

---

49. THE TIES THAT BIND
March 1, 2004

In boxing, a champion keeps the title on a tie, but draw odds in chess is a huge advantage for the simple reason that a draw is the logical outcome of a good game. The history of the world chess championship is a case study in how champions sought to extend their reign by hook or crook.

At Steinitz-Zukertort in 1886, often cited as the first official title match, the rules were simple and fair: the first side to win 10 games without counting draws. Steinitz achieved the goal in 20 games and decreed that in future matches he would retain the crown in case of a 9-9 tie. Now challengers had to win by at least two points (10-8) to overcome this hurdle, a controversy that reared its ugly head 100 years later.

In 1894 Steinitz succumbed to Lasker, who held the title for 27 years after a close call in 1910 when he had to win the last game against Schlechter to tie a short 10-game match 5-5. Each side drew 8 and won once.

The problem with the system was that the champion could duck tough challengers by imposing onerous conditions. Relations soon soured between Capablanca and Lasker, who required him to win by two points in a 30-game match. "The unfairness of this condition is obvious," complained Capa, who probably should have played anyway because even a one-point victory would have established his legitimacy in the court of public opinion. Instead he had to wait for a war to end before dethroning Lasker at Havana in 1921.

The London rules of 1922 ushered in serious reforms. Now one side had to win six games without counting draws in a contest of unlimited duration. In 1927 Capa fell to Alekhine by 6 to 3 with 25 draws. Alas, a revenge match failed to materialize.

In 1935 Alekhine imposed a rematch clause and draw odds with a limit of 30 games against Euwe, who won narrowly by 15½-14½. Two years later Alekhine regained the title by 10-4 with 11 draws. His death in 1946 left the title vacant and FIDE stepped in to fill the void. From now on champions had to defend every three years against a qualified challenger, but it didn't take long for the Soviets to stack things in their favor.

Botvinnik won a rigged event in 1948 and then got draw odds in 24-game matches plus a guaranteed rematch if he lost! Each draw inched him closer to victory and he held the title on a 12-12 tie in his first two outings with Bronstein in 1951 and Smyslov in 1954. Since chess was the national game in Russia where stars were subsidized by the state, prize funds were kept low to discourage competitors from the West. Communist supremacy at chess became a propaganda weapon in the Cold War.

Things changed when a kid from Brooklyn accused the Russians of cheating. Spassky had draw odds against Fischer in 1972, but no rematch clause, and the purse skyrocketed from about 1,500 roubles to $250,000.

After capturing the crown, Fischer, like Steinitz a century earlier, demanded 10 wins with a 9-9 tie clause. He argued that only wins should count, not draws, in a match of unlimited duration. In principle he was right. In practice he was wrong, and I pleaded with him in vain to drop the tie clause and set an example by reducing the number of wins to six.

FIDE granted his conditions but set a limit of 36 games. In effect, this restored draw odds and nullified the requirement to win any games. Although it favored Fischer, who was the defending champion, he stubbornly destroyed his own career by spurning a $4 million purse to face Karpov at Manila in 1975.

Karpov seized the title by default and defended it twice in 1978 and 1981 against Korchnoi. The rules called for six wins, draws not counting, but FIDE restored the rematch clause for Karpov—a bigger mathematical edge than the reclusive Fischer ever demanded.

The first Karpov-Kasparov match in 1984 demonstrated the flaw of an open-ended match in the modern world. After 23 weeks and 48 games neither side could achieve the goal, and FIDE aborted the marathon despite protests by both players.

Kasparov won the rematch and, to his credit, struck a blow for chess justice by renouncing a rematch clause. But he retained draw odds in 24-game matches and in 1987 held the title on a slim 12-12 tie against Karpov, then beat him again in 1990.

Kasparov accused FIDE of mismanaging the title for half a century and, backed by funding from Intel, created the Professional Chess Association (PCA). In 1993 the rules called for 24 games against Short for $2.5 million in London.

Future matches got shorter and shorter, thus increasing the burden on Kasparov's challengers to overcome draw odds. In 1995 he cut the number of games from 24 to 20 against Anand, who took the lead after eight straight draws before losing two in a row. With only nine games remaining, Anand was desperate to regain the lead and succumbed by game 18 in one of history's most disappointing title matches.

When asked whether the chess world would applaud Kasparov if he generously forfeited draw odds, PCA Commissioner Bob Rice replied, "The political views of chess players are so difficult to fathom that attempting to alleviate a negative feeling by doing a particular thing is an extraordinarily dicey proposition. I would be amazed if such an act by Kasparov would have much effect."

At London in 2000 Kasparov shortened the contest against Kramnik from 20 to 16 games, but this time draw odds didn't save him. Clearly out of form, Kasparov failed to win a single game and his reign came to an end.

When will there be a fair match where both sides have equal rights? Today chess fans don't even know who is the champion and who is the challenger because the world championship is in a state of total chaos. In 2006, Kramnik finally unified the title by beating Topalov who made a fool of himself by accusing him of cheating in a stormy match dubbed "Toiletgate." They no longer are no speaking terms.

50. FOOL'S MATE

September 2, 2002

Al Horowitz (1907–1973) was one of the most unforgettable characters I ever met. He was a tireless promoter of chess, which was the love of his life. He founded *Chess Review* in 1933. To keep the magazine afloat, he barnstormed America, giving free exhibitions to subscribers and taking on as many as 70 at once. An obituary in the *New York Times* dubbed him...

A SPINNER OF TALES

His philosophy of chess was that "you must be ruthless and have the killer instinct. Never say that the person you are playing with is your partner. He's not. He's your opponent, and you are not playing with him; you are playing against him. Always remember that he wants to beat your brains out."

"Chess is a great game," he once said. "No matter how bad you are, there is always someone worse. If you lose to a 10-year-old, then try a 9-year-old and go down the line until you find someone slightly worse than yourself."

His books included numerous anecdotes that showed his ability not only to analyze a game, but also to spin a witty yarn. In this encounter he gallantly gave queen odds to a certain lady who frequented the famous Marshall Chess Club at 23 West 10 Street in New York City. Alas, she walked into the notorious Fool's Mate: 1 g3 g5 2 Bg2 f6 3 Bf3 f5?? 4 Bh5 mate.

"Would that I could draw the curtain here," he wrote. "But after five minutes, when Black admits to mate, she inquires, 'Where did I go wrong?' And this was a most puzzling problem. I was tempted to reply, 'Miss Peters, you went wrong when you sat down to play.' But the honesty and sincerity she displayed hardly deserved such gruff manners. 'You should not play the Baton Attack against a master,' I admonished, using the broad 'A' of the English in master."

51. LOOKING BACK
November 24, 2003

I must confess that looking back at bound volumes of defunct chess magazines used to be one of my secret vices. The older, the better.

I still recall a contest in the English magazine *Chess* that ran a cartoon of a master giving a simultaneous exhibition against 20 players by moving pieces with his feet. The winning caption? "They sense de-feet."

Another favorite was *Chess Review*, founded by Al Horowitz in 1933. He couldn't earn a living on Wall Street during the Great Depression despite a business degree from NYU, so he turned to chess on the theory that he could win a quarter a game and "a quarter could buy a meal." He won a good many quarters and became a member of three American world championship teams in the 1930s. Al died in 1973 at age 65.

Unlike the master in the cartoon, he moved pieces with his hands in exhibitions to gain subscribers for his struggling new "picture chess magazine." I still marvel at his success. After winning the U.S. Championship in 1951, I embarked on a similar tour and eked out a profit by charging only $2 a board with a guarantee of 30 boards in each city.

"You can't make money at chess. Find another career," kids were warned back then. Truer words were never spoken.

Many of our leading players sadly gave up chess to support a family. Isaac Kashdan, who helped start *Chess Review*, moved on to greener pastures. So did Arnold Denker, who won the U.S. Championship in 1944. Arthur Dake became a civil servant and Reuben Fine became a psychologist. Meanwhile the USSR subsidized its chess stars and seized control of FIDE, the world chess body.

Yet during all the lean years Al Horowitz promoted the royal game with evangelistic zeal. His *Chess Review* was innovative and outspoken. It pioneered a rating system in 1942 that was refined by Arpad Elo into one that measures performance today. In 1952 a Horowitz editorial blasted the rigged FIDE Interzonal at Saltsjobaden, claiming "undeniable collusion by the Russians in a move to freeze out Western competitors." The same charge, echoed a decade later by Bobby Fischer in *Sports Illustrated*, led to wholesale reform of the way challengers qualified for the world championship.

Chess Review was the largest, slickest and most important source of monthly chess news in America, but it always struggled to make ends meet. Photos of glamorous Hollywood stars and grandmasters graced the cover along with witty and well-written features. Al wrote many books on the game before taking over Herman Helms's long-running weekly chess column in the *New York Times*.

For a while I wrote a column in *Chess Review* dubbed "Odds and Evans." When my book *New Ideas in Chess* came out in 1958, I asked Al to review it. "I don't have time. Review it yourself," he suggested. I was taken aback by this apparent breach of ethics but carried out his orders. He trusted his writers to be fair and expected them to toe the line. In 1994 Dover reprinted this book as part of its inexpensive chess classic series.

In 1969, after a run of 36 years, *Chess Review* merged with *Chess Life*, a house organ of the United States Chess Federation. From now on editors had to answer to a board of directors and lacked genuine editorial independence. One editor was canned for backing 18-year-old Fischer, who was unjustly forfeited in a match against veteran Samuel Reshevsky in 1961, because officials dared not offend a major sponsor. "We have to take back control of our magazine," a board member said.

By 1980 *Chess Life and Review* became *Chess Life* again. Recently a friend gave me the 1964 *Chess Review* annual, which brought back pleasant memories. Unable to resist an old vice, I browsed through it and found some delightful tidbits:

- "I always knew Alekhine couldn't have beaten Capablanca in 1927 without help from the devil," wrote a reader in a letter to the editor.
- "Black adopts a line which Keres likes but, treating it not exactly like Keres, he permits White to reach a position to the liking of Tal. The upshot is a game to the liking of the reader." [Colorful note to a Tal victory by Hans Kmoch who Horowitz hired to analyze games.]
- "The Losin' Defense...When can we see a truly sympathetic book about chess? Nabokov—over many agonizing pages—contrives the Luzhin Defense where his hero jumps out of a window." [A pan of Nabokov's novel, *The Defense*, which many years later was made into a movie.]
- "Two advertising men, Hal Davis and Bob Pliskin, know what

to do with the 38 minutes it takes them each working day to commute to New York City. They play chess on the train. Since they started 15 years ago they completed about 1200 games, with honors fairly evenly divided."

Al Horowitz had real stature and is unlikely ever to be replaced. One of his best efforts, against Salo Flohr, is included in Reuben Fine's *The World's Great Chess Games.*

HOROWITZ vs. FLOHR
Caro-Kann Defense, USA vs. USSR Radio Match, 1945

1 e4 c6 2 d4 d5 3 Nc3 dxe4 4 Nxe4 Nf6 5 Nxf6 gxf6 6 Ne2 Bf5 7 Ng3 Bg6 8 h4 h6 9 h5 Bh7 10 c3 Qb6 11 Bc4 Nd7 12 a4 a5 13 Qf3 e6 14 0-0 Bc2 15 Bf4 Bb3 16 Bd3 e5?! 17 Be3 Bd5 18 Be4 Qb3 19 dxe5 fxe5 20 Rad1 Bxe4 21 Qxe4 Qe6 22 Rd2 Nf6 23 Qf3 Rg8 24 Rfd1 Rg4 25 Nf5 e4 26 Bb6! Rxg2 27 Qxg2 Qxf5 28 Rd8 Rxd8 29 Rxd8 Ke7 30 Qg3 Nd7 31 Bc7 Qd5 32 c4 Qg5 33 Qxg5 hxg5 34 Ra8 Ke6 35 Bxa5 f5 36 Bc3 f4 37 a5 g4 38 b4 f3 39 Bd2 Kf7 40 Ra7 g3 41 Rxb7 **Black Resigns**

52. WHY I PLAY CHESS
may 8, 2006

Recently I spent several pleasant hours looking at back issues of *Chessworld*, a great magazine that folded after just three issues in 1964, the same year it was launched. Editor Frank Brady later penned *Profile of a Prodigy*, a major biography of the enigmatic Bobby Fischer. Brady once served as editor as *Chess Life* and now teaches at St. John's University, a recipient of the Chess College of the Year Award by the USCF.

Bobby was only 21 when he swept the USA Championship in 1964 with 11 straight wins. I was runner-up at 7½-3½, which is normally a winning score.

During this tournament I turned 32, half the number of squares on a chess board. Between rounds Brady caught up with me for an interview in the penultimate issue of his magazine. Some excerpts:

BRADY: Do you expect to win it?

EVANS: No. I'll be happy to finish in the top three. My feeling is that everybody is doing badly here with the exception of Fischer.

BRADY: Why do you play chess?

EVANS: For the spirit of competition. I don't like to have to score the point in order to win the money. I try to make each game a work of art.

BRADY: Do you still get actual pleasure from playing chess?

EVANS: Anybody who does anything well finds pleasure in it.

BRADY: How would you rate Fischer in historical terms?

EVANS: It's been my opinion for a few years now that he's the best player in the world. I'd say he's in the same league as Capablanca or Morphy. Of course it's hard to make a comparison since they didn't have the competition that he has now.

BRADY: Fischer just told me that Paul Morphy would beat anybody alive today in a set match.

EVANS: It's impossible to tell how good Morphy was. He was head and shoulders above others in his age. In the ring anyone looks good against a palooka.

BRADY: Why do you say Fischer is at the top of his form right now?

EVANS: Well, he's been doing nothing but studying chess, I'd estimate five or six hours a day. He's beautifully prepared for every opening and moves quickly. In each game he's about an hour ahead of his opponent on the clock.

BRADY: How would you describe his style of play?

EVANS: He follows the truth on the board. If it calls for a wild move and he can't see it clearly, he'll make that move. Whatever is called for in a given position, Fischer will do.

BRADY: What about your style?

EVANS: Positional. But I'm also alert to tactics and never give up on inferior positions. I subscribe to a theory of the second resource. That is, no matter how bad your position, if it's not totally lost, you will reach a point during the game where you will be presented with an opportunity to win or draw if you take advantage of it.

BRADY: Do you want to become famous?

EVANS: I guess everyone does. Chess is a back door to fame.

53. PRISONER 99432
June 10, 2002

A weird chapter in American chess ended in 2001 when Claude Bloodgood died while serving a life sentence. Just five years earlier he was briefly rated as the nation's number two player.

"The Convict Who Would Be King" in the *Virginian-Pilot* by Marc Davis reports how prisoner 99432 brutally killed his mother in 1969, "Bloodgood jumped her, beat her head with a screwdriver, strangled her with his hands, smothered her with a pillow, rolled her body in a porch rug, then drove 70 miles and gently laid her corpse along a wooded road, placing a pillow under her battered head."

Incredibly, thanks to his chess prowess, guards let him out to play in tournaments. His escape in 1974 led to the resignation of Virginia's director of prisons.

Bloodgood played thousands of games by mail from his maximum-security cell. He also found a flaw in the system that enabled him to beef up his rating solely by beating fellow inmates.

He boasted over 100 wins stretching from 1948 until 1966 against the likes of Humphrey Bogart, Charlie Chaplin, Gary Cooper, Marlene Dietrich, Albert Einstein, Clark Gable, Edward R. Murrow, and John Wayne. They were fake.

He was born in 1937 and thus was only 11 in 1948. The dates don't jibe. To cover his fantasies, including spying for the Nazis during World War II, he insisted he was born in 1924.

The man was a pathological liar. He left behind boxes of records and games that may wind up in the Cleveland Public Library, home of the world's largest chess collection. This bogus game with Bogie was found in his papers. It probably was won against another prisoner and he simply attached the movie star's name to it.

BOGART? vs. BLOODGOOD
Poisoned Spike Gambit, Hollywood, 1955?

1 d4 Nf6 2 g4?! Nxg4 3 f3 Nf6 4 e4 d6 5 Be3 c6 6.Bc4 Qa5 7 Nc3 b5 8 e5 dxe5 9 dxe5 bxc4 10 exf6 exf6 11 Nge2 Bb4 12 Qd4 Be6 13 h4 0-0 14 0-0-0 c5 15 Qe4 Na6 16 Kb1 Bxc3 17 Nxc3 Rab8 18 h5 Rxb2 19 Kxb2 Rb8 20 Kc1 Qxc3 21 h6 Nb4 **White Resigns**

54. FREEBIES FOR FELONS
January 2. 2006

The U.S. Chess Federation (uschess.org) was formed in 1939 to promote the study of chess "for its own sake as an art and enjoyment, but also to improve society." The USCF now offers two basic services: rating tournament players and publishing *Chess Life*, a quality monthly magazine. It also raises funds for sending teams to international events.

Dues are $49 a year but vary for seniors, juniors and various other categories. The USCF takes a loss on each prisoner who joins for only $12 a year, a policy that sparked lively debate years ago in the quarterly newsletter of the Chess Journalists of America (chessjournalism.org). By now it appears that 'the ayes have it.'

NO!
By N. Edward Albaugh

I see no problem with discounts for juniors and students who have not yet acquired the earning power to pay full price, or for seniors who often live on low fixed incomes.

But those who prey upon the rest of us are simply not deserving of such consideration. Why should those who steal, beat, and murder be given a price break? Why should those who play by the rules and pay taxes subsidize them? Am I the only one who can see the lunacy here?

I am tired of coddling prisoners and having them treated as victims. I am tired of seeing the standards of decency in our society eroded. Enough is enough.

Even if chess reduces recidivism, so what? It is not the charge of the USCF to reform a prison system. If chess is so good for rehabilitation, why must we bear the burden?

It is not the business of the USCF to spend money on social programs. I resigned after 11 years because of this outrage. I won't pay dues for inmates who get a 75 percent discount. If they can't afford to join because menial prison jobs don't pay much, that's tough! Many honest people are in the same boat, yet our dues were raised. When do we get a break?

YES!
By Steve J. Frymer

The mission of the USCF is to promote chess in the United States. Prisons have thousands of potential members, some who spend countless hours studying and playing postal chess.

Their education is in our best interest, culturally, economically and for reasons of personal safety. We have a golden opportunity to use chess to benefit society. Here is a letter from an inmate:

"We started working up unofficial ratings for a small group of 25 in here and got recognition from the Recreation Manager, who was very receptive and gave us the nod to form a club (The Captured Pawns). Within a week 50 people signed up, and more came out each day to join the chess club.

It's really rewarding to watch a new player work hard and climb up the rating ladder. Almost all of them are young and I actually see how chess fosters a sense of personal responsibility, analytical thinking and self-esteem. By working hard at chess and seeing results they are far more likely to straighten out their lives and to become productive citizens."

What do you think? Here I must confess to a slight bias. When awarding the Best Question each month in my *Chess Life* contest, if two items have equal value I usually give the book to a prisoner. I figure it's less likely that convicts who study chess will create mayhem after they get out. Studies indicate that rates of recidivism are lower for people who learn how to play in jail, but maybe chess just produces smarter crooks. I still recall that the infamous bank robber Willie Sutton was captured when the book found in his possession was *How to Think Ahead in Chess*.

55. PLAY IT AGAIN, SAM

March 20, 2006

"Before becoming a legend, this star of *The Maltese Falcon* hustled strangers at chess in New York City."
—Question on *Jeopardy*

After the stock market crash in 1929, Humphrey Bogart played for chump change against all comers at penny arcades and parks. He was a director for the U.S. Chess Federation and also the best player in the Hollywood enclave. In *Casablanca*, the Oscar-winning film of 1943, he suggested that putting chess into the script would give more dimension to Rick, a cynical, world-weary loner who fought too many lost causes. Some of the dialogue was autobiographical.

When interviewed in 1945, he said chess was one of those things that mattered to him most. Bogie added that he played every day between those tedious waits between takes when making movies. So did John Wayne and, more recently, Will Smith.

Bogie made 75 movies. In 1999 the American Film Institute dubbed him the Greatest Male Star of All Time. He won the academy award only once for *The African Queen* which was filmed in the Congo where he often passed time playing chess with the crew. Dr. Paul Limbos, who was staying at the same hotel in Stanleyville, recalls their meeting in 1951:

"Bogie challenged me to a game one evening. When I accepted, he asked if I was an amateur. I nodded. 'Then let's play for a dollar a game,' he said. I won easily. In fact, I won $17 that night. There were three draws.

Both Katherine Hepburn and Lauren Bacall tried their best to distract me from the game at hand. They continually poured my glass full of whiskey but I just wouldn't swallow the bait. Bogie never seemed to stop smoking. He must have gone through at least three packs just playing against me.

Generally he played the Italian or Scotch openings as White

and the French Defense as Black, and he knew them well. Bogie never played me again. Whenever our paths crossed in the corridor of the hotel, he would cordially say 'Hello, Doc,' and continue on his way."

Here's one of the games played on the veranda of the Sabena Hotel that night. Bogie made the mistake of weakening his kingside instead of stopping for 9...Re8 or h6. Later 13...Nf6 is indicated.

LIMBOS vs. BOGART
French Defense, Congo, 1951

1 e4 e6 2 d4 d5 3 Nc3 Bb4 4 exd5 exd5 5 Bd3 Nf6 6 Nge2 O-O 7 O-O c6 8 Bg5 Nbd7 9 Ng3 Qc7 10 Nh5 Nxh5 11 Qxh5 g6 12 Qh6 f5 13 Rfe1 Nb6? 14 Re2 Bd7 15 Be7 Bxe7 16 Rxe7 Rf7 17 Rxf7 Kxf7 18 Qxh7 Kf6 19 Re1 Qd6 20 g4 Rd8 21 f4 g5 22 h4 **Black Resigns**

---

56. CHESS BANNED!
February 28, 2005

"I have, in my years of teaching, been fortunate enough to see how beneficial chess is to kids. It's absorbing, it's intellectually productive, it's just the best tool to teach good decision making," said Jim Celone, a math teacher whose after-school chess classes in New Haven, Connecticut, were wildly successful.

Many cities and many countries teach chess in school. Yet at various times throughout history the game was banned along with dice and cards in times of stress. The church once frowned on its diabolical attraction because it might lead to sloth, one of the seven deadly sins.

Muslim nations occasionally exhibit the same hostility. In the 1980s Ayatollah Khomeini banned chess in Iran because "it hurts memory, may cause brain damage, and produces a war-mongering mentality." The Taliban banned it in Afghanistan and the most revered figure in Iraq, Ayatollah Ali al-Sistani, recently proclaimed that soccer is okay but chess is "absolutely forbidden."

IT CAN'T HAPPEN HERE

Someone who prefers to remain anonymous revealed on the Net that chess was just banned at his high school in Louisiana:

> "I'm a substitute science teacher with a master's degree in biology at a small private school that has some remarkably gifted kids. I've also played chess for 42 years and feel as though it greatly enriched my life, so I started letting my students play during breaks or after class. The game caught on and is immensely popular.
>
> Some older students wanted to start a club. One parent bought five sets for them, but administration sent a memo that banned all forms of board games.
>
> I went to a school meeting with a set I bought for $3.99 in 1972 and gave a five minute talk on what value I placed on

chess and why. I pointed to the set and said that I played at least 4000 games on it and wondered how many of their kids would be playing those $40 video games in 30 days, much less in 30 years from now.

I knew what I was up against when a do-gooder pointed out that chess was not appropriate under the new No Child Left Behind Act, since there were definite winners and losers, and educators need to see that everyone succeeds!?

Well, I picked up my set and told them next year's football season would be interesting under that philosophy. I said ignorance never lost an argument, and I don't know if they have figured out what I meant by that. The ban stood."

Banning chess in school is rare but nothing new. In 1997 Oak Mountain Intermediate School in Shelby County, Alabama (a suburb of Birmingham) outlawed chess because it was "too competitive and did not foster the appropriate spirit commensurate with school principles." The parent of student Trey Kennedy argued in vain that the school had not one but two stadiums equipped with night lights for baseball.

Chess too competitive but not baseball? Give me a break!

57. A GREAT SHOWMAN
June 24, 2002

George (Kolty) Koltanowski, the greatest showman and promoter that chess ever knew, died at age 96 in 2000. A diamond cutter by trade, he left Belgium before World War II and created a daily chess column that ran without interruption for 52 years in the *San Francisco Chronicle*.

"Chess is an international language. Everyone in the world can understand it, appreciate it and enjoy it," said Kolty, who spoke eight languages.

Though his tournament results were modest, he wrote more than a dozen chess books and made headlines in 1937 by taking on 34 opponents at once without sight of the board to set a blindfold record with 24 wins and 10 draws. (In 1947 Miguel Najdorf upped it to 45 opponents at once in Brazil, winning 39, losing 2 and drawing 4. Kolty raised it to 56 at San Francisco in 1960, winning 50 and drawing 6.)

He was a tireless exhibitor and raconteur who entertained fans with his specialty, the Knight's Tour. Spectators posted random words and phone numbers in the 64 squares of a giant chessboard. Kolty memorized the hodgepodge in seconds and, while blindfolded, called out the path required for a knight to touch every square just once as he recalled these scraps of information in order.

"I don't know how he does it," said his wife. "He can't even remember to bring home a loaf of bread from the supermarket.

"Pawns are like buttons," Kolty often said. "Lose too many and the pants fall down by themselves." At his newspaper office in San Francisco, while blindfolded, he beat movie star and chess expert Humphrey Bogart by a pawn after Bogie missed a draw with 28...Re2! 29 Rf2 Re1 30 Rf1 Re2, etc.

KOLTY vs. BOGIE
French Defense, 1952

1 e4 e6 2 d4 d5 3 exd5 exd5 4 Bd3 Nf6 5 Ne2 Bg4 6 O-O Bd6 7 f3 Be6 8 Bf4 O-O 9 Nd2 Nc6 10 c3 Ne7 11 Bxd6 Qxd6 12 f4 c5 13 Nf3 Nf5 14 Qd2 Ne4 15 Qc1 Rac8 16 dxc5 Qxc5 17 Ned4 Nxd4 18 Nxd4 Rc7 19 f5 Bd7 20 Bxe4 dxe4 21 Qf4 Re8 22 Rae1 Re5 23 Rxe4 Rxe4 24 Qxe4 Bc6 25 Qe3 Re7 26 Qg3 Re8 27 f6 g6 28 Qh4? h5? 29 Re1 Rxe1 30 Qxe1 Qd6 31 Nxc6 Qxc6 32 Qe7 Qc8 33 h3 Qc6 34 b4 Qxc3 35 Qe8 Kh7 36 Qxf7 Kh6 37 Qe7 Qc1 38 Kf2 Qf4 39 Ke2 Qc4 40 Kf3 Kg5? 41 f7 **Black Resigns**

58. A BLACKBOARD JUNGLE
October 10, 2005

I Choose to Stay: A Black Teacher Refuses to Desert the Inner City by Salome Thomas-El proves that one person can make a difference by using chess as a tool to motivate his students: "It's more than just a game: It's also a great way to learn decision-making and problem-solving," he says. Disney optioned a film to star Will Smith, who is an avid player:

> "My father taught me chess when I was seven and rarely do I run into somebody who beats me. On *Enemy of the State* this old dude beat me bad. The next day I found a master to train me for the next three months so I could beat this dude before the movie was over. I did."

EDUCATION = SALVATION

One of eight children, the author was raised by his mother in Philadelphia. Education was scorned in the ghetto and he constantly was taunted for striving to better himself.

Now a middle school principal, he still spends time coaching chess in the schoolroom. His memoir depicts a valiant struggle to rescue kids from despair and violence. "Every kid needs somebody to be crazy about them. In my first 10 years, 20 of my students were murdered. Nothing prepares you for that."

He chides government mandates that lack proper funding like No Child Left Behind as well as frequent tests that eat into class time. "The pig doesn't get fat by weighing," he quips.

Arnold Schwarzenegger gave the school a $20,000 grant after he was checkmated by a student during one of his visits. In a foreword to the book, he is optimistic that inner-city public schools can succeed and even produce great students. But are there enough great teachers willing to fight the system?

In 2004 the Philadelphia Youth Chess Challenge was launched by the local nonprofit After School Activities Partnerships. Students at more than 70 elementary, middle, and high schools across the city can now stay off the mean streets by participating in after-school chess clubs.

Salome sits on the board of America's Foundation for Chess that was founded in 2000 to make chess part of the curriculum in all schools (af4c. org). Each year they raise nearly $300,000 to save the endangered U.S. Championship.

Salome also has a special message for teenage girls. If a guy hits on them, he suggests they ask him to solve a quadratic equation in exchange for their phone number. "If he's not ON his way, he's IN your way," he is fond of saying.

FIGHTING CRIME

Much the same story is told around the country. We know that chess reaches autistic patients and reduces the rate of recidivism for inmates. But can this ancient pastime also be useful in rescuing troubled teens?

A full page in *USA Today* (June 16, 2004) featured Orrin Hudson, 41, an ex-Alabama state trooper who is married with five children. He won a Martin Luther King Award as well as one for education from the TBS Superstation for teaching chess to intractable black youths in Atlanta.

Out of some 100,000 students in DeKalb County, Georgia, a few dozen expelled for crimes ranging from guns to drugs attend Project Destiny School. Standing in front of a large chess wallboard, Hudson says, "If you lose, you only have yourself to blame. As in life, you may never recover from just one bad move."

Often the message falls on deaf ears. Half the students ignore him. "I'm teaching them to think on their own, because the only thing that can save you is yourself."

Hudson's crusade began after five employees were slain in 2000 at Wendy's for $2,400. He knew the two gunmen and decided to take a hard look at himself. "What do I know how to do? What has made a difference in my life?"

The answer was chess. As the seventh of 13 kids, he learned from his brother and became the first black Birmingham champion in 1999 despite entering with the lowest rating. He figured that what worked for him would work for others.

Since then he has taught chess to 15,000 kids in several states. A motivational speaker, he also founded Be Someone Inc. which has income and expenses of about $50,000 a year. His students have won prizes in regional and national tournaments.

Philadelphia plans to establish chess clubs in all 264 public schools. Many other cities are also discovering it can be an effective antidote to juvenile delinquency. What have they got to lose?

Presidential hopeful Barack Obama also credits chess as a boon for poor blacks. He told *The Chicago Sun* (July 2007):

> "And it's working. Parents in Harlem are actually reading more to their children who are staying in school and passing statewide tests at higher rates than other children in New York City. These kids are going to college in a place where it was once unheard of, and some even placed third at a national chess championship."

In an age of mindless video games, chess not only instills discipline but also is easier than you think. And great fun.

59. COLOR BLIND
April 5, 2004

It had to happen. Someone opened a new frontier in civil rights by claiming that chess is racist!

Bill Ware, who teaches Algebra Chess at Southern University and A&M College in Baton Rouge, Louisiana, thinks it's unfair that White always moves first while Black must fight for equality. "By saying that White automatically is offensive, it states that White is better than Black," said Ware.

He plans on erasing racism and color superiority in chess. Exactly how? So far as I can see by replacing black and white with other colors like red, green, or blue.

I wonder what Ware would say about Yoko Ono's design of a chess set where all the pieces and all the squares are white? There could never be a winner or a loser because no game is possible.

Ware's suggestion is reminiscent of Chris Rock's "The Dark Side With Nat X" skit on *Saturday Night Live*, where a black militant sees racism in every aspect of life. He even rails against pool as a racist game because the object is for the white ball to knock all the colored balls off the table.

Surely it's time to free the game from outdated rules and to demand equality for all Chess-Americans.

60. YOUTH MUST BE SERVED
January 16, 2006

Today it's taken for granted that juniors are perfectly capable of competing with seniors on equal terms. But that wasn't always the case.

Before an international tournament at the Manhattan Club in 1976 a bitter dispute erupted when directors invited 12-year-old Joel Benjamin and 13-year-old Michael Wilder. Some committee members, fearing a bad result could upset the youngsters in the future, argued that players should be picked solely on their merits and qualifications.

"I understand that Benjamin was quite discouraged, losing game after game night after night," said grandmaster Bill Lombardy. "Unfair pressure is put on juniors to win when they are constantly told how talented they are."

Bill Goichberg organized and directed the event without pay largely because he thought nobody would object to setting aside two places for these lads even if their strength was far below the other masters: "There's simply no substitute for experience. Six of the 16 competitors were under age 19. Both Wilder and Benjamin are now better than they were before."

First prize was shared by Norman Weinstein with two Soviet grandmasters who emigrated to America, Anatoly Lein and Leonid Shamkovich (10½-4½). Wilder was next-to-last (3½) and Benjamin (2) landed dead last. Neither seemed harmed by the experience and both later went on to capture the U.S. Championship.

Here's an odd draw by Benjamin and an older guy who tied for sixth, age 16! Why Benjamin agreed to split the point is a mystery. Perhaps he was short of time or lacked confidence. White stands better at the end after 28 Qb4!

BENJAMIN vs. ROHDE
Caro-Kann Defense, New York, 1976

1 e4 g6 2 Nc3 Bg7 3 f4 c6 4 Nf3 d5 5 e5 h5 6 d4 Nh6 7 Bd3 Bg4 8 h3 Bxf3 9 Qxf3 Nf5 10 Be3 h4 11 Bf2 e6 12 0?0 Nd7 13 Nb1 Bf8 14 Nd2 Qc7 15 Qe2 c5 16 c3 Be7 17 Nf3 0?0?0 18 Bxf5 gxf5 19 Qe1 Qb6 20 b3 Rdg8 21 Kh2 cxd4 22 cxd4 Kb8 23 Rd1 Qa6 24 a4 Rc8 25 Bxh4 Bxh4 26 Nxh4 Qc6 27 Nf3 Qc2 **Draw!**

GM Joel Benjamin

61. SCHOLASTIC BOOM
January 10, 2005

Chess began to prosper in America only after Bobby Fischer wrested the title from Boris Spassky in 1972, but interest seemed to wane until the movie *Searching for Bobby Fischer* in 1993. It sparked a scholastic boom, an influx of new players in junior tournaments, while grants and jobs flowed to chess coaches.

"I initially thought it was so boring, and I also thought it would be way over their heads. But kids actually latch onto it so quickly. It's amazing," said a chess mom.

The Associated Press reported:

> "There may be stiff competition from video games, television and computers these days, but the ancient game of kings is enjoying a revival among children. Youth membership in the U.S. Chess Federation has more than doubled since 2000 and sales of chess sets in America have increased steadily. Chess is also being used as an educational tool in schools that use it to teach critical thinking, math, history, and even English skills by having students write out their moves."

Erik Anderson, who heads the respected American Foundation For Chess, stated, "Our goal is to be in every second-grade class in America. The future is incredibly bright."

Yet some critics wonder if all this will rescue the USCF founded in 1939 "to extend the role of chess in American society." Despite nearly 100,000 members (mostly under age 20) the USCF teeters on the brink of bankruptcy after decades of massive mismanagement.

The USCF president avers, "The National Scholastic Championships are worth a lot of money. They have a tremendous potential and we can run them very effectively." Thousands of kids now pay entry fees competing for college scholarships and trophies, making these mega-events a cash cow. Big bucks, even from selling concession rights, but where is it all going?

In a controversial 24-page article "Scholastics and the Soul of Chess," Tom Braunlich argues that all is not rosy for organized chess! He notes that most kids quit after high school while real adult membership in the USCF has steadily declined, and he berates educators who use chess as a learning tool or team sport while ignoring real talent.

Yet why encourage kids to be chess pros when it's not lucrative and a pocket computer can spot the best move in a split second? If most kids lose interest when they enter the real world to earn a living, so what? Once bitten by the chess bug they often return to the game as a hobby after raising a family.

Unlike golf, there are no huge green fees and one chess set lasts a lifetime. That's just fine with me.

62. READY FOR PRIME TIME?
April 24, 2006

Chess and soccer are two of the most popular pastimes in the world. But not in the United States.

Will chess ever be ready for prime time in America? I don't have a clue, but it seems dubious.

A breakthrough came in 1972 when Bobby Fischer wrested the crown from Boris Spassky in an exciting Cold War skirmish that captured global headlines. In 1993 the film *Searching for Bobby Fischer* created a scholastic boom that made parents proud of toddlers who learned chess.

"More than 45 million people in the U.S. play chess and more than half are children," recently said anchor Cindy Hsu of CBS-2.

Unlike bridge, which has trouble attracting youngsters, more and more schools are now adding chess to the curriculum. Despite these fitful stops and starts, will it ever become a mainstream sport?

Ironically, another Russian put chess on page one in 1996 when Garry Kasparov lost the first game to Deep Blue before beating IBM's electronic brain 4-2 in their six-game series. IBM's Web site got six million hits a day and their stock soared from 98 to 125 when it was over. A year later Kasparov lost the rematch.

"I tried everything," sighed a master in Texas. "I even gave exhibitions against 50 opponents at once dressed as a clown. Don't laugh. I was a starving graduate student and it helped pay the bills."

David Letterman played a goofy game with Kasparov on his TV show and Madonna learned how to play before marrying her husband who is a chess buff. But before chess can become popular, celebrities must embrace it. The resurgence of poker is due mainly to a combination of TV coverage and big money.

So will chess ever be ready for prime time? In despair we visited a gypsy fortune teller who predicted it would never replace baseball. For a small additional fee, however, the answer was at last revealed.

TOP 10 SIGNS CHESS HAS MADE IT

1. When the pro tour is on TV Saturday and Sunday afternoons.
2. When Nike offers $40 million to a chess star for a shoe contract (Air Positionals).
3. When membership in the United States Chess Federation reaches one million players.
4. When every newspaper carries a chess column.
5. When all schools teach chess.
6. When a girl becomes world champion.
7. When kids on every block have a Karpov-Kasparov V1 Matching Secret Decoder Ring.
8. When chess pieces are found in crackerjack boxes.
9. When every country club has a chess pro on staff.
10. When groupies mob chess stars.

63. WHEN SAMMY MET CHARLIE
December 12, 2005

Samuel Reshevsky (1911–1992) was a Polish child prodigy who gave an exhibition tour in Europe after World War I. "You play war. I play chess," he told a general. "I just make good moves and wait for the other guys to make mistakes," he told perplexed reporters.

In 1920 his parents settled in America and dispatched the boy wonder on an arduous cross-country tour for two years which drew incredibly large audiences. In 1921 Sammy met the world's most famous movie star and a posed publicity photo showed them playing chess while Charlie Chaplin was editing *The Kid* in his Hollywood studio. *My Autobiography*, penned by him in 1964 at age 75, recalls this encounter.

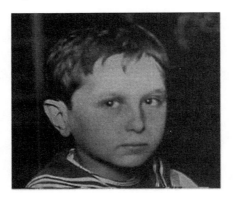

The Boy Prodigy

"He was to give an exhibition at the Athletic Club, playing chess with 20 men at the same time, among them Dr. Griffiths, the champion of California. He had a thin, pale, intense little face with large eyes that stared belligerently when he met people. I had been warned that he was temperamental and that he seldom shook hands with anybody.

After his manager had introduced us and spoken a few words, the boy stood staring at me in silence. I went on with my cutting, looking at strips of film.

A moment later I turned to him. 'Do you like peaches? 'Yes,' he answered. 'Well, we have a tree full of them in the garden; you can climb up and get some—at the same time get one for me.' His face lit up. 'Ooh, good! Where's the tree?' 'Carl will show you,' I said, referring to my publicity man.

Fifteen minutes later he returned, elated, with several peaches. That was the beginning of our friendship. 'Can you play chess?' he asked. I had to admit that I could not. 'I'll teach you. Come see me play tonight. I'm playing twenty men at the same time,' he said with braggadocio.

I promised and said I would take him to supper afterwards.

'Good, I'll get through early.'

It was not necessary to understand chess to appreciate the drama of that evening: twenty middle-aged men pouring over their chessboards, thrown into a dilemma by a child. To watch him walking about in the center of the U-shaped table, going from one to another was a drama in itself.

There was something surrealistic about the scene as an audience of 300 or more sat in tiers on both sides of a hall, watching in silence a child pitting his brains against serious old men. Some looked condescendingly, studying with set Mona Lisa smiles.

The boy was amazing, yet he disturbed me, for I felt as I watched that concentrated little face flushing red, then draining white, that he was paying a price with his health.

'Here!' A player would call, and the child would walk over, study the board a few seconds, then abruptly make a move or call 'Checkmate!' and a murmur of laughter would go through the audience. I saw him checkmate eight players in rapid succession, which evoked laughter and applause.

And now he was studying the board of Dr. Griffiths. The audience was silent. Suddenly he made a move, then turned away and saw me. His face lit up-and he waved, indicating that he would not be long.

After checkmating several other players, he returned to Dr. Griffiths, who was still deeply concentrating.

'Haven't you moved yet?' said the boy impatiently.

The doctor shook his head.

'Oh, come on, hurry up!'

Griffiths smiled.

The child looked at him fiercely. 'You can't beat me! If you move this, I'll move that!' He named in rapid succession seven or eight moves ahead. 'We'll be here all night, so let's call it a draw.'

The doctor acquiesced."

Sammy won 15 and drew 5 against some of the best players in Los Angeles. At an earlier exhibition in a department store he won 9, drew 2, and lost to Don Mugridge, age 16. Referee Harry Borochow recalls that Sammy burst out crying and sobbed, "I wouldn't mind if I lost to an older man, but to a little boy..."

How well did Sammy play in those days? Exhibition games don't mean all that much, but take a look at his draw with Borochow in the Athletic Club.

RESHEVSKY vs. BOROCHOW
Old Indian Defense, Simultaneous Exhibition, 1921

1 d4 Nf6 2 c4 d6 3 Nc3 Bf5 4 f3 Nbd7 5 e4 Bg6 6 Nge2 e5 7 Be3 Be7 8 Rc1 0-0 9 Ng3 Re8 10 Bd3 c6 11 Qd2 Bf8 12 0-0 Qc7 13 f4 exf4 14 Bxf4 Nh5 15 Nxh5 Bxh5 16 c5 f6 17 Qf2 a6 18 Qg3 Rad8 19 Kh1 Bg6 20 cxd6 Qb6 21 Na4 Qxd4 22 Rc4 Qa7 23 R4c1 Bxe4 24 Bc4 Bd5 25 Bxd5 cxd5 26 Qd3 d4 27 Rc7 Ne5 28 Bxe5 Rxe5 29 Qb3 Kh8 30 Rxb7 Qa8 31 d7 Re7 32 Qd5 Re5 33 Qc6 Re6 34 Qxe6 Qxb7 35 Rxf6 Qb4!
Draw

Borochow said: "Here Sammy demonstrated the draw by 36 h3 Qxa4 37 Rxf8!+ Rxf8 38 Qe7 Qd1+ 39 Kh2 Qf1 40 d8/Q Qf4 with perpetual check."

Alas, Sammy finished last in New York in 1922, his first real tournament with five masters. The victor Edward Lasker said that after two days the boy was pale and his eyes seemed lifeless. A month later his parents were charged with "undue exploitation." The case made headlines but was dismissed when the court appointed a guardian to oversee the boy's education. His benefactor was Julius Rosenwald, founder of Sears & Roebuck. Sammy finally attended public school at 12 and later graduated from the University of Chicago.

In 1935 he resumed his chess career at Margate, England, where he created a sensation by taking first in a field of 10 ahead of the legendary Capablanca. Sammy went on to capture the U.S. Championship eight times, but he couldn't earn a decent living from chess. He worked as a certified public accountant and an insurance salesman when he realized the Soviets would always block his path to the world championship.

RESHEVSKY vs. CAPABLANCA
Queen's Gambit Declined, 1935

1 d4 Nf6 2 c4 e6 3 Nc3 d5 4 Bg5 Nbd7 5 cxd5 exd5 6 e3 Be7 7 Bd3 0-0 8 Qc2 c5 9 Nf3 c4 10 Bf5 Re8 11 0-0 g6 12 Bh3 Nf8 13 Bxc8 Rxc8 14 Bxf6 Bxf6 15 b3 Qa5 16 b4 Qd8 17 Qa4 a6 18 b5 Re6 19 Rab1 Rb8 20 Rb2 Be7 21 bxa6 Rxa6 22 Qc2 Ne6 23 Rfb1 Ra7 24 a4 Nc7 25 Ne5 Qe8 26 f4 f6 27 Ng4 Qd7 28 h3 Kg7 29 Nf2 Ba3 30 Ra2 Bd6 31 Nfd1 f5 32 Nb5 Ra5 33 Nxc7 Bxc7 34 Nc3 Qd6 35 Qf2 b6 36 Qf3 Rd8 37 Rab2 Qe7 38 Rb4 Rd7 39 Kh1 Bd8 40 g4 fxg4 41 hxg4 Qd6 42 Kg1 Bc7 43 Kf2 Rf7 44 g5 Bd8 45 Ke2 Bxg5 46 Rxb6 Qa3 47 Kd2 Be7 48 Rb7 Rxa4 49 Qxd5 Ra5 50 Qxc4 Rh5 51 Kd3 Qa8 52 Qe6 Qa3 53 Rd7 Rhf5 54 Rb3 Qa1 55 Rxe7 Qf1 56 Kd2 **Black Resigns**

---

64. THE BOY WONDER
february 6, 2006

Child prodigies exist in only three fields: chess, math, and music. My article about Sammy Reshevsky meeting Charlie Chaplin prompted readers to ask for more details about the boy wonder who came to America in 1920 at age 9 after he embarked on a worldwide exhibition tour.

A yellowing copy of *The Literary Digest* dated December 18, 1920, featured personal glimpses of the wunderkind. Some highlights:

- "When Sammy's father's linen business in Lodz, Poland, ceased because of the war, he spent much of the ensuing leisure playing chess with his cronies. At 5, Sammy was allowed to play and beat his father within a week. In six months he beat the champion of Poland and it occurred to his parents that it would not be a bad idea to exhibit the boy wonder throughout Europe. But money wasn't as plentiful as it once was and they came to America."

- "His head is flat on top and wide above the ears, while his chin is small and pointed. His eyes are small, bright, and shrewd, his features are small, and his expression is in some ways older than his father, who is stout, bearded and jovial. The boy has never been to school but speaks Yiddish and German, a word or two of French and is learning English. Every day he reads a chapter in the Talmud, but isn't allowed to read parts about sex relations. He can write his name in Yiddish script."

- "He is an excellent judge of time and distance, as he shows in boxing. He likes grand opera and symphonies, but has no use for jazz. He sings arias from several operas in a pleasant childish voice but cannot read music."

- "He is a good sport at chess and neither bites and gouges nor crows over a loser. Mostly he whistles very softly while playing. If his opponent makes a bad move, he is likely to ask, 'Do you want to make it?' If yes, Sammy probably will give one more chance. On a second affirmative reply, he will shrug his shoulders with the remark, 'I am sorry for you,' and go on to victory."

• "Sammy does not like to be shown off. It is not that he is bashful or sullen, but that he has had too much of it. Some experts believe he is a good visualizer and, being a child, his powers of attention are greater than older persons with many more things on their minds to distract them."

In his first tournament at New York 1922 Sammy won once, lost twice, and drew twice in five games. Here he gets demolished by Jacob Bernstein who later ran a chess club on Fourteenth Street. I visited once or twice in 1946 when I began attending Stuyvesant High School in that neighborhood and vaguely remember a haze of smoke, noise, and squalor, plus a bunch of seedy characters playing pinochle. Jacob or "Yankele" as everyone called him, was short, fat, and balding with a winning smile who served hot tea in glasses with ornate silver holders.

BERNSTEIN vs. RESHEVSKY
Cambridge Springs Variation, New York, 1922

1 d4 Nf6 2 Bg5 d5 3 c4 e6 4 Nc3 Nbd7 5 e3 c6 6 Bd3 Qa5 7 Bh4 Bb4 8 Nge2 Ne4 9 Qc2 f5 10 f3 Nxc3 11 bxc3 Bd6 12 0–0 Qc7 13 Bg3 Nf6 14 e4 fxe4 15 fxe4 dxe4 16 Bxe4 0–0 17 Rae1 Bd7 18 Bd3 Rae8 19 c5 Bxg3 20 Nxg3 b6 21 Ne4 Nxe4 22 Bxe4 h6 23 Qe2 Qd8 24 cxb6 axb6 25 Rxf8+ Rxf8 26 Bxc6 Bc8 27 Ba4 Qf6 28 Bb3 Kh8 29 Rf1 Qxf1+ 30 Qxf1 Rxf1+ 31 Kxf1 Kg8 32 g3 Kf7 33 Kf2 Bb7 34 Ke3 Ke7 35 c4 g5 36 c5 b5 37 a3 Bc6 38 Bc2 Bd7 39 Be4 Be8 40 Kd3 Kd8 41 Kc3
Black Resigns

Sammy, 11, competing in his first tournament at New York 1922

65. THE JOY LUCK CLUB
June 7. 2004

The Joy Luck Club by Amy Tan, an acclaimed novel and film, is about four Chinese mothers in San Francisco who form a club that meets once a week to play mah jong and swap tales. One of their daughters is a rebellious chess prodigy whose mother urges her to be quiet, obey rules, and develop "invisible strength."

Waverly must do dishes every time she loses a chess game. Suddenly she stops playing but decides to start again. "One day quit, next day play. Everything for you is this way: so smart, so easy, so fast. Not so easy anymore," chides her mother.

At age 14, Waverly starts to lose games and her self-confidence:

> "What she said, it was like a curse. This power I had, this belief in myself, I could actually feel it draining away. All the secrets I once saw, I couldn't see them anymore...the best part of me just disappeared. In her hands, I always became the pawn. I could only run away. And she was the queen, able to move in all directions, relentless in her pursuit, always able to find my weakest spots. But I can't put it all on my mother. I did it to myself. I never played chess again."

In an interview, Amy Tan explained she didn't play chess yet felt a bond with Waverly:

> "What amazed me was I wrote about a girl who plays chess and her mother is both her worst adversary and her best ally... By the end of this story I was practically crying because I realized that—although it was fiction—it was the closest thing of describing my life. Of the feelings that I had, of these things that my mother had taught me that were inexplicable or had no name. This invisible force that she taught me, this rebellion that I had. And then feeling that I had lost some power, lost her

approval and then lost what had made me special. It was a magic turning point for me. I realized that was the reason for writing fiction. Through that, this subversion of myself, of creating something that never happened, I came closer to the truth. So, to me, fiction became a process of discovering what was true, for me. Only for me."

The book offers seven cryptic "secrets" that stumped readers of my monthly *Chess Life* column. I'm clueless. A Chinese fan tried to decipher them (see parenthesis) but perhaps they were invented by the American-born author who said that she doesn't play chess.

1. Double attack from easy and west shores (thrust on both flanks at once?)
2. Throwing stones on the drowning man (exploiting an advantage by going for the kill?)
3. The sudden meeting of the clan (when two bitter enemies meet, a clash of force?)
4. The surprise from the sleeping guard (a hidden piece suddenly joins the attack?)
5. The humble servant who kills the king (power of the lowly pawn?)
6. Sand in the eyes of advancing forces (a quiet sneak attack?)
7. A double killing without blood (perhaps stalemate or an equal trade of pieces?)

66. UNRULY KIBITZERS
January 23. 2006

A reader asked if it was cheating when his opponent got up and hovered behind his back to peek at the board during a tournament game. I said "no, just tell him to stop. If he refuses, then complain to the director he's disturbing you—that's against the rules."

The same goes for unruly kibitzers. The urge to kill them stems from their passion to meddle in your games, though it usually doesn't happen in tournaments.

For the benefit of the uninitiated, a kibitzer is a pest who offers unwanted advice. Years ago a frustrated player sent me a list of rubberneckers based on a lifetime of suffering. Some truths are eternal.

Cibicus Nefarious: His efficiency is manifested by forming a bond with you, sitting close, often casually nudging you clandestinely under the table, driving you to desperation as you don't know what he wants you to move.

Cibicus Accessorius: The fertile soil this species thrives on is that of coffee houses where routine comments fly from all directions. He hates your opponent as much as you do, and he is jubilant in your victory and desolate if you lose. To secure his job he may call you a genius; it boosts your ego and you tolerate him as a mascot. You are even apt to buy him a cup of coffee.

Cibicus Migrans: This wandering kibitzer rushes from board to board to find out where the next great explosion is about to take place. When the death blow has been struck, he hastens to the next thrill.

Cibicus Expertus: This master is self-appointed. He doesn't play anymore but knows simply everything about chess. Often he devotes a brief glimpse at the board and lets you feel in silent disgust that you are an ignoramus.

Maybe you recognize some of these types. The other day I ran into one at a local bookstore when two players pored over the board in a trance without making a move for almost 10 minutes. A stranger stared at the board with the same intensity but left for a few minutes to answer his cell phone. When he returned, he asked what happened.

"Can't you see that nothing has changed?" replied an irritated player. "Sir," said the stranger, "I know nothing about this game. I saw you both staring so I also stared to find out what you were staring at."

Perhaps the last word should go to poet Lawrence Ferlinghetti who, in "Deep Chess," wrote the following: "And if you take too much time for one move, you have that much less for the rest of your life."

67. ALEKHINE'S LAST MEAL
January 19, 2004

Alekhine's Death Photo

The death of world champion Alexander Alekhine at age 53 refuses to die. Although it didn't look suspicious, rumors are still circulating that he either killed himself or was murdered.

The AP reported that he choked to death on a piece of meat on March 24, 1946, in Estoril, Portugal: "Intimates said Alekhine was accustomed to eating with his friends, never using knives or forks when he could avoid them, and that he would eat alone when he wanted complete enjoyment from a meal."

Alas, nobody was around to administer the Heimlich maneuver. A famous police photo shows the great man slumped in a chair wearing an overcoat to keep warm on a cold day. Also visible is a room service tray with empty dishes and a peg-in set ready for another game.

A waiter found the body when he brought in breakfast. "He was slumped at the table and yesterday's supper had not been touched, although his napkin was already tucked in," he said—a statement that conflicted with the photo showing empty dishes, thus giving rise to various conspiracy theories (take your pick).

A policeman barred the door, waiting for the coroner to arrive. Foul play was suspected. The police chief allegedly hinted that Alekhine hung himself, but there was pressure to hush it up. I don't buy it.

It's true that Alekhine was despondent, desperate, and broke. His health was eroded by heavy drinking and smoking as well as a recent bout with scarlet fever. But why commit suicide after just learning that London was about to organize a title match against Mikhail Botvinnik? Alekhine was overjoyed at the prospect and eager to prove himself over-the-board.

"He had such a political reputation that a Soviet player could not meet him at the board," wrote Botvinnik, who pulled strings to persuade the Kremlin to let him play. Indeed, Alekhine was in such bad odor that Alekhine's Defense was renamed the Moscow Defense in the USSR.

In his book *Alexander Alekhine* (1975), Soviet GM Alexander Kotov supports the view that his hero died of natural causes. He explains why Alekhine was reviled after the war and why people tried to strip him of the title and ban him from international tournaments. Alekhine stood accused of writing a series of articles called "Jewish and Aryan Chess" in 1941 and of collaborating with the Nazis.

The Oxford Companion to Chess notes that Alekhine was anti-Nazi:

> "When the Second World War began Alekhine was then in Buenos Aires playing for France in the Olympiad; as captain, he refused to allow his team to play Germany. Returning to France, he joined the army as an interpreter and when France fell in 1940 he fled to Marseilles. In the autumn of 1940 he sought permission to enter Cuba, promising, if permission were granted, that he would play a match with Capablanca. This gambit failed, and in April 1941 he went to Lisbon, seeking a visa to the USA. In September 1941 he went to Munich to play in a chess tournament and, somewhat out of practice, could do no better than share second place with Lundin one and a half points after Stoltz."

Kotov continues the story:

> "Nevertheless, when Alekhine was taken prisoner things were not too unpleasant for him. This is, no doubt, because the directors of fascist propaganda immediately understood they would be able to exploit the fact that the world champion was taking part in tournaments in occupied Europe. Alas, they were not mistaken. Alekhine was later to pay dearly for this.

As soon as the guns had been silenced, chess life began to return to normal. It was the English who decided to organize the first postwar international tournaments in London and the traditional Christmas tournament at Hastings at the end of 1945 to the beginning of 1946. The world champion was not forgotten—official invitation to both tournaments for Alekhine arrived from England...His head was full of new chess ideas, while opening innovattions were written in his notebooks. 'Wait till I get to London, they will see that I can still play!'

And then, suddenly, terrible news arrived by telegraph: the English, the strict, sporting, and conservative English, had withdrawn their invitation. At first Alekhine could not believe it. How was it possible? It was pitiless, inhuman."

What happened is that Reuben Fine, Arnold Denker, and other stars threatened to withdraw unless Alekhine was excluded. The Brits caved. Decades later GM Denker apologized for his role in this sorry affair. He also recalled with awe his first glimpse of Alekhine giving a six-board blindfold exhibition: "Seeing him play these lower echelon masters really opened my eyes. It was just not describable."

Many historians believe that Alekhine's health had deteriorated to the point where several contenders could have vanquished him. "It is very doubtful if he could have re-imposed the discipline that won him those matches with Capablanca and Euwe. But he would still have posed formidable problems," opined IM Robert Wade in *Soviet Chess* (1968).

The rightful challenger was Paul Keres, an Estonian who earned that right by virtue of his stunning victory at AVRO 1938 followed by his defeat of ex-world champ Max Euwe in a 1940 match. However, as noted in *The Oxford Companion*, Keres returned home to his wife in Soviet-occupied Estonia when the war ended "but not before making a deal with the Soviet authorities. He would be 'forgiven' for playing in German tournaments, i.e., collaborating with the enemy. In return he promised not to interfere with Botvinnik's challenge to Alekhine." In fact, Keres did not take part in either London 1946 or Groningen 1946.

Kotov continued:

"Hopelessly ill, abandoned by all, and rejected by people together with whom he had trodden a great path and who now did not even wish to see him and question him personally, Alekhine was slowly dying in a small room of the hotel Park, half closed for the winter, in Estoril. He had no prospects, no means, and no friends to support him. He either spent the time in bed, or else paced about the room like a lion in a cage. 'One day he phoned me,' writes Lupi. 'I have absolutely no money,' said the fading world champion with difficulty. 'I need just a few escudos to buy a cigarette. This loneliness is killing me. I must live, I must feel life around me. I have already worn out the floorboards in my room. Take me somewhere."

Old players never die—they just check out. A few years after he died Russia honored him as its greatest star and requested that his grave be moved to Moscow, but his widow refused. His ideological rehabilitation was fully completed by the Alekhine Memorial Tournament at Moscow in 1956 where Kotov interviewed a Belgian violinist named Neuman who lived in the same hotel as Alekhine.

Neuman said he rushed to the room that morning when a waiter told him Alekhine was dead. "'You can't go in there,' said a policeman, barring my way. 'We are waiting for a forensic specialist. We have to establish that death was from natural causes. What? Yes, you may have a look.' I opened the door, the curtains were still drawn and the light was on, although outside it was sunny. On the table were plates, while to the side, on a support for suitcases, was a chess board with the pieces set out. My friend was sitting in an armchair...as though still listening intently to my violin."

The Oxford Companion says Alekhine "died of a heart attack" and that "for three weeks his body lay unburied at Esoril, Portugal." Ominous rumors surfaced that the police photo was doctored and that he was murdered! In December 1999 Canadian GM Kevin Spragett cited Alekhine as "the world champion who died under the most mysterious circumstances."

On his Web site Spragett wrote:

"What is wrong with the official story? (I mean, apart from the fact that if a 'normal' person was sitting down and choking he would get up and become quite frantic, possibly even overturning the board and pieces in the process!?)

The doctor who wrote the official death certificate (Dr. Antonio Ferreira, just by chance an avid chess player himself) later told friends that Alekhine's body was found on the street, in front of his hotel room! He had been shot! He said that government pressure had forced him to complete the death certificate as it now exists. (Portugal was neutral during World War II, and might have wanted to avoid any controversy.)

According to well placed sources (including Spassky, who

is married to a French woman who worked in the diplomatic services) the French Resistance created a super secret 'Death Squad' after the second world war to 'deal' appropriately with those people on a blacklist who had collaborated too willingly with the Nazis once France was over run by Germany. Apparently the list was not less than 200,000 names!

Correspondence of Alekhine, shortly before his untimely demise, mentioned that he felt he was being followed! Alexander Alekhine's initials were AA, so that would put him at the top of any list! Alekhine died within a day or two of the British Chess Federation voting to hold the Botvinnik-Alekhine match...so if there was an assassin then he had to move quickly since Alekhine was about to go to England!...The truth is out there!!"

The reason I discount these rumors is that an American doctor, who was then a medical student, wrote a letter to my column in *Chess Life* saying that he witnessed the actual autopsy and that Alekhine died by choking on a piece of meat. So did Dr. Antonio Ferreira, who allegedly signed the death certificate. But he was also a student then, as he attested in the following letter to George Koltanowski:

"His body was sent to the Medical School of Lisbon, where an autopsy was performed. As reported in 1946, Alekhine died of 'asphyxia due to an obstruction in his breathing channels, due to a piece of meat.' And how do I know? I was at the time a student of medicine there and like other students I had to attend a number of autopsies...In one of those routine attendances the subject was Alekhine." (Quoted in "Everything You Always Wanted To Know About Alekhine—But Didn't Know Enough to Ask" by this writer and Larry Parr in *Chess Life*, May 1993. Also see "The Tragedy of Paul Keres" by me in *Chess Life*, October 1996).

In the final analysis, Alekhine was a true artist who left a legacy of masterpieces that still delight and astound us. Here is his last match game in official competition played at Estoril in January 1946 (in 4 games he beat Francesco Lupi twice, lost 1 and drew 1).

LUPI vs. ALEKHINE
Petrov Defense

1 e4 e5 2 Nf3 Nf6 3 Nc3 Bb4 4 Nxe5 0-0 5 d3 d5 6 a3 Bxc3+ 7 bxc3 Re8 8 f4 dxe4 9 d4 Nd5 10 c4 Ne7 11 Be2 Nf5 12 c3 Qh4+ 13 Kf1 e3 14 Qe1 Qxf4+ 15 Kg1 Nxd4 16 cxd4 Qxd4 17 Rb1 Qxe5 18 Bb2 Qf5 19 Rd1 Nc6 20 Rd5 Qc2 21 Ba1 Bf5 22 Bd1 Qb1 **White Resigns**

---

68. HE BEAT ALEKHINE
January 9, 2006

"Our relations had always been good but after this game Alekhine would not speak to me for three days. Great chessplayers do not like to lose."

—Vladas Mikenas

We tend to forget that many strong tournaments took place long ago and far away. In 1937 Mikenas was tenth in a field of 18 at Kemeri, a Latvian resort. Salo Flohr, Vladimir Petrovs, and Samuel Reshevsky tied for first at 12-5, half a point ahead of Paul Keres and Alexander Alekhine, who was in training to regain his crown from Max Euwe. America's Reuben Fine lost five games, barely achieving a plus score (9-8) before his stunning performance at AVRO a year later. In the British magazine *Chess*, Mikenas reminisced about his victory over Alekhine:

"This game was preceded by an interesting episode. To my surprise he sat down at my table while I ate in a restaurant. Alekhine, though he looked cheerful, had still not been able to get himself together after losing his title in 1935. I suggested a glass of liquor. My companion flatly refused. 'Only milk. You see, I lost to Euwe because of that damn alcohol,' he replied.

From the bottom of my heart I wished him good luck. We parted good friends. But then suddenly I noticed Alekhine coming back. 'Who are you playing tomorrow?' he asked in an agitated tone. 'With you, doctor,' I replied with a smile.

After my 16...Nef4! Alekhine winced. It came as a surprise. He composed himself, adjusted his spectacles and thought for 40 minutes. I was satisfied he would decline the sacrifice. Quite frankly I did not calculate everything, but analysis after the game confirmed my intuition. On 17 gxf4 Nxf4 18 Qe4 Qg4 19 Nd4 Bxe5! wins.

Only nervousness can explain why he played 23 Ne4? He

should defend by 23 Rac1. At precisely this moment an official brought him coffee. Alekhine thanked him, while all the while staring at the board. Then, instead of sugar, he absent-mindedly put a White pawn into the cup! It was not clear to me why he was so ruffled. After my 23...Bxe4? it is hard to communicate just how overjoyed Alekhine now became. With a trembling hand he pointed to the c2 square and, smiling, said, 'Young man, you could have won at once with 23...Rc2!'

There and then I noticed 24 Qxc2 Qxf3+ 25 Kg1 Bh3 with unstoppable mate. 'Not to worry. I will find a way to win against you a second time!' Such a lack of self control was of course out of order but I was angry with myself, and after the game was over Alekhine reprimanded me."

ALEKHINE vs. MIKENAS
Gruenfeld Defense, 1937

1 d4 Nf6 2 c4 g6 3 g3 Bg7 4 Bg2 d5 5 cxd5 Nxd5 6 Nf3 0-0 7 0-0 c5 8 e4 Nf6 9 e5 Nd5 10 dxc5 Na6 11 a3 Nxc5 12 b4 Ne6 13 Bb2 a5 14 b5 Qd7 15 Qe2 Rd8 16 Nbd2 Nef4! 17 Qc4 Nxg2 18 Kxg2 Qh3 19 Kh1 Be6 20 Qe4 Bf5 21 Qe2 Qg4 22 Rfe1 Rac8 23 Ne4? Bxe4? 24 Qxe4 Qxe4 25 Rxe4 Rc2 26 Bd4 Rc4 27 Re2 g5! 28 h3 h5 29 Bb2 g4 30 hxg4 hxg4 31 Nd4 e6 32 Re4 Nc3 33 Bxc3 Rxc3 34 Rxg4 Kf8 35 Re4 Rd5 36 Ne2 Rc2 37 f4 Rdd2 38 Re1 Ke8 39 a4 Bf8 40 Kg2 Bb4 41 Kh3 Ra2 42 Kg4 Rdb2 43 Rc1 Rxe2 44 Rc8 Ke7 45 Rec4 f5 46 exf6 Kxf6 47 R4c7 e5! 48 Rxb7 exf4 49 gxf4 Rg2 50 Kf3 Rgf2 51 Ke3 Rae2 52 Kd3 Re6 53 Rc6 Rf3 54 Kd4 Rxf4 55.Kd5 Rf5 56 Kd4 Rxc6 57 bxc6 Ke6 58 Rb5 Rxb5 59 axb5 Kd6 60 Kc4 Kc7 61 Kb3 Kb6 62 Kc4 Bd6 63 Kd5 Bb8 64 Kc4 Bc7 **White Resigns**

69. WHAT CAN WE TRUST?
April 3, 2006

Recently FIDE disciplined several people for submitting results of a phony tournament in Hungary with high-rated players that never took place!

Chess statistics, like virtually everything else, are fraught with innocent errors and outright fraud. Even Alexander Alekhine, world champion for almost 20 years, was not above doctoring moves in some of his games for aesthetic reasons.

Alekhine with his cat named "Chess"

His notes are terrific but can't always be trusted. For example, when annotating Reti-Tartakower in his tournament book of New York 1924, after 1 e4 c5 2 Nf3 d6 3 d4 cxd4 4 Nxd4 Nf6 5 Nc3 g6 6 Be2 Bg7 7 0-0 Nc6 8 Be3 Alekhine suggested 8...Ng4 which is a horrible blunder because White can simply gain a piece by 9 Bxg4.

An obituary of Peter Manetti, who died March 2006, stated that he drew with me in the last round at Lone Pine 1972. I don't recall ever playing him, but "our" game is cited in Fritz's Mega Database. This innocent error is likely to survive forever in other places.

The truth is I never played the last round that year because I rushed to the hospital after my wife had an auto accident. Research reveals that Manetti's actual opponent was Roy Ervin, who is famous for showing up at a Roy Ervin Memorial tournament after he had been reported dead. Let's hope that Peter Manetti does the same thing.

Meanwhile there's little hope the record will be corrected so that my name can be erased from this awful draw. Errors in chess, alas, often are passed along from hand to hand like the Olympic torch.

MANETTI vs. ERVIN
Dutch Defense, Lone Pine, 1972

1 d4 e6 2 c4 f5 3 Nf3 Nf6 4 g3 d5 5 Bg2 c6 6 O-O Bd6 7 b3 O-O 8 Ba3 Bxa3 9 Nxa3 Nbd7 10 Qc1 Qe7 11 Ne5 Qd6 12 Qb2 g5 13 e3 a5 14 Rac1 Qe7 15 Nc2 Qg7 16 Ne1 Kh8 17 N1d3 g4 18 Nf4 Nxe5 19 dxe5 Ne4 20 Bxe4 fxe4 21 Nh5 Qg6 22 Nf6 Kg7 23 Qa3 Rxf6 24 exf6 Qxf6 25 Qd6 Qf8 26 Qxf8 Kxf8 27 Kg2 Bd7 28 h3 gxh3 29 Kxh3 Be8 30 f3 exf3 31 Rxf3 Ke7 32 Rcf1 Bg6 33 g4 a4 34 cxd5 axb3 35 axb3 exd5 36 R3f2 Kd6 37 Kg3 Ra3 38 Rb2 Kc5 39 Rf4 Be4 40 Rf7 Ra7 41 g5 Kb4 42 Kf4 Kc3 43 Rh2 Kxb3 44 Rhxh7 Bxh7 45 Rxh7 Ra1 46 Rxb7 Kc4 47 g6 Rg1 48 g7 c5 **Draw**

---

70. CHESS SWINDLES
September 19, 2005

A swindle is the only form of larceny that's legal over-the-board. It's a clever way to rob an unsuspecting opponent of a sure win.

Frank Marshall, USA champion for 25 years, was notorious for extricating himself from hopeless positions and even titled a book of his games, *Marshall's Swindles.*

They say the hardest thing to win is a won game because we all tend to relax when victory is within our grasp.

In today's lingo swindles are called "cheapos" because the bait is hidden in plain view. The bigger they are, the harder they fall.

SWINDLE OF THE CENTURY

We all dream of saving a lost game by a miracle. This Houdiniesque-escape was dubbed "swindle of the century" by *Chess Review.* My victim was Sammy Reshevsky, our premier player until Bobby Fischer swept the 1963–1964 championship with 11 straight wins, the stuff of legend.

I was runner-up with the great score of 7½-3½ prompting a wag to quip that Fischer won the exhibition but Evans won the tournament. In this game I missed 16 Bc3! and saw too late that 27 Rxa6? Qc8! launches a double attack on a6 and c2.

So I had to plod on and fight for a draw. My chance came at the end when Reshevsky snatched the bait instead of 48...Qg6! He still had no inkling of my plot as I reached across the board to pitch my queen. He started to shake my hand and accept my resignation when it dawned on him I had escaped. If 50...Kxg7 is stalemate then so is 50...Kf8 51 Rf7 Kxf7.

He blanched and smiled wryly. With unseemly glee, I strained to hear him curse himself under his breath. He muttered just one word: "Stupid!"

EVANS vs. RESHEVSKY
Nimzo-Indian Defense, 1963

1 d4 Nf6 2 c4 e6 3 Nc3 Bb4 4 e3 c5 5 Bd3 0-0 6 Nf3 d5 7 0-0 dxc4 8 Bxc4 Nbd7 9 Qe2 a6 10 a3 cxd4 11 axb4 dxc3 12 bxc3 Qc7 13 e4 e5 14 Bb2 Nb6 15 Bb3 Bg4 16 Ra5 Rac8 17 c4 Nbd7 18 h3 Bxf3 19 Qxf3 Rfe8 20 Rd1 Ra8 21 c5 Rad8 22 Ba4 Re7 23.Rd6?! b5! 24 Bc2 Nxc5 25 Rxd8 Qxd8 26 Qe3? Ncd7 27 Qd3 Qb6 28 Bc1 h6 29 Be3 Qb7 30 f3 Nb8 31 Ra2 Rd7 32 Qa3 Kh7 33 Kh2 Qc7 34 Bd3 Nh5 35 Rc2 Qd8 36 Bf1 Rd1 37 Rc1 Rd6 38 Qa2 Qf6 39 Rc7 Nd7 40 Ra7 Nf4 41 Qc2 h5 42 Qc8 Rd1 43 Bxb5 Qg5 44 g3 axb5 45 Rxd7 Re1 46 Rxf7 Rxe3 47 h4 Re2 48 Kh1 Qxg3?? 49.Qg8!! Kxg8 50 Rxg7 **Draw by stalemate!**

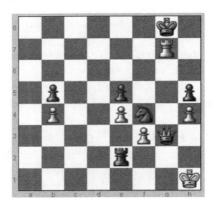

Final Position

71. BLIND SPOTS
June 5, 2006

Everyone makes mistakes. The annals of chess are strewn with oversights, bungles, botches, blunders, boners, goofs, and gaffes in every conceivable size and shape.

Even champions see gremlins. Every passing year provides another example of famous players resigning without realizing they were on the verge of victory. Popiel-Marco, Monte Carlo 1902 is a classic mishap.

Black Resigns

Thinking his bishop was lost, Marco overlooked a saving resource that turns the tables: 1...Bg1! threatens Qxh2 mate. White has nothing better than 2 Kxg1 Rxd3 3 Bxd3 Bxe4 and the queen is boss.

Moral: You can't win by resigning.

Klaus Darga also was the victim of an optical illusion against Levente Lengyel at the Amsterdam Interzonal in 1964. Here is the position just before the time control on move 40 when Black, with seconds to spare, made what I dubbed "the winning mistake."

225

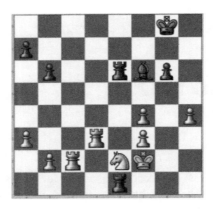

Black to move

Instead of simply 40...Bxh4+ 41 Ng3 Re7 with some slight winning chances, Lengyel blundered with 40...R/6xe2+? Darga, convinced his game was hopeless, missed 41 Rxe2 Bxh4+ 42 Ke3! with a decisive material advantage. They both harbored the delusion that the (nonexistent) rook on e6 still controlled e3.

I watched in horror as Darga extended his hand in the customary gesture of resignation before striking his forehead: "Oh, Gott—Ich habe eine gewinnstellung!" (My God—I have a winning position!) But it was too late to change the result. "If grandmasters can do that, there's still hope for me," chuckled a spectator.

How can such hallucinations be explained?

Dr. Siegbert Tarrasch, a championship contender himself, once observed that an unexpected shot can produce a kind of chemical reaction that beclouds calm and clear thought. His theory covers blunders committed under the influence of sacrificial shock.

The good doctor diagnosed it as amaurosis schacchistica, or chess blind spots, a malady that strikes even in perfectly ordinary positions without prodding from the clock. Alas, there is no known cure.

In an interview with *Playboy* (November 1989), world champion Garry Kasparov dismissed flimsy excuses for losing. "Chess is the most violent of all sports, and there's no luck involved," he said. "I lose because I make some stupid moves. I can't forgive that. I hate myself at that moment."

It's easy to understand garden-variety errors that sprout up in the heat of battle where anyone can overlook an unexpected move. Yet there is also an inner game where mistakes are self-inflicted. If we are troubled, it could reveal itself in our play.

A good example is this contest between the stars of Cuba (Jesus Nogueira) and England during the fifth GMA World Cup in Rotterdam. Nigel Short had a blind spot because of eye strain rather than nervous strain.

In a level position, Short embarked on a faulty combination based on a pin along the e-file, but suddenly realized his bishop sat on e8 instead of a rook. Without waiting for White to snap up the gift by 22 exd4 he threw in the towel.

Reports didn't indicate whether Short, then ranked #3 in the world, was fitted for a new pair of glasses.

NOGUEIRAS vs. SHORT
Bogo-Indian Defense, GMA World Cup Rotterdam, 1989

1 d4 e6 2 c4 Bb4+ 3 Bd2 a5 4 g3 d5 5 Nf3 Nc6 6 a3 Bxd2+ 7 Nbxd2 Qf6 8 e3 Nge7 9 Bg2 0–0 10 0–0 a4 11 Qc2 Bd7 12 Rfe1 Nf5 13 Qc3 Rfd8 14 Rac1 Rac8 15 h4 g6 16 Ng5 Be8 17 Rcd1 Qg7 18 Ngf3 h5 19 Rc1 b6 20 cxd5 exd5 21 Rc2 Ncxd4?? **1–0**

Final Position - Black Resigns

72. A GLORIOUS FAKE
October 17, 2005

"The mad gyrations of White's queen stamp this game as one of the finest ever played."

—*The Golden Treasury of Chess*

Players have been known to doctor moves and fabricate masterpieces, yet outright forgeries are rare. This famous fake was inspired by an offhand game where neither side kept a score sheet. White overlooked a series of brilliant strokes and 16-year-old Carlos Torre recorded his analysis during the postmortem lest the glorious theme be lost to posterity. It's the classic example of an overburdened queen.

The putative winner was Edwin Ziegler Adams, an unknown New Orleans amateur. As fate would have it, he gained immortality with this single effort. Curiously, Torre listed himself as the victim when he submitted the game for publication. Why did he do it?

Years later, when Torre became Mexico's most prominent chess star, he told friends it was not so important who had won or the authenticity of the record, only that it was a beautiful game. But someone who knew them both offered an alternate theory, stating, "I always believed that Adams slipped the kid some cash, even if only 10 or 20 bucks, to say the game was actually played rather than a post-mortem joint analysis."

Most anthologies include this gem. Like everyone else, Reuben Fine assumed it was real. In *The World's Great Chess Games* he noted:

"Torre [1904–1978] might have become world champion had his health held out. In 1926 he suffered a nervous breakdown and had to retire from chess. In 1934 I met him in Monterey, Mexico. Two exhibition games were arranged. He was no longer the old Torre and seemed rather disinterested in what was going on."

One of the most famous games in chess history was never played, but who cares if it's fake?

"Full many a chess master is born to blush unseen. Occasionally we come across games that bear the unmistakable stamp of real creative genius, and yet the winner has never been heard of," noted Fine. "Wonderful. What else can we say of this brilliancy that glistens with six queen sacrifices in succession," raved Chernev. "The final combination is unique in the annals of chess," gushed Horowitz.

Simply 14...h6! was necessary to avoid the back rank mate.

ADAMS vs. TORRE
Philidor Defense, New Orleans, 1920

1 e4 e5 2 Nf3 d6 3 d4 exd4 4 Qxd4 Nc6 5 Bb5 Bd7 6 Bxc6 Bxc6 7 Nc3 Nf6 8 0-0 Be7 9 Nd5 Bxd5 10 exd5 0-0 11 Bg5 c6 12 c4 cxd5 13 cxd5 Re8 14 Rfe1 a5? 15 Re2 Rc8 16 Rae1 Qd7 17 Bxf6 Bxf6 18 Qg4! Qb5 19 Qc4! Qd7 20 Qc7! Qb5 21 a4 Qxa4 22 Re4 Qb5 23 Qxb7 **Black Resigns**

Final Position

73. A PAPAL HOAX
May 23, 2005

Why anyone would forge chess games escapes me, but from time to time your humble scribe has been deceived by an elaborate hoax. The death of Karol Józef Wojtyla (1920–2005), better known as Pope John Paul II, exposed a myth that I unwittingly perpetuated.

In his student days the Polish pontiff was an athlete, playwright, actor and, legend has it, an avid chess player. *The Quarterly for Chess History* once printed a game he won as Black that began 1 d4 d5 2 Nc3 Nf6 3 Bg5 Nbd7 4 Nf3 e6 against a lady allegedly named Wanda Zartobliwy "the wife of the ambassador of the Malta Knights visiting Poland in 1946."

Europe Echecs took the bait in January 1979, soon after the Pope was elected, and printed the bogus game along with a nice problem attributed to him (diagram below). Later the editors were fooled again by the same prankster who sent another chess problem "not published until now." To make the cheese more binding, he pretended to be the Pope himself on fake stationary of the Holy See.

Enter Tomasz Lissowski, a Polish researcher. His suspicions were aroused because Zartobliwy means "facetious" in Poland. "My interest was caused when the renowned author Larry Evans reprinted the problem in the *Washington Post*. It appeared in countless chess publications, but I was convinced Evans had become a victim of mystification," he said.

Lissowski contacted a Polish priest who recalled that the Pope did play chess, but not to the extent of distracting him from his spiritual duties, during their seminary days. Lissowki then wrote to the Pope asking if he composed the problem and gave it to the papal nunciature in Warsaw who forwarded it to the Vatican. In early 1995, to his great surprise, Lissowski got a reply in the Pope's own handwriting showing his sense of humor and understanding.

"Greetings and God's Blessing," it said in Polish. This part, which was in Latin, is from the Bible (Isaiah 9:9-6): "For a child will be born to us, a Son will be given to us." It was the Pope's witty way of saying that he never spawned a chess problem.

White mates in 2 moves.

The problem was attributed falsely to Karol Wojtla with the intended solution of 1 Qa7! But there are two "cooks": 1 Nc5+! Nxc5 2 Kxc5 mate. So is 1 Qc3! Nd6 2 Qc6.

74. STRANGER THAN FICTION
July 11, 2005

Chess problems that require checkmate in a fixed number of moves are the product of some composer's fertile imagination. These devilish brainteasers often are scorned by practical players who prefer to solve real positions.

Composed endgame studies, on the other hand, actually help us improve our game. They employ valuable themes, and it's hard to see how anyone could improve on the simplicity and purity of this study which looks real.

So real, in fact, that in 1925 the composer dubbed it Pape vs. Roth when submitting it to a chess magazine. Was he inspired by watching a skittles game between those players, or was it a hoax?

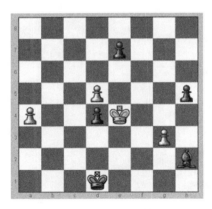

White to play and draw

REINCARNATION
It was composed by George Bernhard (1892–1964) and took on a life of its own over the years. The latest incarnation was in the *Encylopedia of Combinations*, which cited #1487 as Pape vs. Roth played in West Germany

1974! White is a piece behind and his plight seems hopeless. A natural try is 1 a5 aiming for a queen. It fails owing to 1...Bxg3 2 a6 Bb8 and Black wins. But salvation is at hand. The exquisite solution features a rare stalemate in the very center of the board.

I believed it was a real game when I first wrote a column about Pape vs. Roth years ago. The finale was so beautiful that a reader wondered if it was real. He asked to see the complete score of the game leading up to the diagram. A search revealed that such a game doesn't exist!

Ah, well. I never subscribed to the notion that truth is stranger than fiction anyway.

Solution: 1 d6! exd6 2 Kd3! Bxg3 3 a5 d5 4 a6 Bb8 5 a7! Bxa7 Stalemate!

75. VIVA STALEMATE!
July 26. 2004

If neither side makes a serious error, then a draw is the logical outcome of a game. Yet some critics advocate rule changes to reduce the great number of draws. A pet target of the draw-haters is stalemate. This rule states, "The game is drawn when the king of the player whose turn it is to move is not in check and the player cannot make a legal move. This immediately ends the game."

A crude proposal that keeps popping up is to award a loss to the player who is stalemated. This would radically alter centuries of tradition and make chess boring.

How many players would dare to risk gambits in the opening or embark on sacrificial attacks if there were no hope of salvation in the endgame? You're a pawn up! Trade down! Brute force invariably would decide the issue.

We can't destroy chess to save it. Many beautiful, subtle themes would vanish without stalemate as a saving resource. And those who get careless no longer would be punished for letting the underdog escape with a surprising draw.

WHEN RULES CLASH

Another rule states, "The game is won by the player whose opponent declares that he resigns. This immediately ends the game."

Suppose a player fails to notice he is stalemated and resigns by mistake? Is it scored as a win or a draw? Which rule takes priority?

The consensus seems to be a draw because stalemate happened first, but it's still a gray area that needs to be resolved. "Law should be clear, concise and consistent. To interpret it is to corrupt it," said Napoleon, who was an avid chess player.

This game from Italy, between Mario Sibilio and Sergio Mariotti, holds the record for the shortest stalemate in 27 moves.

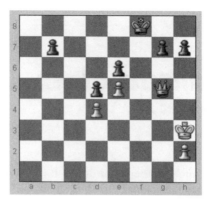

Final Position

SIBILIO vs. MARIOTTI
French Defense, Ravenna, 1982

1 e4 e6 2 Nf3 d5 3 e5 c5 4 b4!? cxb4 5 d4 Nh6 6 a3 bxa3 7 c3 Nf5 8 Nxa3 Nc6 9 Nb5 a6 10 g4 Bd7 11 Bg5 Be7 12 gxf5 axb5 13 fxe6 fxe6 14 Rxa8 Qxa8 15 Rg1 Qa3 16 Bxb5 Bxg5 17 Rxg5 Qxc3 18 Kf1 O-O 19 Bxc6 Bxc6 20 Kg2 Ba4 21 Qe2 Bc2 22 Ne1 Be4 23 f3 Rxf3? 24 Nxf3 Bxf3 25 Qxf3 Qd2 26 Kh3 Qxg5 27 Qf8! Kxf8 **Draw!**

76. A PHANTOM OFFER
December 5, 2005

The rules are quite specific about draw offers. You may offer a draw once during a tournament game by making your move and then starting the opponent's clock. "The latter may accept or reject it either orally or by completing a move."

A reader wondered why the word "offer" is used. "You can't offer what you don't have. So let's replace it with the draw proposal," he wrote. Another fan suggested that to "proffer" a draw, presenting it for acceptance, is just as neutral and a tad more elegant.

Be that as it may, most European players simply ask to draw just by saying "remis"? No more words are necessary. Of all the rivals I ever faced, the legendary Samuel Reshevsky had the most unique way to proffer a draw. "Are you playing for a win?" he would ask. One of his opponents, who didn't understand that Reshevsky wanted a draw, replied, "Well, I'm certainly not playing to lose!"

But a new kind of draw offer surfaced this year at the third Staunton Memorial in London. It was dubbed "the phantom offer" by Jonathan Levitt in his brilliancy prize victory over 14-year-old British prodigy David Howell, his former student.

This bizarre incident took place during a time scramble that ended on move 40. Earlier, at move 24, Howell had rejected a draw. In the British monthly magazine, *British Chess*, Levitt described what happened:

"After playing 40...Qa1+ I said (or possibly mumbled), "That's move 40" as I leaned over to see his scoresheet. The arbiter confirmed he heard me say that too...I went off to the toilet and was surprised to find David still thinking when I returned. After 10 more minutes he stopped the clock and put out his hand. Naturally I assumed he was resigning. The arbiter was there and we soon realized we were shaking hands but not agreeing on the result.

Somehow David imagined that he had heard me offering

a draw! In nearly 30 years of tournament chess no opponent of mine has ever attempted to agree to a phantom draw offer. I immediately stated that I had not offered a draw and David seemed to accept it quite readily and without much fuss...When he resigned I said the position was a forced win for me after move 40 and he replied that he still thought I had offered a draw and only changed my mind when I went to the toilet.

Not only would he not take my word for it, or the word of the arbiter who witnessed the entire episode, but it is also entirely apparent from the position and the run of the game that there would have been no [second] draw offer."

I found the whole episode very upsetting (especially the comment at the end of the game, tantamount to accusing me of cheating) since for many years I have been a friend to the whole Howell family as well as having been David's teacher.

HOWELL vs. LEVITT
French Defense, 2005

1 e4 e6 2 d4 d5 3 Nd2 c5 4 exd5 Qxd5 5 Ngf3 cxd4 6 Bc4 Qd6 7 Qe2 Nc6 8 Nb3 Be7 9 Bd2 a6 10 0?0?0 Nf6 11 Kb1 b5 12 Bd3 Bb7 13 Rhe1 0?0 14 g4 g6 15 g5 Nh5 16 Be4 Rfe8 17 Bc1 Qc7 18 Nbxd4 Nxd4 19 Rxd4 Bxe4 20 Qxe4 Bc5 21 Rd3 Rad8 22 Rc3 Qb6 23 Ne5 Rd5 24 Ng4 Red8 25 Rf3 R8d7 26 a3 Bf8 27 Rh3 Bg7 28 Rg1 Qd4 29 Qf3 Kf8 30 Ne3 R5d6 31 Rg4 Qa7 32 Rgh4 Qb7 33 Qe2 Qh1 34 Rxh5 gxh5 35 Qxh5 Rd1 36 Nxd1 Rxd1 37 Rf3 Rxc1 38 Ka2 Ra1 39 Kb3 Rxa3 40 Kxa3 Qa1 41 Kb4 Qa4 42 Kc5 Bd4 43 Kd6 Qb4 44 Kc6 Qc5 45 Kd7 Qa7 46 Kc6 Ke8 **Black Resigns**

Position after 40...Qa1

77. CROWNING GLORY
September 16, 2002

White to play and win

A checker is crowned when it reaches the opposite end of the board, just as a pawn also can be queened upon reaching its eighth rank. Yet chess has the option of replacing this pawn with any piece, except a king. The main reason for not always creating a queen, the most powerful piece on the board, is to prevent the opponent from escaping with a draw.

The most famous example of under-promotion was found by Fernando Saavedra (1847–1922) a Spanish monk whose claim to fame is one miraculous move in a game printed in an 1895 Scotch newspaper that was drawn after 1 Kb5 Rd5 2 Kb4 Rd4 3 Kb3 Rd3 4 Kc2 Rd4! 5 c8/Q? (if 5 Kc3 Rd1! 6 c8/Q? Rc1 snares the queen) Rc4! 6 Qxc4 stalemate.

Immortality can come in strange ways. At the Glasgow Chess Club, Saavedra showed the astonished audience how White missed a win by under-promotion, inspiring the chess editor to note, "This position is one of the most remarkable end games we have seen for years."

However, on the same day (May 25, 1895) another paper in Ireland alleged that Saavedra had seen this theme while stationed in Dublin several years earlier. James Porterfield Rynd, a barrister and Irish chess champion, claimed he won a similar ending against Colonel William Lynam, president of their local chess club.

But does it really matter whether Saavedra found the move himself or merely recalled it from his days in Dublin? His crowning glory forever will be known as The Saavedra Position.

The correct solution is 1 Kb5 Rd5 2 Kb4 Rd4 3 Kb3 Rd3 4 Kc2 Rd4! 5 c8/R!!! Ra4 6 Kb3! With the double threat of Rc1 mate or Kxa4.

Upon reaching the eighth rank you can make a second queen, if the original one is still on the board, by replacing the pawn with an upside-down rook. At a Dutch tournament a dispute arose between two grandmasters when Hans Ree queened a pawn. He punched his clock without bothering to replace the pawn with a queen, expecting Miguel Najdorf to resign on the spot. But his veteran opponent promptly protested that now he had the right to designate which piece Ree could select! Since Ree's intention was clear, the referee rejected Najdorf's claim. A FIDE tribunal upheld the referee's decision.

A similar incident happened in Karpov-Kasparov, Linares 1993:

Black to move

Kasparov promoted a pawn by 24 cxd1 and said "queen" while looking to the referee for a second queen without receiving any response. "Karpov immediately said that my pawn on d1 was a bishop! It was quickly straightened out, and they even added a few more minutes to Karpov's clock. I didn't object, as it gave me more time to savor the picture in front of me until he resigned three moves later. It was also an important game because at the time Karpov and I were tied for first with four rounds to play. That win was part of a five-game stretch that I consider the best consecutive tournament rounds of my life," wrote Kasparov.

There's an old adage that every soldier carries a marshal's baton in his haversack. Still, the notion of promoting a pawn into any piece we desire would have sounded strange to medieval ears.

The rules have evolved over time. *A Short History of Chess* by Henry Davidson states:

> "Pawn promotion had a troubled history. Moralists were disturbed that someone could have two or more queens on the board. At various times the promoted pawn could become only the piece on whose file it started from. In Italy during the 18th century the pawn could be promoted only to a piece which had been lost. If a player already had a queen, he could not earn another by advancing the pawn."

78. HOW TO WATCH A CHESS GAME
August 29, 2005

Robert Benchley wrote, directed, and acted in many short satirical films. In a 1923 article for *The Humorist*, he revealed how to watch a chess game.

"We will suppose that you have found two people playing chess somewhere. They probably will neither hear nor see you as you come upon them, so you can stand directly behind the one who is defending the south goal without fear of detection.

At first you may think they are both dead, but a mirror held to the lips of the nearest contestant will probably show moisture. Soon you will observe a slight twitching of the lips and then, like a greatly retarded moving picture of a person passing the salt, one of the players will lift a chessman from one spot on the board and place it on another spot.

It would be best not to stand too close to the board at this time, as you are likely to be trampled in the excitement. The players may even forget themselves to the point of shifting their feet or changing the hands on which they are resting their heads. Almost anything is liable to happen.

When the commotion has died down a little it will be safe for you to walk round and stand behind the other player and wait there for the next move. You will perhaps find it hard at first to keep your attention on the board. It can be accomplished by means of several little optical tricks.

For instance, if you look at the black and white squares on the board very hard for a very long time, they will appear to jump about and change places. The black squares will rise from the board about a quarter of an inch and slightly overlap the white ones. If you suddenly change focus, the white squares will do the same thing to the black ones.

And finally after doing this until someone asks you what you are looking for, if you shut your eyes tight, you will see an exact reproduction of the chessboard in pink and green in your mind's eye. By this time the players will be almost ready for another game."

Alas, we are unable to obtain the game that Benchley was watching. Instead we submit this comedy of errors between two of Thailand's best players who competed on their Olympic team. But don't ask how to pronounce their names, which are jawbreakers.

White missed a crusher with 20 Nf6+! exf6 21 gxf6. His disastrous twenty-ninth move cost him the game.

SUNTHORNPONGSATHORN vs. FUFUENGMONGKOLKIT
Sicilian Defense, Bangkok, 1985

1 e4 c5 2 Nf3 d6 3 d4 cxd4 4 Nxd4 Nf6 5 Nc3 g6 6 Be3 Bg7 7 f3 Nc6 8 Qd2 Bd7 9 0-0-0 0-0 10 g4 Rc8 11 Kb1 a6 12 h4 h5 13 g5 Ne8 14 Nxc6 Rxc6 15 Nd5 Be6 16 Bh3 Qd7 17 Qg2 Nc7 18 f4 b5 19 f5 gxf5 20 Nb6 Rxb6 21 Bxb6 fxe4 22 Bxc7 Qxc7 23 Bxe6 fxe6 24 Qxe4 Qc4 25 Qg6 Rf2 26 Rc1 Kf8 27 Rh3 Rf1 28 Rh1 Rf2 29 Qd3?? Qxd3 30 cxd3 Rxb2+ 31 Ka1 Rb3+ **White Resigns**

---

79. FIRST INSTANT TV REPLAY
August 15, 2005

In tournaments it's not enough to make the right move. We must also write the move.

Chess, like golf, is one of the few games requiring a score sheet. Former world champion, Tigran Petrosian, often wrote down his move before making it and then crossed it out if he changed his mind. This practice irked Bobby Fischer, who protested to officials in vain.

But recently FIDE decreed that we must record a move only after making it on the board. In the good old days we could exchange a volley and fill in the blanks later. Today each move must be written down immediately if we have more than five minutes left on our clock.

Keeping a running tally is clearly a burden, especially in severe time-pressure. We've all heard horror stories about clerical errors or sloppy penmanship, but both players should sign a score sheet to verify the result and keep the carbon copy.

Some grandmasters have been penalized for turning in the carbon and selling originals to collectors. Now that score sheets of classical games are valuable commodities, it appears that FIDE officials have been selling them to private investors.

Technology may free us from the distraction of writing down moves. "Intelligent boards" wired to the game can track moves and also flash the time consumed by each side on giant demonstration boards for the benefit of spectators. But players may still have to rely on manual clocks and score sheets due to power failures and Murphy's Law.

The first time I saw intelligent boards used was in a $100,000 blitz event won by Mikhail Tal at the 1988 World Chess Festival in Saint John, Canada. The crowd also watched the first instant TV replay in chess history.

In blitz each side has only five minutes for the entire game and nobody has to write down moves. The diagram is from Rafael Vaganian vs. Kiril Georgiev and White's two extra pawns should win if he can do it before his time runs out.

White found the only illegal move!

Normally in blitz a player is disqualified for making an illegal move. At lightning speed, play proceeded 61 f4?? Rxg3. Black snatched the king and claimed the game. But the contestants all agreed at a meeting held before this event began that an illegal move could be corrected if it was done before punching the clock. So now the outcome hinged on a technicality.

Fortunately TV cameras were running and an instant replay proved Vaganian did not punch his clock. Saved by the bell, he was allowed to substitute 61 Kg4 (for f4??) and then proceeded to win the disputed position.

All's well that ends well.

80. BISHOP MURDER CASE
November 14, 2005

Movies often use chess as a prop to hint that characters who play the game are smart. Actors usually mutter something memorable, like "check," and there's a good chance the board will be set up wrong with a dark square instead of a light one in the lower right hand corner.

Black mates in 4 moves

One of the few films that actually integrates chess into the plot was *The Bishop Murder Case* (1930) based on S.S. Van Dine's best-selling mystery novel of the same name. Basil Rathbone plays Philo Vance, an aloof chess-playing sleuth who is called upon to solve a series of murders by a killer who leaves a Black bishop and warning notes in rhyme at the scene of each crime signed "The Bishop."

It turns out the victims all knew each other and they all played chess. The prime suspect is John Pardee, an eccentric millionaire who promotes the Pardee Gambit. For years he bankrolled tournaments featuring his opening, but analysis has showed his brainchild to be flawed. He is on edge and bitter about the fate of his gambit. At least one victim publicly ridiculed it. Did Pardee kill him to get even?

But Pardee had an alibi. He was playing chess with the great Akiba Rubinstein at the Manhattan Chess Club. Could he have slipped away and committed this murder while his opponent pondered a complex move for 45 minutes?

Pardee later is also found dead, slumped over the board in the position he just lost to Rubinstein (diagram) with a bullet in his head and a gun in his hand. The search for the killer resumes when another murder occurs after Pardee's apparent suicide.

Philo Vance finally pins the murder on a professor who was jealous over his niece's loss of affection for him and led the police on a merry chase to implicate one of her suitors (a leading player). A real-life model for Pardee was Isaac Leopold Rice, the patron saint of American chess until he died at age 65 in 1915.

Rice taught law at Columbia and got rich by accident after a client talked him into taking a business case outside of his field. At first Rice refused but was persuaded by his client's argument: "We played a game of chess 13 years ago and I like the way you played."

Rice won the case and became a prosperous corporation lawyer, but chess always remained his first love. He tirelessly promoted the Rice Gambit: 1 e4 e5 2 f4 exf4 3 Nf3 g5 4 h4 g4 5 Ne5 Nf6 6 Bc4 d5 7 exd5 Bd6 8 0-0!? Bxe5 9 Re1 Qe7 10 c3. He sponsored tournaments and international postal events where each game had to begin with this precise sequence.

In 1903 he financed a match with Lasker as White against Chigorin to test the position. Black won 3½-2½ but Rice, like Pardee, was undaunted and refused to abandon his gambit. His analytical team always found a way to bolster White's resources before the next great test. Interest abounded as long as his checkbook stayed open, and over 30 players were honored by variations named after them in the course of this vast odyssey.

His gambit died when he did because at best White could only draw. Today the Rice Gambit, alas, is interred in a footnote of most opening manuals.

If Rice never existed, could a novelist conjure up an odd character like John Pardee?

Solution: 1...b1/Q!+ 2 Kxb1 Kd3 3 Ka1 Kc2 4 d4 Bb2 mate

81. TV OR NOT TV
September 5, 2005

Poker became a surprising hit on TV once big bucks entered the picture. But many people doubt that chess is ready for prime time.

Chess has no bouncing balls, as in tennis, that glue you to the tube. To follow the action you must have enough knowledge to savor its nuances. There's the rub.

True, the Fischer-Spassky title match in 1972 captured high ratings. But who has the patience to watch lesser mortals huddled motionless over a board for hours on end?

Bringing chess to the masses requires superb technology, faster games and skilled commentators to captivate a largely untutored audience. A two-hour pilot pitting Russia against the USA took place in July on four boards over the Net with music by Bering Strait, a Nashville band of young Russians who earned a Grammy award in 2002 for Best Country Music.

Each player had 20 minutes per game plus five seconds a move and faced the same rival twice. The jury is still out on this noble experiment that was syndicated on TV via satellite by Martin Broadcasting.

All four members of the American squad were immigrants! The American team consisted of Polgar (2577), Onischuk (2628), Gulko (2589), and Stripunsky (2565), while the Russian team comprised Khalifman (2658), Sakaev (2672), Aleksey (2625), and Vitiugov (2519).

Russia won 6-2. This odd game by former Russian champion Boris Gulko (now an American), against Evgeny Alekseev seems destined for the anthologies. After spurning a draw by 19 Qd8 Re8 20 Qd3 he pitched his queen to tree Black's queen on a2 but couldn't seem to trap it but then missed a win by 35 Kb5! Black later overlooked 42...Qc7! Take a look!

GULKO vs. ALEKSEEV
English Opening, July 11, 2005

1 Nf3 c5 2 c4 Nc6 3 d4 cxd4 4 Nxd4 e6 5 Nc3 Nf6 6 g3 Qb6 7 Nb3 Ne5 8 e4 Bb4 9 Qe2 d6 10 Bd2 0-0 11 0-0-0 a5 12 f4 a4!? 13 fxe5 axb3 14 a3 dxe5 15 axb4 Ra1 16 Nb1 Qa7 17 Qd3 Qa2 18 Bg2 Re8 19 Bc3 Re7 20 Kd2! Rd7 21 Na3 Rxd1 22 Rxd1 h5 23 Bf3 Rxd3 24 Kxd3 Nd7 25 c5 Kf8 26 Kc4 Ke7 27 Rc1 f5 28 Bd1 b5 29 Kxb5 Nb8 30 Kc4 Nc6 31 Bxb3 Ba6 32 b5 Na5 33 Bxa5 Qxb2 34 bxa6 Qxc1 35 Kb4?? Qe1 36 Ka4 Qxe4 37 Bb4 Qc6 38 Ka5 f4 39 Nc4 f3 40 Ne3 Kd8 41 Bc2 Kc8 42 Bd3 Kb8? 43 Bb5 Qe4 44 Nf1 Qd4 45 c6 e4 46 Bd2 Qd8 47 Ka4 Qd4 48 Kb3 Qd5 49 Kb4 Qd4 50 Ka5 **Draw**

Final position

82. THE CHESS PLAYER'S BIBLE
July 25, 2005

"A chess library of any standing must possess *MCO*. It is the standard by which other opening references are judged."
　　　　　　　　　　　—John Graham in *The Literature of Chess*

Modern Chess Openings, now in its 14th edition, is known as the "chess player's bible" because it's one of the most trusted books in the chess world. Since the original edition by Griffith and White about 100 years ago, this one-volume reference work has been updated nearly every decade to reflect the changes and advances in opening theory.

I felt entrusted with the keys of the kingdom when Walter Korn (who owned the rights to *MCO*) invited me to revise the Tenth edition of the gospel. My manuscript embodied key opening innovations right up to the end of 1964 and was published in the fall of 1965—expanded to more than 500 pages compared to 360 in the ninth edition and 317 in the eighth. My announcement of a new edition appeared in *Chess Life* in 1964 and is still valid today.

> We can never know whether a particular variation belongs to the past or the future; things often have an uneasy way of stirring in their grave, and I disinterred a great deal of material which was, at best, buried in a footnote (the pauper's grave) in previous editions. I also felt a pang of regret whenever it became necessary to prune and expunge outmoded lines, thereby diminishing the immortality of bygone masters.

> Although I tried to retain valuable lines, which are merely unfashionable, the sheer physical limitations required extreme compression. Space is space. True, we run the risk of being surprised by old novelties whose sole virtue is having been forgotten. But progress walks a tightrope—often we go forwards by glancing backwards—and I tried to strike this delicate balance within the strict framework of a crowded, bustling encyclopedia.

No game as organic as chess can withstand the wash of experience. The last decade has produced more novel and important material than the whole preceding century. Improvements came fast and thick—a veritable tornado in the Nimzo and King's Indian, Sicilian, Ruy Lopez. The greater official support enjoyed by chess in many countries yields a rich tournament harvest. As a result, even as my 10th edition reaches you, part of it will be outdated.

While it is the avowed duty of the compiler to compile—not anticipate trends—I was unable to resist the temptation of indicating in the footnotes where the student might profitably seek and expect reinforcements. When no source is quoted, evaluation reflects solely my judgment and responsibility. It is axiomatic that chess should end in a draw with best play. In every case where a game was lost, one can find a weak move or sequence that was responsible.

Apparently White has no forced win and his "jump" or "serve" tends to evaporate as the middle game approaches. Yet the advantage conferred by the first move ranks with the ancient belief in the soul or the modern belief in the atom. Strange, this tyranny of the unseen!

POOR BLACK

Theoreticians have thus sentenced Black to a term of hard labor for 15 or 20 moves to achieve that elusive thing called equality. Poor Black, is it any wonder that he suffers from an inferiority complex? The function of theory is to restore justice. One may now offer this definition: "White: Since recent Supreme Court decisions, not so big an advantage as it once was."

But with the refinement of technique, a slight edge in the opening now looms larger than ever. The better the player, the smaller the edge he needs to win. Black is always skating on thin ice—one slip is fatal, whereas White can trip and still survive. As Fischer succinctly stated my theory, "White, having the advantage of the first move, is allowed one minor blunder per game."

Playing the Black pieces has its compensations however. Once White makes the first move he commits himself to a fixed posture. In a sense Black chooses the defense which determines the course and character of the struggle. Thus there is a growing tendency for White to adopt those namby-pamby "reverse" openings (English, Reti) on the theory that what is adequate for

Black may be even more effective with an extra move. This has the effect of postponing the hand-to-hand battle.

JUGGLING VOLATILE ELEMENTS

In *New Ideas in Chess* I tried to demonstrate how the elements of Time, Space, Force, Pawn Structure, combine and interact like volatile chemicals; how an advantage in one element can be converted into another, similar to the principle of conservation of energy in physics. Surely the chessboard, even more than the universe, is a "closed system."

The gambit, for example, poses the clean-cut question: "Does White (or Black) have sufficient compensation for the sacrifice of material?" The answer to this and even more subtle positional problems must be viewed organically in the light of actual game continuations stemming from these positions. What happened here? There? Why? Did the decisive mistake come later? What comes after forges our evaluation of what comes before? Creative evolution, if you will.

Many theoreticians like Pachman, Euwe and Horowitz had some poor tournaments results because they approached a position stale. Improvements are usually hatched in actual contests when there is something at stake—not in pre-tournament preparation. The "heat of battle" and "mind over matter" are not just empty clichés. We vote with our feet. What we do determines our real belief. The move a master actually plays in an important tournament game is the one he believes best, the one he puts his money on—not the move he suggests while coldly annotating the game of a fellow master.

Every position examined with new eyes actually becomes new because you are involved in living it, in the process of playing for a win. In practice this means both players tacitly cooperate to create a dynamic imbalance. White tacitly agrees to avoid known equalizing lines; Black, the specter of easy simplification. The player who exchanges queens at the first opportunity or who forces a quick book draw (particularly with White) is often scorned by fans. Paradoxically the best way to play for a draw is to play for a win. Of course this is less true in postal chess which lacks suspense, spontaneity, and the time clock.

HOMEWORK

Nowadays, unfortunately, how much you know counts almost as much as how far ahead you see, especially with valuable minutes ticking away. If you want to make chess your career, a profound grasp of the opening is every bit as vital as natural talent. When asked to comment on Fischer, Tal quipped: "Who can play against Einstein's theory?"

The average player using *MCO* wants a place of reference, a watering hole. He wants to see where he went wrong or what move a grandmaster made when challenged with the same position or the same problem. This book satisfied that need.

MCO is not intended to be memorized or to encourage a slavish generation of players with an obedient reverence for authority. The important thing is not how I evaluate a given position, but the feeling of comfort you experience. If we disagree too often, alas, then one of us is wrong.

MY BEST ADVICE

The best advice I can give is not to detour from a recommended theoretical highway merely for fear of meeting with a prepared variation or an opponent's pet line. A good player must learn to cope with all positions—open, closed, quiet, wild—with equal dexterity. This willingness to follow the truth wherever it leads, without prejudice, however inimical to your personal style, is the main way to improve your game.

I tried to make this tenth edition stand the test of time by basing it on lasting values. If it serves you for the next five or ten years, a constant companion, then my job has been done. This kind of book is really a task for a computer and a team of chess analysts. After more than two years of research forgive me for heaving a sigh of relief. For better or worse *MCO* is now in your hands.

83. EMANUEL'S MANUAL
October 31, 2005

Emanuel Lasker held the crown for 27 years (1894–1921) longer than anyone in history. His classic *Manual of Chess* is as fresh and rich today as when he first translated it to English in 1932.

Lasker advises us to trust our common sense and not to rely on memorizing fashionable openings. "I have applied at least 30 of my 57 years to forgetting most of what I learned or read," he said in the original German edition of 1925. Above all, Lasker saw chess as a struggle. "Some ardent enthusiasts have elevated chess into a science or an art. It is neither. Its chief characteristic seems to be—what human nature delights in—a fight."

His indomitable will and fierce independence were reflected in his games. Unlike many of his fellow masters who lived only for the 64 squares, he penned books on philosophy and mathematics as well as chess.

Albert Einstein wrote a foreword to Lasker's biography recalling long debates in their youth about the theory of relativity. Lasker argued there was no proof the speed of light in a vacuum was infinite. Einstein said he couldn't wait indefinitely for proof, especially since no way to verify his theory was available at the moment.

Einstein noted that his friend's persistent skepticism derived from chess which was, after all, just a trivial pursuit. Thus he echoed George Bernard Shaw who scribbled, "Chess is a foolish expedient for making idle people believe they are doing something very clever when they are only wasting their time." But Lasker maintained that playing games is necessary and no less worthy than building bridges or making bombs.

Despite the anguish of exile after fleeing Nazi Germany and the loss of all his wordly goods, Lasker remained cheerful. "Everything in the long run changes for the better," he wrote.

After long layoffs away from the arena, he did well at Nottingham 1936, his last tournament. Two rounds before the end he bumped the reigning world champion out of the lead when Euwe stumbled trying to win a dead draw from the grand old man. Lasker died as a charity case at New York in 1941.

LASKER vs. EUWE
Queen's Gambit Declined, Nottingham, 1936

1 d4 d5 2 c4 c6 3 Nf3 Nf6 4 e3 Bf5 5 Bd3 e6 6 cxd5 Bxd3 7 Qxd3 exd5
8 Nc3 Bd6 9 0-0 0-0 10 Re1 Nbd7 11 e4 dxe4 12 Nxe4 Nxe4 13 Qxe4
Re8 14 Qxe8 Qxe8 15 Rxe8 Rxe8 16 Kf1 Nb6 17 Bd2 f6 18 Re1 Rxe1
19 Nxe1 Kf7 20 Ke2 Ke6 21 h3 Nc4 22 Bc1 Bc7 23 Kd3 Ba5?? 24 b4!
Bxb4 25 Nc2 Bd2 26 Bxd2 Nb2 27 Ke2 Kd5 28 Bc1 Nc4 29 Kd3 Nb6
30 Ne3 Ke6 31 Nc4 Nc8 32 Na5 Nd6 33 Bf4 **Black Resigns**

---

84. THE GENDER GAP
March 21, 2005

Nobody knows why chess is dominated by men or how to lure more women to the game.

"One of the most virulent debates in chess circles these days is over women's tournaments. One side says they encourage more women to compete; the other argues they promote the idea of women as second-class chess citizens," reported the *New York Times*.

The traditional view was offered by Harry Golombek, the late dean of British chess. He said, "This may sound ungallant, but I think chess is really a game for the masculine imagination."

However, there is no hormonal divide. Unlike weightlifting, you don't need big muscles for mental combat. No events are closed to women, including a shot at the world championship, and you can go as far as your ability takes you.

Scholastic coaches observe that up until age 13 children compete in equal numbers, yet most girls lose interest in high school. My hunch is that the girls discover that beating boys doesn't make them too popular with the boys they beat.

An assault on the male citadel was launched by an experiment in Hungary in the 1970s when three sisters named Polgar—Susan, Sofia, and Judit—were taught chess before age five and molded into champions by remarkable parents.

The girls became grandmasters in their teens by competing solely in mixed events. They received a well-rounded education, fluent in several languages, yet constantly had to battle bureaucrats and Communist apparatchiks who tried to restrict them to weak women's tournaments. Even world champion Garry Kasparov called them "trained dogs."

Men who play vastly outnumber women. To remedy this imbalance FIDE holds segregated events and maintains separate rating lists based on gender, but does this policy help or hinder women? Some critics contend that rewarding mediocrity or lowering the bar is not the answer.

USCF treasurer Timothy Hanke wrote, "I, for one, am sick of the whining. If organizers want to offer inducements to encourage more women, so be it. But if chess isn't a level playing field, I don't know what is. So let's not pretend barriers exist."

One reader noted, "I'm just as offended by women's chess as by using dice to determine which move we make. It's a slap in the face to intellectual merit." Another reader agreed, "Clearly, you can't support separate titles and prizes for girls and then blather about equality."

Walter Tevis, author of *The Hustler* and *The Queen's Gambit* opined: "I think it would be good if women don't play in women's tournaments at all. Doing so only reinforces the notion of their inferiority. I would like to see chess be a sexless game."

Indeed, everyone knows you can only get good by facing the best. Chess doesn't need affirmative action.

Jennifer Shahade, two-time USA women's champ, wrote
Chess Bitch: Women in the Ultimate Intellectual Sport

85. THE BRILLIANCY PRIZE

Monday, February 27, 2006

"A win by an unsound combination, however showy, fills me with artistic horror."

—Wilhelm Steinitz

My book *Modern Chess Brilliancies* had several lives after its publication by Simon & Schuster in 1970. Hypermodern Press produced an algebraic edition in 1994 that went digital, with added material in 2002 by Hardinge Simpole Publishing.

These 101 annotated games are mostly from the 1960s, yet they are likely to stand the test of time. This excerpt from my preface traces the history of a proud tradition: The Brilliancy Prize.

THE CLOCK

Modern chess had its inception in the great international tournament at London 1851, and already Staunton complained that championship matches were dragging endlessly and threatening public interest in professional competition.

"When a player upon system consumes hours over moves when minutes might suffice and depends, not upon out-maneuvering but out-sitting his antagonist, patience ceases to be a virtue."
—Howard Staunton

Consequently Staunton proposed a sandglass to limit each separate move. Crude mechanical clocks were introduced officially at Paris 1867 where players were fined for overstepping the time limit. The twentieth century opened with the now familiar double-faced push-button clock, heralding an equally significant development: allotting each side two hours for the first 40 moves (or some such equivalent) and punishing noncompliance with an outright forfeit instead of merely a fine. The clock had an obvious effect on not only the popularity but also the quality of chess; modern tournaments would be inconceivable without it.

THE PRIZE

The Brilliancy Prize is an institution that has survived intact. Traditionally after each major event an august body of critics selects those games with the greatest aesthetic appeal, as manifested by original, striking, intentional, and successful combinations.

At Carlsbad 1907 Cohn was awarded a Brilliancy Prize against Tchigorin "for a beautiful combination starting from an extraordinary deep pawn sacrifice." Later Cohn conceded (presumably with the award tucked safely in his pocket) he did not intend to sacrifice the pawn—he lost it and was forced to play energetically to compensate for his material inferiority. Needless to say, the victims received no share of the swag even when the board was "showered with golden pieces" (a phrase attributed to Lewitzsky-Marshall, Breslau 1912).

The loser's lot is negative immortality. But that's not so bad.

THE PROBLEM

The convulsive combination that destroys the enemy on the spot is easily understood by duffer and grandmaster alike. In his classic work, *The Art Of Sacrifice*, Spielmann wrote, "The beauty of a chess game is assessed, and not without good reason, according to the sacrifices it contains."

This pretty much expresses the feeling of the ages.

But one problem has persistently plagued the judges: must a combination, to merit the crown, be correct in all variations and withstand rigorous postmortem analysis? Historically the answer has been yes, though many a red-faced jury has seen its selection posthumously exploded, especially now by computers. The recipient of the award is concerned only that his brainchild worked over-the-board. What is often overlooked, however, is the performance of the loser, without whose unwitting cooperation no masterpiece is possible. This consideration raised its specter at Majorca 1968, where one of the judges reported:

> "After a long and heated discussion nobody could remember a drawn game ever having won a brilliancy prize. The question was: which of the players was responsible for the brilliancy; and if it was sound, why did he not win the game? On the other hand, if the brilliancy was sound but served only to save a lost game, should that player receive an award despite his having

reached a lost position? An uproarious discussion (rather, melee) followed."

When the smoke cleared they decided both players would share the prize jointly with another game.

THE ACCIDENT

Since a brilliancy is essentially an accident, we can't start any given game with the conscious intention of creating one. The opponent, the tension, the ticking of the clock—above all, the opportunity—must be present. Because combinations cannot always be calculated with precision and often are subject to surprising hazards, a master must have implicit faith in his own judgment.

With typical candor, Najdorf confessed, "When I play chess, I hardly ever calculate the play in detail. I rely very much on an intuitive sense which tells me what are the right moves to look for."

Players who strive to keep the draw in hand (the modern tendency) are not held in such high esteem as the gamblers whose games are filled with thunderbolts, errors, flashes of insight, tension and luck. As Reti observed, "The pleasures to be derived from a chess combination lie in the feeling that a human mind is behind the game, dominating the inanimate pieces and giving them the breath of life."

THE COMBINATIONS

"A combination is a blend of ideas—pins, forks, discovered checks, double attacks—which endow the pieces with magical powers."
—Irving Chernev

"Combinations have always been the most intriguing aspect of chess. The master looks for them, the public applauds them, the critics praise them. It is because combinations are possible that chess is more than a lifeless mathematical exercise. They are the poetry of the game; they are to chess what melody is to music. They represent the triumph of mind over matter."
—Reuben Fine

Anderssen and Morphy, whose combinations have almost without exception withstood a century of criticism, loom as the towering masters of a swashbuckling era filled with naïve delight in the sacrifice as an end in itself. Even young Steinitz reveled in the fiery excitement of combinations, admitting that he "did not play with the object of winning directly, but to sacrifice a piece."

Later in his career Steinitz discovered what we now know, that positional play is the best possible preparation for releasing accumulated energy in the explosion of a combination. But in those days the romantics were so enraptured with aesthetics that they almost felt cheated when good defense frustrated a brilliancy.

The sacrifice was a ritual act by which mighty paladins revealed their superiority; it was understandable and even expected that their benighted opponents would take umbrage: "What, you dare to sacrifice against me? I will refute your puny offer. I will devour everything and you shall lose miserably!"

In *The Chess Sacrifice*, Vukovic remarks that "mature technique has long since blown away any such ideas; now the content of the position is weighed objectively and not arrogantly."

When Anderssen was reproached by his admirers for not exhibiting his customary flair in his match against Morphy (1858) he replied, "No, Morphy won't let me. He always plays the very best move. He who plays Morphy must abandon all hope of catching him in a trap, no matter how cunningly laid, but must assume that it is so clear to Morphy that there can be no question of a false step."

This magnanimous tribute failed to credit Morphy's revolutionary new approach, because Anderssen himself did not fully appreciate why he lost—note how he displays a certain unease in dismissing his own attacks as mere traps. Morphy's attacks always flowed from the position organically; Anderssen's were usually inspirations of the moment. Morphy knew not only how to attack but also when to attack. And that is why he won.

THE DEFENSE

Indeed, how are bold and risky ventures to be assessed? That they work against inferior defense is no reason to reward them; and that they fail does not necessarily mean they are incorrect. It seems to me that an unclear sacrifice, apart from its beauty, should be evaluated by two criteria: (a) it should contain no obvious flaw; (b) it should serve the end for which it is intended even if only a draw.

Of course, the sacrifice must not be a wild trap based solely on the hope that the defender will overlook the refutation and go astray; there should always be an acceptable line in case the right defense is found. It is unlikely that any master will employ such a wild weapon if he sees the hole in it, unless he is prompted by sheer desperation. Such an exigency is aptly termed a swindle, and chess literature is replete with these saving resources.

Obviously a rise in the quality of defense necessitated a corresponding adjustment in the standard of attack. In modern chess most of the beauty resides in the annotations; brilliancies exist chiefly as grace notes, unheard melodies, because the enemy anticipates and thwarts them with appropriate rejoinders. Naturally, the brilliancies of yore are impossible when an opponent refuses to stumble into the silly pitfalls which render them possible. To the uninitiated, some of the most hard-fought struggles seem devoid of all bravura. This is comparable to the jazz buff claiming that Bach bores him.

THE MATADORS

The chess pro on the tournament circuit earns his crust of bread, to be sure, but his burning ambition is to create a few masterpieces. It is a tribute that he still is able to forge fresh material despite adverse conditions and the reams of analysis to which all phases of the game, particularly the opening, have been subjected. There is even talk of two world championships: one for machines, the other for humans.

In *The Royal Game*, Stefan Zweig sums up the agony and ecstasy of the chess master:

> "It stands to reason that so unusual a game, one touched with genius, must create out of itself fitting matadors. This I always knew, but what was difficult and almost impossible to conceive of was the life of a mentally alert person whose world contracts to a narrow, black-and-white, one-way street; who seeks ultimate triumphs in the to-and-fro, forward-and-backward movement of 32 pieces; a being who, by a new opening in which the knight is preferred to the pawn, apprehends greatness and the immortality that goes with casual mention in a chess handbook; of a man of spirit who, escaping madness, can unremittingly devote all of his mental energy during ten, twenty, thirty, forty years to the ludicrous effort to corner a wooden king on a wooden board!"

86. WHAT IS A SECOND?
May 16, 2005

"My wife is my second."

—Danish GM Bent Larsen

Modern chess largely requires team effort. When Mark Taimanov won his last round game at the 1970 Interzonal, thus earning the dubious honor of being mauled 6-0 by Bobby Fischer a year later in an elimination match, he embraced Evgeny Vasiukov, his second. In fact, each of the four Russians had his own separate second (Paul Keres for Vasily Smyslov).

But unlike Garry Kasparov, who employed a stable of analysts before he recently retired from tournaments, neither Larsen nor Fischer relied too much on helpers. Their brand of chess was a triumph of chess over committee.

Kasparov publicly accused an aide of spying before firing him. And Anatoly Karpov, his arch-rival, once blamed one of his rare short losses on his team.

I was Fischer's second in 1970 at Mallorca. The night before each round we prepared for his next opponent, a session often lasting three hours. But I never actually knew which opening Bobby would choose (and neither did he!) until he reached the board. I like to think he varied his play and broadened his repertoire thanks to my influence.

Games were adjourned after five hours in those days and players barely had time to eat, sleep, and resume play in the morning. Bobby and I always worked together except when time was short and he wanted me to double check a particular variation on my own. One of our triumphs was an ending where Bobby sacrificed a pawn against Taimanov to demonstrate the absolute supremacy of a bishop over a knight. However, Vlastimil Hort sealed an inferior move we had scarcely considered and Bobby had to work out an intricate win over-the-board.

A lot of nonsense has been written about the role of seconds. In the Yugoslav magazine *MAT*, Rudolf Maric extolled his job:

"Your boy must sleep, rest his mind, and everything you show him must be exactly calculated. If the enemy finds a hole in the analysis, you are treated as a traitor by your own side. But there is one thing you must always remember: a player is as good as the second! When your man's zero is finally forgotten and replaced by many wins, then the friendship is stronger than ever."

My main job was waking Fischer up and seeing to it that he got to the duel on time.

87. THE ART OF CHESS
May 9. 2005

"*Chess*: an art appearing in the form of a game."
—*The Great Soviet Encyclopedia*

"Not all artists are chess players, but all chess players are artists," said Marcel Duchamp, who took the art world by storm in 1913 with his Nude Descending a Staircase.

"In those days my freedom was complete," recalled the renowned art dealer D.H. Kahnweiler. "In the morning I would visit painters, and in the afternoon I would play chess with Braque, Derain and Vlaminck."

Marcel Duchamp

A generation of artists is still influenced by Duchamp's theories. A founding father of Dada, he laid down his brushes for many years after World War I to pursue a new obsession, "Chess is more than pure mathematics. If anything, it is a struggle. It has no social purpose. That above all is important," he declared.

Expatriate American Man Ray, a photographer, explained how chess wrecked his friend's first marriage:,"Duchamp spent the one week they lived together studying chess problems. His bride, in desperate retaliation, got up one night when he was asleep and glued the chess pieces to the board. They divorced three months later."

Duchamp aspired to reach the heights of chess, but he started too late. Known as "the painter who never painted" he competed on four French Olympic teams and also designed a chess book in 1932 before settling in America.

He donated several valuable works to the American Chess Foundation and died at 81 in 1968. Newspaper editors often sandwich chess between obituaries and comics, and Le Figaro in France printed his death notice in its chess column!

The Passionate Pastime - Evans vs Duchamp

Duchamps Spiel by art historian Ernst Strouhel contains 84 of his best games. *Duchamp: A Biography* by Calvin Tomkins in 1996 is the definitive book about his career.

I met Duchamp as he puffed away on his ubiquitous pipe in the 1948 New York State Championship. A few years later we played again in a pool for Hans Richter's surreal film, *The Passionate Pastime*.

DUCHAMP vs. EVANS
Queen's Gambit Declined, 1948

1 d4 d5 2 c4 e6 3 Nf3 c6 4 e3 Nf6 5 Nc3 Nbd7 6 Bd3 dxc4 7 Bxc4 b5 8 Bd3 a6 9 0-0 c5 10 b3 Bb7 11 Bb2 cxd4 12 Nxd4 Be7 13 Rc1 0-0 14 Be2 Rc8 15 Bf3 Bxf3 16 Qxf3 Ne5 17 Qe2 Qa5 18 Rc2 Ba3 19 Bxa3 Qxa3 20 Nb1 Qd6 21 Rfc1 Rxc2 22 Rxc2 Neg4 23 Nf3? Ne4 24 Nc3 Ngxf2 25 Nxe4 Nxe4 26 Nd4 h6 27 Rc6 Qa3 28 Qc2 Nf6 29 Qb1 Nd5 30 Nc2 Qe7 31 Qe1 Qb7 32 Rc5 Qb6 33 b4 Rd8 34 Nd4 e5 35 Nf5 Qf6 36 e4 Nf4 37 Rc3 Qb6 38 Kf1 Kh7 39 g3 Nd3 40 Qe2 Nxb4 41 a3 Nc6 42 Qg4 g6 43 Ne3 Ne7 44 Qf3 Kg7 45 Ng4 Qd6 46 Kg2 h5 47 Nf2 Nc6 48 Nd3 Nd4 49 Qe3 a5 50 Nc5 b4 51 axb4 axb4 52 Rc4 Rc8
White Resigns

---

88. TOUCH MOVE!
April 25, 2005

Chess is perfect. People aren't.

The rules of the game are clear, concise, and consistent. If you touch a piece, you must move it. If your hand quits the piece, the move stands. If your hand is still on it, then you can change your mind and move it elsewhere. But move it you must.

Enforcing touch move in the heat of battle isn't always easy. A case in point was the first encounter in 1994 between Judit Polgar, then 17, and world champion Garry Kasparov, then 31, at a major tournament in Linares, Spain.

Judit Polgar

After a tough fight Polgar threw in the towel because 47 Kg1 e2 49 Re1 Qd4 49 Kh1 Nf2 50 Kg1 Nh3 51 Kh1 Qg1! 52 Rxg1 Nf2 leads to smothered mate.

Afterwards she complained that Kasparov took back a move. At first he played 36...Nc5 but then saw it refuted by 37 Bc6 and instead he placed the knight on f8.

Since the rules specify that a protest must be lodged during play, nothing could be done after the game was over. "I didn't want to cause unpleasantness during my first invitation to such an important event," she explained. "We were both in severe time pressure. I was also afraid I would be penalized on the clock if my protest was rejected."

"Kasparov did not take his hand off the knight, so he had a perfect right to change his move," said the chief arbiter. "My conscience is clear. I have the feeling my hand was still on it," added Kasparov.

Yet we all know the naked eye can be fooled. A camera crew was filming the game and a replay revealed that Kasparov removed his hand for exactly ¼ of a second! Deliberate foul or did he try to change his grip in order to reverse direction? Who can say for sure?

His enemies promptly called it cheating. But Robert Solso, a noted cognitive psychologist, said that a time span of 250 milliseconds might be too short to make such a conscious decision.

POLGAR vs. KASPAROV
Sicilian Defense, 1994

1 e4 c5 2 Nf3 d6 3 d4 cxd4 4 Nxd4 Nf6 5 Nc3 a6 6 f4 e6 7 Be2 Be7 8 0–0 Qc7 9 Qe1 Nbd7 10 a4 b6 11 Bf3 Bb7 12 Kh1 Rd8 13 Be3 0–0 14 Qg3 Nc5 15 f5 e5 16 Bh6 Ne8 17 Nb3 Nd7 18 Rad1 Kh8 19 Be3 Nef6 20 Qf2 Rfe8 21 Rfe1 Bf8 22 Bg5 h6 23 Bh4 Rc8 24 Qf1 Be7 25 Nd2 Qc5 26 Nb3 Qb4 27 Be2 Bxe4 28 Nxe4 Nxe4 29 Bxe7 Rxe7 30 Bf3 Nef6 31 Qxa6 Ree8 32 Qe2 Kg8 33 Bb7 Rc4 34 Qd2 Qxa4 35 Qxd6 Rxc2 36 Nd2 Nf8 37 Ne4 N8d7 38 Nxf6 Nxf6 39 Qxb6 Ng4 40 Rf1 e4 41 Bd5 e3 42 Bb3 Qe4 43 Bxc2 Qxc2 44 Rd8 Rxd8 45 Qxd8 Kh7 46 Qe7 Qc4 **White Resigns**

---

89. TURNER STYLE
March 14, 2005

"If I lost 25 pounds I think I could beat anybody in the world."
                —Abe Turner interviewed by Johnny Carson (1962)

Someone just sent me a tape of that show and listening to it brought back pleasant memories. Abe was the closest thing to a chess coach I ever had.

He learned the game at a naval hospital in 1943 while recovering from shrapnel wounds inflicted during World War II. We met at a dive on Times Square where anyone could walk in and play chess for ten cents an hour. Hustlers fleeced the rubes. The official name was The New York Academy of Chess and Checkers but habitués fondly called it "the flea house." It was the main alternative to the staid Manhattan and Marshall club or outdoor tables in Central Park or Washington Square Park. Bobby Fischer also hung out there.

Playing "Turner style" meant grabbing a pawn and then trying to grind out a win, even if it took forever, by swapping pieces to reach an endgame. He seldom erred, always played safe, and was usually content to draw with strong players. But he could bite if they tried to crush him. Looking back, Abe had the best score of any American in tournaments against the up-and-coming Fischer (two wins and a draw).

Abe looked like the stocky movie actor William Bendix. Always colorful and in good spirits, he left an indelible impression on all who knew him. His corpulence framed the role of the buffoon which he chose to play in life. Here is some of his repartee with Johnny Carson.

CARSON: Why would losing 25 pounds help you win at chess? Would it bring you closer to the board, or what?

TURNER: No, it just would make me mentally alert and give me vim and vigor.

CARSON: Why not go on a diet?

TURNER: I don't eat much anyway.

CARSON: So how do you account for your weight? You're pretty heavy.

TURNER: I drink lots of soda pop every day. It keeps me going. You see, Johnny, when you play chess every day like I do, I'm always on the go.

CARSON: What do you do to relax?

TURNER: I go to the zoo. I like to watch the monkeys. It makes me feel superior to them, puts me at ease.

TURNER: Did you ever win the championship of the United States?

TURNER: No, but I came fourth in the U.S. Open championship.

CARSON: That's pretty good. What do you do for a living? Is this your living?

TURNER: Yes, well mainly. I write and lecture on the game, I give exhibitions and I also play for money.

CARSON: Chess for money? Who do you play for money?

TURNER: Mostly lots of people in the city, but mainly these out-of-town people from around the country who come to New York and try to establish a reputation.

CARSON: Can you make good money playing chess?

TURNER: Not too much. Not in this country.

The audience cracked up when Abe explained why he didn't like to play a certain lady." She's young and beautiful. She has an enormous chest and knocked over a piece every time she bent to make a move. Between a low-cut dress and exotic perfume, how can you concentrate on a game of chess? I'm only human. Sometimes I didn't notice when she knocked off one of my pieces with her whatchamacallit."

"I know what to call it," quipped Johnny. "So I can't understand why chess isn't more popular."

In 1962 a co-worker at *Chess Review* stabbed Abe in the back nine times and stuffed his body in a safe. Abe died at age 38.

TURNER vs. FISCHER
King's Indian Defense, New York, 1956

1 d4 Nf6 2 c4 g6 3 g3 Bg7 4 Bg2 0-0 5 Nc3 d6 6 Nf3 Nc6 7 0-0 a6 8 e3
Rb8 9 Nd2 e5 10 Nb3 Bg4 11 f3 Bd7 12 d5 Ne7 13 c5 Ne8 14 e4 f5 15
Be3 f4 16 Bf2 fxg3 17 hxg3 g5 18 Nd2 Ng6 19 Nc4 h5 20 Qb3 h4 21 g4
h3 22 Bh1 Nh4 23 Bg3 b5 24 cxb6 cxb6 25 Ne3 b5 26 Nf5 b4 27 Nd1
Nxf5 28 gxf5 Nf6 29 Ne3 Nh5 30 Kh2 Rc8? 31 Qxb4 Nxg3 32 Kxg3
g4 33 fxg4 Bh6 34 Rf3 Bb5 35 Qd2 Bf4 36 Rxf4 exf4 37 Kxf4 Qf6 38
g5 Qe5 39 Kg4 Rf7 40 g6 Rfc7 41 Bf3 Kg7 42 Rh1 Rh8 43 Rxh3 Rcc8
44 Rxh8 Rxh8 45 Qc3 Qxc3 46 bxc3 Kf6 47 Kf4 Rh3 48 Bg2 Rh4 49
Ng4 Kg7 50 Kg5 **Black Resigns**

90. THE KING OF SWING
January 17. 2005

Two music legends, both chess buffs, died in 2004: singer Ray Charles at 73 and bandleader Artie Shaw at 94. I had the pleasure to play chess with both of them.

My afternoon with Ray was brief, but I had several chats with Artie aboard a cruise when I gave a chess class and he lectured on serial monogamy, a subject he knew well after having had eight wives.

Both Lana Turner and Ava Gardner described him as overbearing, pedantic, and brilliant. He badgered Ava to read books and even hired a master to teach her chess. When she beat him, he stopped playing her.

Newlyweds Ava and Artie Shaw, 1945

His companion on the ship was a skinny girl barely out of her teens who didn't join him in my chess class. His powers of recall were amazing and he talked a blue streak about the past.

I couldn't resist asking why he married so many times. His fame attracted women, he explained. "But you just couldn't shack up in those days so you had to get married," he said. "Success is an opiate. Money pours in, people throw themselves at you. It made me nuts and I couldn't handle it."

He was the first white bandleader to tour the South with a black vocalist, Billie Holiday. "Back then she was very young and healthy. She didn't use hard drugs except some marijuana now and then, but most musicians did that."

After a stint in the navy during World War II he grew bored with the same old popular songs and switched to classical clarinet. In 1954 he gave up jazz for good.

During the "Red Scare" of the 1950s a congressional committee demanded to know why he signed a peace petition on behalf of the Communist Party. He cooly replied that if the Republican Party submitted one, he'd gladly sign it too.

Persecuted and facing tax problems, he moved to Spain where he married his last wife, actress Evelyn Keyes. She said after they were divorced that chess and crafting chess boards were among his favorite hobbies. Towards the end Shaw remarked that being freed of the need for sex was like finally dismounting a wild horse.

When a reporter asked if he believed in God, Artie said: "If there's such a force, it's like a microscopic cell in the left toenail of Garry Kasparov in the middle of a chess match. That cell has as much awareness of what he's doing as we do of God. The most one can hope for is to live a good life and try to leave things a little better than you found them."

91. ADDICTED TO CHESS
December 06, 2004

"I love chess. You can wake me up at night and say, 'Hey, let's play some chess' and I get up and do it."

—Ray Charles (1930–2004)

HIT THE BOARD, JACK!

The movie Ray has a stunning performance by Jamie Foxx as well as one chess scene. When Ray's wife learns of his heroin addiction and threatens to leave him, he composes "Hit the Road, Jack" and enters rehab in 1965.

Ray loses to his therapist on a special peg-in set for the blind. Just the last move is shown, and he appears to be the victim of a famous trap (1 e4 e5 2 Bc4 Bc5 3 Qh5 Nc6?? 4 Qxf7 mate). He sweeps the board to the ground, but later replaces heroin with an addiction for chess and takes control of his own empire by firing friends who are cheating him.

MY AFTERNOON WITH RAY

"He was an avid chess player, because it challenged his mind," said his manager. "He felt the pieces with his hands. He sometimes got so involved in a game he didn't want to go on stage."

We played chess in his office as I asked him questions during an interview I conducted for *Chess Life* (September 2002). I took it easy but was in for quite a surprise—he missed a likely draw by 17 fxe4! I was impressed by his natural ability, alertness, and quick sight of the board. If Ray Charles had devoted himself to chess instead of music (God forbid!) he might have been the first world-class blind player.

RAY TALKS CHESS

"One of the other patients in the hospital taught me how to play. We'd sit up late at night and he beat the hell out of me. But I learned. You always learn when you lose 'cause you pay attention and find out why. The beautiful thing about chess is that there are so many ways. You can't learn it all. I find the game truly intriguing.

I'm nowhere near what you call a master. I'm just a person who loves chess. I don't care if I lose. I try not to, but I just love to play.

I not only see the pieces moving in my mind's eye but I also try to think two or three moves ahead. As you know, you just don't move pieces. You have to have a reason. So you say to yourself, if I do this and he does that, then what will I do? That type of thing.

I never took any formal lessons. A bunch of us cats would get together every Sunday and just play rise and shine. Quick chess. Not where you spend hours to make a move. Like I say, I play chess strictly for fun. Not seriously. I beat Willie Nelson yesterday. He tells me that I turned the lights out on him.

But I once played Dizzy Gillespie and he beat the hell out of me. Diz wouldn't give me a chance to get even. We really didn't have time for another game, to be truthful. He was a good player. Trust me."

CHARLES vs. EVANS
Four Knights' Game, Los Angeles, March 8, 2002

1 e4 e5 2 Nc3 Nc6 3 Nf3 Nf6 4 d4 exd4 5 Nxd4 Bc5 6 Nxc6 bxc6 7 Qe2 O-O 8 Be3 Bxe3 9 Qxe3 Re8 10 f3 d5 11 Qd3 a5 12 O-O-O Ba6 13 Qd2 Bxf1 14 Rhxf1 dxe4 15 Qxd8 Raxd8 16 Rxd8 Rxd8 17 Rd1? Rxd1 18 Kxd1 exf3 19 gxf3 Kf8 20 Kc1 Ke7 21 Kd2 Ke6 22 Ke3 Nd5 23 Kd4 Nxc3 24 Kxc3 Kd5 **White Resigns**

92. HOW TO SPOT AN ADDICT
february 2. 2004

Most woodpushers play chess for fun, not blood. They spend an hour or two at the board for the challenge.

Real addicts are easier to spot. Ex-world champ Mikhail Botvinnik said playing chess was the only time he felt truly alive because it forced him to use the full power of his brain.

Some novelists have explored the nature of this addiction. In *The Defense*, Vladimir Nabokov spoke of the "abysmal depths" of chess. In *The Royal Game*, Stefan Zweig wondered how sane men could dedicate 20, 30, 40, 50 or 60 years to "the ludicrous task of cornering a wooden king on a wooden board." In his essay "Concerning Chess", H.G. Wells wrote in 1901:

> "There is a class of men who gather in coffee-houses and play with a desire that dieth not, and a fire that is not quenched. The passion for playing chess is one of the most unaccountable in the world. It is the most absorbing of occupations, the least satisfying of desires, an aimless excrescence upon life. It annihilates a man.
>
> You have, let us say, a promising politician, a rising artist, that you wish to destroy. Dagger or bomb are archaic, clumsy, and unreliable - but teach him, inoculate him with chess! Our statesmen would sit with pocket boards while the country went to the devil, our army would bury itself in checkered contemplation, our breadwinners would forget their wives in seeking after impossible mates. There is no remorse like the remorse of chess. No chessplayer sleeps well."

Today millions of people gather to play and discuss chess on the Net. Some diehards compiled a list of telltale signs that distinguish addicts from the rest of the world, and chess widows will immediately recognize these 15 symptoms:

- Names first born child either Bobby, Garry, Judit or Fritz.
- Looks at a newspaper's chess column before any other section.
- Keeps a chess book and chess set in the bathroom.
- Always keeps a chess set at the office or in a backpack.
- Asks all new acquaintances if they know how to play chess.
- The first question they ask other players is "What's your rating?"
- Goes directly to the game and chess section in a bookstore.
- Owns more books about chess than any other subject.
- Owns more chess clocks than watches.
- Mumbles "J'adoube" when bumping into someone or something by accident.
- Multiplies 8x8 faster than 7x7.
- Pays more attention to a chess game than the dialogue in a movie.
- Squawks the board was wrong with a dark square in the lower right-hand corner.
- Panics for an instant when a cashier says "Check?"
- Thinks the Olympics take place every two years.

93. WHEN NOT TO QUIT
December 22, 2003

Why did Black resign?

Each year yields a bumper crop of fresh blunders. But nothing can equal resigning in a won position!

It's quite rare, but this debacle occurred again in round seven of the European Team Championship in Bulgaria (won by Russia among 37 nations). When Switzerland was matched against Belgium, Viktor Korchnoi on board one wrongly advanced his rook from g4 to g6 with a flourish (see diagram). After this bolt from the blue, as his final seconds ticked away, Belgium's Van der Stricht gave up because he saw no way to save his queen or defend his king. Indeed, if 1...fxg6 2 Qxh6 mate.

Yet when Korchnoi got back to his room, he found a flaw in his own combination (see solution below). We all know that nobody ever won by resigning, but how can such oversights be explained?

Black was the victim of what Dr. Siegbert Tarrasch once diagnosed as "sacrificial shock," an affliction prevalent even among grandmasters that can take place in perfectly ordinary positions. Tarrasch noted that an unexpected sacrifice often contains an element of shock that renders calm and clear thought difficult even without any prodding from the clock.

Most resignations are justified. Still, should we play each and every game to the bitter end no matter how painful, or quit gracefully when facing inevitable defeat?

If you think your position is hopeless it usually is hopeless. And different players cope with loss in different ways. They say there are two types of losers: bad sports and good actors.

One grandmaster resigned by tossing his king across the room and shouting, "Why must I lose to this idiot!" As a teenager, Bobby Fischer sometimes burst into tears when he lost. Later he analyzed the game with his opponent in a postmortem session.

Austria's Rudolf Spielmann indicated his disgust by grimacing, closing his eyes, shaking his head, and pushing the pieces away from him as if they were poison. Ernst Gruenfeld tipped his king, shook hands, and left the table without even glancing at the winner. The British style is a hearty handshake and a happy smile, best exemplified by the almost superhuman sportsmanship of Sir George Thomas.

Capablanca confessed, "There have been times in my life when I came very near thinking that I could not lose even a single game. Then I would be beaten, and the lost game would bring me back from dreamland to earth. Nothing is so healthy as a thrashing at the proper time, and from few won games have I learned as much as I have from most of my defeats."

Solution: The saving grace is 1...Nxe5! 2 Rxe6 Nxd3! (threatening Nf4+) 3 Rxh6+ gxh6 (check!) 4 Kf1 Rg6 with more than enough material for the lost queen.

94. THE SEVENTH SEAL
August 9, 2004

The Seventh Seal (1957) is a somber, cryptic film directed by Ingmar Bergman. The title is from the Book of Revelation in the *New Testament*: "And when He broke the seventh seal, there was silence in heaven for about half an hour."

A fourteenth-century medieval knight returns from the Crusades after 10 years to find Europe ravaged by plague and despair. "I want God to put out his hand, show his face, speak to me. I cry out to him in the dark but no one is there," he tells a hooded figure, who turns out to be Death waiting to claim him.

To forestall his fate, the knight challenges Death to a chess game that lasts throughout the entire film. "As long as I resist you, I live. If I win, you set me free." Death, who never loses, readily agrees. Play is interrupted as the knight continues on his quest to find knowledge.

We all live and die without ever really knowing the reason why. But can the knight use the delay to find faith or outwit Death? Alas, his quest is futile. He finds only silence, realizing, "We must make an idol of our fear and call it God. If you scare the people, then they fall into the arms of priests."

When he sees that losing is inevitable, the knight knocks over the pieces hoping to start anew. But Death restores the position and announces mate in one move.

Since then, playing games with Death has been parodied in other films. Woody Allen, a huge fan of Bergman, called *The Seventh Seal* "a brilliant, sinister fairy tale" and made a short spoof of the famous chess scene where a young couple challenges Death to a badminton match.

Another spoof appeared in *Bill & Ted's Bogus Journey* where they beat Death at various games. But the Grim Reaper then changes the terms to make it the best of two out of three, or three out of five.

The Seventh Seal is considered a masterpiece, though some critics see it as a pretentious allegory. Chess allows us to pass time agreeably, but Death always wins the endgame.

95. THE LOSING DEFENSE

February 16, 2004

WHAT'S WHITE'S BEST MOVE?

Very few movies deal seriously with chess. Some notable exceptions are *Dangerous Moves* about a world championship match (it won an Oscar as best foreign film of 1984) and *Searching For Bobby Fischer* (1993) a true story about a father who pushes his talented son too hard.

Night Moves (1975) uses chess as a device to shed light on the leading man's character. *Fresh* (1994) depicts chess as the only gem in the violent life of a 12-year-old drug pusher in the inner city. And *Hatley High* (2003) is a low budget spoof about chess mania in a small town.

Chess itself plays a central role in *The Luzhin Defense* (2000) by Dutch director Marleen Gorris (who won a 1995 Oscar for Antonio's List). Except for a hokey ending, her film doesn't stray far from Vladimir Nabokov's novel, *The Defense*, about the obsession and "abysmal depths" of chess.

Nabokov noted, "Luzhin is uncouth, unwashed, uncomely, but something in him transcends both the coarseness of his gray flesh and the sterility of his recondite genius. He has been found lovable even by those who understand nothing about chess."

This visually exquisite period piece takes place during a chess tournament in the 1920s at an Italian resort. John Turturro is well cast as the nerdy Alexander Luzhin, a Russian contender whose one-dimensional life is disrupted when he meets the first woman who ever showed him affection. Within a few days he proposes marriage, and she accepts. Still, it's hard to fathom the girl's attraction for Luzhin. Maybe she just wants to spite her aristocratic parents, who strongly oppose her union with such a narrow fanatic.

When Luzhin suffers a nervous breakdown, a doctor advises him to sacrifice chess and marry the girl. But he is torn between his love for her and his passion for chess. In his torment, he jumps out of a window.

"At the instant when Luzhin unclenched his hand, at the instant when icy air gushed into his mouth, he saw exactly what kind of eternity was obligingly and inexorably spread out before him," wrote Nabokov, who supposedly based it on his friend Curt van Bardeleben, a famous Berlin player who committed suicide in 1924. Recently, Lembit Oil, an Estonian grandmaster distraught over the breakup of his marriage and his failure to receive invitations to elite tournaments, ended his own life in the same way.

In his foreword to the novel, Nabokov writes:

> "My morose grandmaster remembers his professional journeys not in terms of sunburst luggage labels and magic-lantern shots but in terms of the tiles in different hotel bathrooms and corridor toilets—that floor with the white and blue squares where he found and scanned from his throne imaginary continuations of the match game in progress; or a teasingly asymmetrical, commercially called agate pattern with a knight move of three harlequin colors interrupting here and there the neutral tint of the otherwise regularly checkered linoleum... or certain large glossy black and yellow rectangles whose h-file was painfully cut off by the ocher vertical of the hot-water pipe..."

In his spare time Nabokov collected butterflies and composed chess problems. Certain recurring motifs lead to Luzhin's "sui-mate" (as Nabokov calls it) but these nuances are virtually impossible to film.

The novel contains no chess games and no dialogue. Nabokov wrote it in Russian in 1929 but waited 35 years to see an English edition after he rejected a publisher's suggestion to make Luzhin into a demented violinist by replacing chess with music.

Despite a depressing theme, the film captures the tension and drama of tournament chess. As Luzhin analyzes a position, chess pieces glide into a pattern etched in his mind's eye; and those antique chess clocks are a joy to behold.

Before the film was released, a preview audience of chess experts in New York burst out laughing toward the end. "For an hour and fifty minutes we all sat enthralled, hanging on every development. Unfortunately the last ten minutes presented a farfetched, totally contrived ending that nearly destroyed the previous hard-earned credibility of the movie," wrote GM Ron Henley.

However, GM Alexander Shabalov recently called it "simply the best chess movie ever" on an Internet newsgroup. "It was much more sensible than the novel," he said. "At no moment did they show nonsense at the chessboard. It is true that the movie made Natalia's character bigger than Nabokov intended, but that is what you do when you get Emily Watson in the cast. And John Turturro was just magnificent. There were moments when I looked at the screen and I saw Ivanchuk, Ehlvest, Micky Adams."

Be that as it may, former *Chess Life* editor Burt Hochberg lambasted the way chess was handled in *Games* magazine (September 2001):

"In desperate time pressure Luzhin sealed 1...Nxf4 (see diagram) and the game is adjourned as he slouches dejectedly out of the playing hall. Although his sacrifice was in fact the start of a winning combination, he clearly doesn't realize it. How do we know? Because he discovers the brilliant point of the combination only later.

Luzhin suffers a breakdown and is cared for in a sanitarium. We're not told how much time has elapsed since the adjournment, but it had to have been several days. This in itself is irregular, to say the least. A game is to be resumed at the appointed time. If one of the players does not appear, he is forfeited. But after Luzhin's suicide, his fiancee Natalia finds his chess notes. She shows them to a friend who, incredibly, manages to convince Turati and the match officials to resume the game.

Natalia plays the winning moves in Luzhin's place and checkmates Turati. Very pretty, very noble, and very much against the rules. Can you imagine officials permitting this? First, a player is required to make his own moves. Second, it is flatly illegal to use notes during a game.

As chess lovers we are supposed to be grateful when a chess position is shown in a movie with a white square in the right corner, but I think we need to raise our standards. Blatant illegalities and absurdities in the portrayal of chess in a popular medium should not be glossed over and tolerated but should be loudly denounced."

I have one quibble. The sacrifice is not the start of a winning combination as Hochberg claims (see solution) nor is it the sealed move because we see Turati playing 1 exf4? over the board before the game is adjourned. This move is the losing defense.

The last word really must go to Dutch writer Tim Krabbe. "It takes a sad sort of guts to turn a novel about the tragic enchantment of chess into a feminist pamphlet; man is too weak, woman must finish his work for him."

Solution: The fictitious game was composed for the movie by British GM Jon Speelman. Black is a pawn down and won after 1 exf4? Re3+ 2 Kg4 f5+ 3 Kg5 Kg7 4 Nd5 Rh3! 5 gxh3 h6+ 7 Kh4 Bf2 mate! But the best defense is 1 Nd1! (even 1 Bxa6 works) Ne6 2 Bxa6 gaining a second pawn with a winning position.

96. PROVING THE OBVIOUS
September 6, 2004

When the great Capablanca was asked how many moves he saw ahead, he always said: "Just one. The best one."

But how do you find it? Countless books were written to help lesser mortals answer this question.

"Maybe it's not romantic to think that avoiding mistakes is the way to improve, but it's far more important to avoid doing anything stupid than to create brilliant combinations. Don't just look at what you threaten–look at what threatens you! In other words, assume your move is a blunder until you check it out carefully," I noted in *The 10 Most Common Chess Mistakes*.

How players think continues to fascinate scholars. At the 2004 meeting of the Cognitive Science Society in Chicago, Ruth Byrne and Michelle Cowley of Trinity College Dublin in Ireland presented their study of 20 players who varied in skill from novice to grandmaster. Each was given six positions where neither side had a clear advantage and told to think aloud while deciding on a move.

The responses were graded by a powerful chess computer and there were no surprises; the experiment merely proved the obvious. We already knew that weaker players are more likely to pick weak moves because they can't predict the opponent's best reply. And we already knew that stronger players pick strong moves because they can see further ahead.

"People who know their area are more likely to look for ways that things can go wrong for them," said Ruth Byrne. That's precisely what good players do, so what's new? "The chess master is the chemist of a dimension that is geometrically bounded by 8x8. The elements he works with are Pawn Structure, Space, Force, and Time," I wrote many years ago.

The researchers concluded that chess masters and scientists think alike because they use a process of elimination and don't seek the desired outcome when testing their hypothesis. Byrne and Cowley plan to devise more chess experiments.

Unlike science, however, chess strategy employs psychology. The object is to win, not to find the truth.

97. LAST WORDS
November 25, 2002

Every language has a word for surrendering. "I resign" is common in English. In Sweden they say "upgivvet." In Holland "geef het op." In Italy "abbandona." In German "aufgegeben" conveys just the right ring of disgust.

Yet few linguistic crises arise because these dreaded words are seldom uttered. A simple handshake will usually suffice to surrender a lost game. Many players also concede defeat by tapping their king, then stopping the clock and signing the score sheet.

In 1972 Boris Spassky resigned the last game of his title match with Bobby Fischer in Iceland by phone. The American, reluctant to believe his ears, feared a trick and showed up at the board anyway just to make sure Spassky had put it in writing.

At Hastings in 1895, a landmark international tournament, Kurt von Bardeleben endeared himself to his colleagues by refusing either to resign or to play out hopeless positions. At the moment of truth he often walked away from the board and forfeited on time without showing up again.

Having to concede defeat is bad enough, but every so often someone gives up when the game may still be saved. This occurred at the Nice Olympiad in 1974.

To make matters worse, this same game was played before—and Black suffered from the same delusion by resigning on move six! He didn't see how to stop 7 Qxf7 mate without losing a piece. But 6...Nh6! 7 Bxh6 0-0! saves the day. If 8 Bc1 (better is 8 Bxg7 Kxg7 9 Nxc3) Nb4! 9 Qh5 d5 10 Bxd5 Nd3 11 Ke2 Nxc1 12 Rxc1 cxb2 wins for Black!

Of course there is a sure cure for premature resignation: never give up the ship. Though dragging out lost games to the bitter end is considered poor sportsmanship, you can't win by resigning.

MITFORD vs. SHARIF
Hungarian Defense, 1974

1 e4 e5 2 Nf3 Nc6 3 Bc4 Be7 4 d4 exd4 5 c3 dxc3 6 Qd5 **Black Resigns?**

---

98. MODERN TIMES
December 23, 2002

Long before the Internet, a statesman observed that a lie gets halfway round the world before truth has a chance to get its pants on. Thanks to the speed of information, anyone can spread lies via cyberspace in seconds.

Recently the rumor mill buzzed about a contender for the world title killed in a car crash. No one was more stunned to learn of his death than Hungary's Peter Leko, 23, when he awoke the next morning.

But was it ever really possible to trust the printed word? When Mark Twain's demise was published in American newspapers, he cabled his editor from Europe that the reports of his death were greatly exaggerated.

We tend to forget that people lived in a five-mile-per-hour world before the invention of the telegraph and railroads. Reuters used carrier pigeons as well as couriers to transmit news. Postal chess games took months and even years to complete, but now countless games take place each and every day over the Net.

Contests usually are now conducted at a fast clip in cyberspace. Last week fans were treated to a four-game rapid match that took place over two days in New York where Anatoly Karpov upset Garry Kasparov 2.5-1.5. Each side had only a half hour per game, which is to real chess what popcorn is to real food.

RICHMOND PEARSON'S LEGACY

A single room, called The Chess Game, exists at the Richmond Hill Inn in Asheville, North Carolina. A chess set is still included in the decor to honor what used to be the home of congressman Richmond Pearson, ambassador to England, and chess enthusiast.

After the transatlantic cable was laid, Pearson arranged a match in 1897 between the U.S. House of Representatives and the British House of Commons. A press release by the Richmond Hill Inn states, "This contest attracted much interest and excitement in both countries because telegraphic communication between continents was still a recent innovation.

"The games were designed to interest congress in ways to speed and cheapen communications. The match lasted seven days and ended in a draw, with each side winning 2½ games apiece. As a memento the cable company gave each player a trophy in the form of a metal "castle" that enclosed a piece of the cable over which the games were played."

99. SLIPS OF THE HAND
August 25, 2003

Think with your head—not your hands.

If you touch a piece, you must move it. If you merely want to adjust a piece by centering it on a square, you must first say J'adoube (I adjust). This is basic chess etiquette.

When a renowned grandmaster collided with a stranger on the street, he said J'adoube, by way of apology. "Sir," sniffed the stranger, "you know as well as I do that one is supposed to say J'adoube before making a move—not after!"

At the Sousse Interzonal in 1967, shocked spectators saw Yugoslav grandmaster Milan Matulovic lift a piece and put it back after discovering that moving it would cost him the game. He stuttered, "J'adoube," and moved another piece instead, which is commonly known as cheating. His opponent Istvan Bilek squawked, but the referee took no action because he didn't see the incident. The game was eventually drawn.

A few months later, as fate would have it, Matulovic got away with the same stunt against the same opponent! Thenceforth his colleagues dubbed him J'adoubovic.

Even without touching a piece you can still get into hot water. Jan Ehlvest nearly forfeited for sealing an illegal move in a winning position against Lubomir Luboyevic at the 1989 World Cup series in Rotterdam.

Luboyevic missed an easy draw by 39...Rc5 40 Rb7 Bf5. He was clearly lost at adjournment on move 62 and resigned without bothering to show up when play was resumed next day.

That's when the fun began. When officials opened the envelope, they found that Ehlvest wrote down 62 Rf2-a2?? (illegal) instead of sealing his intended 62 Rc7-h7 (if 62...Rxc5 63 Rh4+ Kd5 64 Rh5+ Kd6 65 Rxc5 wins). He had rotated the board in his mind's eye!

This hallucination might have cost Ehlvest the game—had his opponent not already resigned! So his slip of the pen was erased by Luboyevic's slip of the lip.

EHLVEST vs. LUBOYEVIC
French Defense, 1989

1 e4 e6 2 d4 d5 3 Nc3 Be7 4 Bd3 dxe4 5 Nxe4 Nf6 6 Nf3 Bd7 7 0-0
Nxe4 8 Bxe4 Bc6 9 Bd3 Nd7 10 Re1 0-0 11 Bf4 Bd6 12 Ne5 Nxe5 13
dxe5 Bc5 14 Qg4 Qd4 15 Qh4 h6 16 Rad1 g5 17 Bxg5 Qxf2 18 Qxf2
Bxf2 19 Kxf2 hxg5 20 b4 b5 21 Re3 a5 22 a3 axb4 23 axb4 Ra4 24
Rb1 Kg7 25 Rg3 f6 26 exf6 Kxf6 27 Ke3 Rh8 28 h3 Rh4 29 Rf1 Rf4
30 Rxf4 gxf4 31 Kxf4 Rxb4 32 Ke3 Bd5 33 Rg8 Kf7 34 Rc8 Bxg2 35
Rxc7 Kg8 36 Rh7 Bf1 37 Bg6 Rc4 38 h4 Bh3 39 Bd3 Rb4? 40 Rh5 Bf5
41 Bxf5 exf5 42 Rxf5 Rxh4 43 Rxb5 Kf7 44 Re5 Rc4 45 Kd3 Rc8 46
c3 Kf6 47 Re3 Rd8 48 Kc2 Kf7 49 Kb3 Rb8 50 Kc4 Rc8 51 Kb5 Rb8
52 Kc6 Rc8 53 Kd7 Rc4 54 Kd6 Rc8 55 Re7 Kf6 56 Rc7 Rd8 57 Kc6
Ke6 58 c4 Ke5 59 c5 Kd4 60 Kb7 Rd5 61 Kb6 Kc4 **Black resigned
without, alas, waiting to see White's (illegal) sealed move.**

Final position after 61...Kc4

White sealed 62 Rf2-a2. Chief arbiter Gijssen accepted it as 62 Rc7-
h7 since the intention was clear. Nowadays, fortunately, sealed moves are
no longer consigned to envelopes held by the arbiter overnight because all
games are played to a finish in a single session.

100. SPARKLING MEMOIR
November 3, 2003

The Bobby Fischer I Knew and Other Stories by Arnold Denker as told to Larry Parr, aptly subtitled "Anecdotes from the Front Line of American Chess," won several awards as Chess Book of the Year in 1996. This classic with over 300 games was just reprinted by a fledgling British publisher, Hardinge Simpole.

In 1944, at age 30, Denker won the USA Championship. He was in an ad for Camel cigarettes—the first time I recall a chess player getting paid for an endorsement. Somehow it left a lasting impression on me, and I was honored a half century later when asked to write a foreword to this splendid book.

Denker is a superb raconteur whose career spans the decades from Alekhine to Kasparov. This sparkling memoir contains pen portraits of many raucous and colorful figures in twentieth-century chess. Sections on Capablanca, Chernev, Euwe, Dake, Fine, Flohr, Helms, Horowitz, Marshall, Pinkus and numerous others are rendered with Dickensian precision. I knew a few of them and often catch myself saying, "Yes, he got it just right!"

A NOTORIOUS INCIDENT

My only quibble is that the stories are so good I wish they lasted longer. Take L. Walter Stephens's one claim to fame. Denker recalls:

> "I scored 4½-½ in the 1942 U.S. Championship and met Sammy Reshevsky in round six. It featured my maddest time scramble and his flag fell on move 45 or so. L. Walter rushed up, grabbed the clock from behind, turned it around so the dial was on my side and without the slightest hesitation forfeited...me!"

A near riot broke out. When several witnesses tried to reason with L. Walter, he retorted with his now famous query, "Does Kenesaw Mountain Landis ever reverse himself?" That supremely stupid statement ended all possible discussion. For Judge Landis, the czar of baseball who had been appointed to clean up the sport after the White/Black Sox scandal of 1919, was notorious for never changing a decision. I played the rest of the tournament, to use Bernard Shaw's memorable image, like a squashed cabbage leaf.

THE REST OF THE STORY

Curious, I asked Denker what Sammy did after the referee made this mistake. "I asked Sammy why he didn't say something? He said, 'It's not my decision' and zoomed out. We weren't friends for years after but finally made up when our team went to Moscow in 1946."

At Buenos Aires in 1960 Reshevsky overstepped on time against me and started to protest about his defective clock. With the forfeit safely tucked in my pocket, I took a leaf from Sammy's book and vanished from the playing hall in case the decision was reversed on appeal. In a way I was paying him back for what he did to Denker.

101. FAREWELL, ARNIE
January 31, 2005

Arnold Sheldon Denker, the Dean of American chess, died this month at age 90. Born in 1914, he was friendly with every world champion since Emanuel Lasker.

**Denker (right) beating Reuben Fine in the
1944 USA Championship**

Chess kept him out of trouble on the streets of New York City during the Depression. After attending NYU he turned to boxing and then to chess when "winning a quarter a game could buy you a meal." The chess scene in New York was vibrant because so many masters couldn't find jobs.

The 1930s were America's glory days, our international teams won gold medals four times running. Yet players were penniless and people held them in low esteem. "Chess is as elaborate a waste of human intelligence as you can find outside of an advertising agency," sneered novelist Raymond Chandler.

In 1944 Arnie captured the USA Championship and gave exhibitions at military bases. After the war, when the USSR crushed the USA in a 1945 radio match, he lamented, "Chess requires you full-time, but it doesn't assure you anywhere near an adequate income. The sooner we realize this, the sooner America will regain its prestige as the leading chess nation."

Arnie had to go into business to support his family, then retired to

Florida with a bundle and financed scholastic chess. "Passing the torch on to the next generation was his great passion. It was his life, after his family," said one of his sons.

"I love to travel, and chess is spoken around the world," Arnie said. "I've known thousands of players and never found one who had Alzheimer's. Chess is great because it exercises the mind."

He was the first grandmaster to drop a celebrated four-game match to a machine in 1988. He graciously conceded his electronic foe played "brilliantly" and that he "learned a great deal."

His first book *If You Must Play Chess* (1947) shows how he was always torn between a desire to make risky sacrifices and a desire to be sound. "I still like to attack. If this be treason, then make the most of it!"

His greatest regret was turning against world champion Alexander Alekhine because of some anti-Semitic articles he wrote under pressure from the Nazis while trapped in war-torn Europe. Arnie said:

> "I knew both German and his handwriting. He wrote those infamous articles. I endorsed a world wide ban of Alekhine, a grave error. Alekhine had been my friend. You do not desert a friend. I should have stuck with him as he was dying in Lisbon and try to find the facts, the pressures of war on him. Nowadays I agree with Larry Evans who wrote in Chess Life that you have to be awfully careful about banning people in chess...people change, have horrendous mental problems sometimes...war time duress. We are all sinners and you can take that to the bank. Holier than thou does not work!"

Never one to mince words, Arnie always fought for the players against the chess bureaucrats. "Because I had just retired as a successful businessman people wanted me to inspect the US chess federation books. There was then no question that the USCF was run by crooks and thieves... they simply stole with phony contracts, took money for years of service and the like...all the time while leaving players destitute. Even Fischer was playing for peanuts while living in near poverty in New York."

His second book, *The Bobby Fischer I Knew And Other Stories* (1995), is a sheer classic by a superb raconteur about the many colorful characters he met through chess. "How fortunate for us that he and his collaborator have the rare gift to tell it like it was," I noted in the foreword.

"He was a hail-fellow-well-met kind of guy," said his coauthor Larry Parr. "Arnie loved everything he did, right down to crossing streets by running through traffic with a saint's faith that he would make it to the other side." At last he crossed to the other side. Hail and farewell, Arnie.

INDEX OF GAMES
By Chapter